"The book of Psalms is green pastures and still waters for real people in hard times. *More Precious Than Gold* provides what no money can buy—direct personal access to the refreshment God gives only through his Word."

—Ray Ortlund, Pastor, Immanuel Church, Nashville, Tennessee

"Sam Storms lays the pieces of our contemporary world down on the template of the Psalms, and the result is what it has always been: the power of the Psalms to illumine, interpret, and direct our lives in the ways of the Lord. This book is a particularly insightful exposure of that power."

—C. Hassell Bullock, Franklin S. Dyrness Professor of Bible Studies, Wheaton College

For MAGDA

"Delight yourself in the Lord!"

Ps. 37:4

Sam Storms

More Precious Than Gold

Crossway books by Sam Storms

*To the One Who Conquers: 50 Daily Meditations on the
Seven Letters of Revelation 2–3* (2008)

The Hope of Glory: 100 Daily Meditations on Colossians
(2008)

*Signs of the Spirit: An Interpretation of Jonathan Edwards's
"Religious Affections"* (2007)

Chosen for Life: The Case for Divine Election (2007)

More Precious Than Gold

50 Daily Meditations on the Psalms

SAM STORMS

CROSSWAY BOOKS

WHEATON, ILLINOIS

More Precious Than Gold: 50 Daily Meditations on the Psalms
Copyright © 2009 by Enjoying God Ministries
Published by Crossway Books
    a publishing ministry of Good News Publishers
    1300 Crescent Street
    Wheaton, Illinois 60187

Design and typesetting: Lakeside Design Plus
Cover design: Jon McGrath
Cover illustration: iStock
First printing 2009
Printed in the United States of America

Unless otherwise indicated, Scripture quotations are from *The Holy Bible, English Standard Version*®, copyright © 2001 by Crossway Bibles, a publishing ministry of Good News Publishers. Used by permission. All rights reserved.

Scripture references marked NIV are from *The Holy Bible: New International Version*®. Copyright © 1973, 1978, 1984 by International Bible Society. Used by permission of Zondervan Publishing House. All rights reserved.

    The "NIV" and "New International Version" trademarks are registered in the United States Patent and Trademark Office by International Bible Society. Use of either trademark requires the permission of International Bible Society.

Scripture quotations marked NASB are from *The New American Standard Bible*®. Copyright © The Lockman Foundation 1960, 1962, 1963, 1968, 1971, 1972, 1973, 1975, 1977, 1995. Used by permission.

All emphases in Scripture quotations have been added by the author.

Trade paperback ISBN:	978-1-4335-0261-3
PDF ISBN:	978-1-4335-0561-4
Mobipocket ISBN:	978-1-4335-0562-1

Library of Congress Cataloging-in-Publication Data
Storms, C. Samuel, 1951–
    More precious than gold : 50 daily meditations on the Psalms / Sam Storms.
        p. cm.
    ISBN 978-1-4335-0261-3 (tpb)
    1. Bible. O.T. Psalms—Meditations. I. Title.

BS1430.54.S76 2008
242'.2—dc22

                          2008038696

VP			19	18	17	16	15	14	13	12	11	10	09
15	14	13	12	11	10	9	8	7	6	5	4	3	2	1

To

Glen Burns
Steve Carpenter
David Lightfoot

Board members of Enjoying God Ministries,
without whose faithful and prayerful support this book would
never have been written

Contents

Acknowledgments

I am extremely grateful for the editorial skills of Lydia Brownback. This is the third in a series of meditations on Scripture that she has edited for me, and I am profoundly thankful for her excellence in making these volumes better than they otherwise would have been.

No one has exerted a greater influence on my understanding of the Psalms than the nineteenth-century Baptist preacher Charles Haddon Spurgeon (I quote his *Treasury of David* countless times in this series of meditations). It seems only appropriate to mention him in particular and to share briefly my experience upon visiting the tiny chapel where he was brought to faith in Jesus Christ.

At first we couldn't find it. We walked a long way down Artillery Street in a less than thriving area of Colchester, England. I was the guest of Graham Stevens and Abbeyfield Community Church, where he is the senior pastor. I had spoken there on Saturday night and Sunday morning (February 23–24, 2008), and we took the opportunity that afternoon to go in search of the tiny chapel where Charles Spurgeon was converted.

Graham insisted he knew where it was, having been there before. But it had been a while, and there was nothing in the area that alerted us to its presence. We passed several taverns where local soccer (they call it "football") fans were overheard debating the matches of the previous day.

Finally, Graham remembered. It was easy to miss. Set back from the street amidst rows of attached homes, the only clues as to the location of the chapel were a few small signs indicating the place at which Charles Haddon Spurgeon had been saved.

In one of the many magazines to which I subscribe there was recently an article describing, together with color photos, several of the larger and more innovative church buildings here in the United States. Trust me, Artillery Street Chapel in Colchester would never have qualified, then or now. There is still a very small congregation meeting there. Before Pastor Derek Hale arrived in 1991 it had three members. When he died of cancer in October 1999, the church had grown to eight. By 2006 the membership had grown to fourteen.

The chapel is quite small, perhaps capable of holding seventy-five people. There is nothing to distinguish it physically, but spiritually, well, that's another matter. As I walked in, I immediately noticed a large bronze plaque on the wall indicating the supposed spot where young Spurgeon had sat on January 6, 1850, although he never planned on being there.

Spurgeon had lived a few miles away in the village of Hythe. On that Sunday morning in 1850 he was intent on attending another service, desperate as he was to be rid of the guilt of sin that burdened his soul. "I sometimes think," wrote Spurgeon, that "I might have been in darkness and despair until now had it not been for the goodness of God in sending a snowstorm."[1] The unexpected shift in weather forced him to seek shelter in what was then a nondescript Primitive Methodist chapel where no more than a dozen people were in attendance.

Said Spurgeon, "I had heard of the Primitive Methodists, how they sang so loudly that they made people's heads ache; but that did not matter to me. I wanted to know how I might be saved, and if they could tell me that, I did not care how much they made my head ache."

The minister was not present, evidently snowed in. Finally, a thin-looking man went up into the pulpit to preach. "Now, it is well that preachers should be instructed, but this man was really stupid [Spurgeon's words, not mine!]. He was obliged to stick to his

text, for the simple reason that he had little else to say." The text he
selected was: "Look unto Me, and be ye saved, all the ends of the
earth." There was, Spurgeon thought, "a glimpse of hope for me in
that text." The "preacher" continued:

> Now lookin' don't take a deal of pain. It ain't liftin' your foot or your
> finger; it is just, "Look." Well, a man needn't go to College to learn
> to look. You may be the biggest fool, and yet you can look. A man
> needn't be worth a thousand a year to be able to look. Anyone can
> look; even a child can look. . . . Look unto Me; I am sweatin' great
> drops of blood. Look unto Me; I am hangin' on the cross. Look unto
> Me; I am dead and buried. Look unto Me; I rise again. Look unto
> Me; I ascend to Heaven. Look unto Me; I am sittin' at the Father's
> right hand. O poor sinner, look unto Me! Look unto Me!

After about ten minutes, "he was at the end of his tether," noted
Spurgeon. He recalled:

> Then he looked at me under the gallery [which, by the way, is still
> there but has long since been boarded up], and I daresay, with so few
> present, he knew me to be a stranger. Just fixing his eyes on me, as if
> he knew all my heart, he said, "Young man, you look very miserable."
> Well, I did, but I had not been accustomed to have remarks made
> from the pulpit on my personal appearance before. . . . He continued,
> "and you always will be miserable—miserable in life, and miserable
> in death—if you don't obey my text; but if you obey now, this mo-
> ment, you will be saved." . . . I saw at once the way of salvation. . . .
> Oh! I looked until I could almost have looked my eyes away. There
> and then the cloud was gone, the darkness had rolled away, and that
> moment I saw the sun; and I could have risen that instant, and sung
> with the most enthusiastic of them, of the precious blood of Christ,
> and the simple faith which looks alone to Him. Oh, that somebody
> had told me this before, "Trust Christ, and you shall be saved." Yet
> it was, no doubt, all wisely ordered, and now I can say—
>
> > E'er since by faith I saw the stream
> > Thy flowing wounds supply,
> > Redeeming love has been my theme,
> > And shall be till I die.

Who would have expected that life-giving, sin-cleansing, soul-redeeming grace could be found in that little chapel? Who would have expected that God might use the solemn words of an incredibly simple and stammering man?

Grace cares little of where it is needed. It simply goes and saves and delivers and sanctifies. God doesn't need a spacious sanctuary or multi-media technology or cutting-edge sound equipment. His grace is sovereign and not the least concerned about the surroundings in which it does its work.

Make no mistake about it. On that day the breath of God blew and a blizzard turned aside a searching young soul into an out-of-the-way chapel. That same breath confined a minister to his home and stirred an uneducated layman to ascend a pulpit. And that same, saving breath brought life to the dead, dry bones of a fifteen-year-old boy. And we are all the better for it. Spurgeon too.

Sam Storms
September 2008

Preface

First among Equals

Confidence, or assurance, most often comes in degrees, which is another way of saying that I'm not as certain about some things as I am about others. I say this only to point out that few things are more settled and assured in my soul than the immeasurable value and life-changing power of the written Word of God. That alone accounts for why I have written this series of meditations on the book of Psalms.

There is a measure of satisfaction that comes from reading and deciphering a John le Carré spy novel or, for some (not me), tracking with J. K. Rowling and the many exploits of Harry Potter. But the Word of God is unparalleled and unsurpassed in its capacity to enthrall, empower, and enlighten the mind concerning those truths on which I have built my life and staked my eternal destiny.

The psalmists themselves undoubtedly concur. On numerous occasions they affirm without hesitation the priceless and incomparable value of God's inspired Word. "In the way of your testimonies," wrote David, "I delight as much as in all riches" (Ps. 119:14). If that language isn't sufficiently exalted, he goes on to declare that "the law of your mouth is better to me than thousands of gold and silver pieces" (v. 72), and again, "I love your commandments above gold, above fine gold" (v. 127). The written rules and precepts of the Lord are more desirable "than gold, even much fine gold" (Ps. 19:10a). Or if you prefer an even more tangible image, David insists that God's words are "sweeter . . . than honey and drippings of the honeycomb" (v. 10b).

This is perhaps the principal reason why, if you were to ask a typical group of Christians what their favorite book of the Bible is, I suspect more than half would cite the Psalms. While happily confessing that all Scripture is inspired by God and profitable for our lives, there's something special about the Psalter that makes it the *first among equals* in the biblical canon.

Perhaps it's the fact that no one struggles to find the Psalms relevant. There is something here for everyone in whatever walk of life, however old or young one may be, regardless of circumstance, whether in triumph or trial, joy or sadness. Rarely will you hear someone say, after reading the Psalter, "I just can't identify with this. It doesn't speak to me where I am in life right now."

Among countless other characteristics of the Psalter, many would point to the fact that whereas most of Scripture speaks *to* us, the Psalms also speak *for* us. In the Psalms we find inspired examples of what we can and should and must say to God. They are a perpetual reminder that God welcomes our deepest desires, our most unnerving of fears, our anxiety and adoration, our celebration, and our confusion.

Some point to the passion of the psalmists, or their praise, or their brutal and sometimes painful honesty as they wrestle through the confusion and loss and disappointment that life so often casts our way. As Don Williams put it, "The full range of human emotions is displayed in these living prayers, without the hypocrisy and pretense so often characteristic of the modern church."[1]

The Psalter is also undeniably God-centered. When I asked my wife, Ann, what impressed her most about the Psalms and how she might put this in one simple statement, she replied, "Woe is me! Wow is Thee!" I couldn't agree more. Human beings in all their weakness and misery and sin are here confronted with the wonder and mercy and splendor of God.

Well, that's enough, lest I delay any longer your exploration of this marvelous collection of prayer, praise, and passion. I have kept these meditations brief. Each can be read in five to ten minutes. I encourage you to first read the biblical text itself, slowly meditate upon it, perhaps even memorize portions of it, and only then turn to my comments. I trust that in doing so you, too, will find God's words to be more precious than gold and sweeter than honey.

Psalms 1–19

from Book 1 of the Psalter

1

God's Prescription for Happiness

Psalm 1:1–3

Blessed is the man
    who walks not in the counsel of the wicked,
      nor stands in the way of sinners,
  nor sits in the seat of scoffers;
but his delight is in the law of the Lord,
    and on his law he meditates day and night.

He is like a tree
    planted by streams of water
that yields its fruit in its season,
    and its leaf does not wither.
In all that he does, he prospers.

—Psalm 1:1–3

In most instances I like to leave myself a little theological wiggle room, a loophole, if you will, a measure of flexibility that affords me the opportunity of qualifying some statement that I've made. In fact, it's often the failure to provide nuance and clarification to our declarations that gets us in trouble or boxes us in to a position that on more mature reflection clearly calls for less inflammatory language or more charity to those who might take a different stance.

I say this only to prepare you for something Jonathan Edwards declared in a remarkable sermon entitled, "Nothing upon Earth Can Represent the Glories of Heaven." It is utterly lacking in nuance. Its boldness is breathtaking and its ramifications are profound. And it provides a perfect introduction to our series of meditations on selected psalms. Said Edwards, "God created man for nothing else but happiness. He created him only that he might communicate happiness to him."[1]

Would you have preferred that he not say "nothing else" but happiness? Or would it have been easier to swallow had he chosen a word other than "only"? Well, that's Edwards for you.

I'm convinced that once we understand what Edwards meant by "happiness" and how our experience of it relates to the glory of God, objections will cease. By "happiness" Edwards didn't mean giddiness or frivolity or fame or fortune. Few of the things that constitute happiness for people today were in view when Edwards wrote and preached this sermon.

Let me define the term by appealing to what I wrote in chapter 1 of my book *One Thing*.[2]

When I speak of human happiness I'm not talking about physical comfort or a six-figure salary or emotional stability or the absence of conflict or sexual gratification or any such earthly or temporal achievement. That's not to say such things are inherently wrong. In their proper place they may well be expressions of divine benevolence. But we greatly err if they become foundational to human happiness. We should be grateful for them, but happiness is still within our grasp despite their absence.

The happiness for which we are eternally destined is a state of soul in which we experience and express optimum ecstasy in God. Happiness is the whole soul resting in God and rejoicing that so beautiful and glorious a Being is ours. Happiness, as John Piper says, is the privilege of being enabled by God's grace to enjoy making much of him forever. I'm talking about the ineffable and unending pleasure of blissful union with and the joyful celebration of Father, Son, and Holy Spirit. This is a joy of such transcendent quality that no persecution or pain or deprivation can diminish, nor wealth or success or prosperity can enhance. It's what Paul had in mind in Philippians 4:11 when he spoke of a satisfaction in Christ that was beyond the reach of either adversity or abundance.

In another of Edwards's sermons (actually, the first formal sermon he ever preached), he put it this way:

> The pleasures of loving and obeying, loving and adoring, blessing and praising the Infinite Being, the Best of Beings, the Eternal Jehovah; the pleasures of trusting in Jesus Christ, in contemplating his beauties, excellencies, and glories; in contemplating his love to mankind and to us, in contemplating his infinite goodness and astonishing loving-kindness; the pleasures of [the] communion of the Holy Ghost in conversing with God, the maker and governor of the world; the pleasure that results from the doing of our duty, in acting worthily and excellently; . . . these are the pleasures that are worthy of so noble a creature as a man is.[3]

I've gone to the trouble of making this point because I believe this is what the psalmist had in mind when he wrote of being "blessed" (Ps. 1:1a), a word that occurs twenty-six times in the Psalter. In fact, Psalm 1 begins with the word *blessed* and God's prescription for its attainment.

Believe it or not, happiness or blessedness *can* be found in something negative! There *is* joy in saying *no*. But to whom or what do we respond with a resolute *no*? According to the psalmist, it is to the counsel of the wicked (a reference to what we believe), the way of sinners (a reference to the way we behave), and the seat of scoffers (a reference to the place we belong).

The psalmist speaks of the "counsel" of the wicked, not of their "error" or "falsehood." "The wicked" are often careful to cast their system of thought and their advice for life in ways that initially appear wise and coherent. But there is a fundamental flaw in their thinking, and their values are warped. Happiness is contingent, therefore, on discernment.

Sinners have a "way" that, again, often appears clever and insightful on first glance. Rarely do the wicked exert an influence by taking on the overt barbarism of a Jeffrey Dahmer or a Saddam Hussein.

More often they are quietly pragmatic in their methods, morally slippery in their lifestyle, and cool rather than openly resistant toward any notion of biblical authority.

Yes, there are those who are more explicit and unashamed in their denial of the faith. These are the "scoffers," the "mockers," seen most recently in the brazen atheism of Richard Dawkins, author of *The God Delusion*; and Sam Harris, author of *The End of Faith* and *Letter to a Christian Nation*.

The psalmist is not suggesting that we cease to engage "the wicked" in dialogue, far less that we decline to pray for their conversion. But beware of too close association with such folk. Be wary of lingering long in their presence. Don't be a party to their parties.

But simply saying *no* to the ways of this world is only half the prescription for happiness, and not even the better half. When our *no* stands alone and isolated, our resolve to rejoice in God will gradually erode under the incessant force of temptation and trial. God's prescription for our happiness, to his glory, is dependent on a *yes* to the beauty and splendor of his Word.

We can't afford to stop with detesting the ways of the world. We must "delight" in the "law of the Lord"! Refusing to eat the food of folly and wickedness will not in itself fill our spiritual bellies. We need the meat of God's Word, the balanced diet of the whole counsel of God. That feast awaits us in the next meditation.

2

Read to Rejoice

Psalm 1:1–3

Blessed is the man
    who walks not in the counsel of the wicked,
    nor stands in the way of sinners,
nor sits in the seat of scoffers;
but his delight is in the law of the LORD,
    and on his law he meditates day and night.
He is like a tree
    planted by streams of water
that yields its fruit in its season,
    and its leaf does not wither.
In all that he does, he prospers.

While in England in February 2007, I had the privilege of speaking yet again at the Life in the Spirit conference. During one of the messages given by fellow speaker Dave Smith, he made passing reference to my book *Pleasures Evermore*, and articulated in a most refreshing and poignant way its principal theme. "When it comes to living a successful Christian life," said Dave, "and resisting the power of temptation, simply saying 'No! No! No!' won't suffice. We must learn to say 'Oh! Oh! Oh!'"

I like that. His point was that, by itself, *fear* has limited capacity to deter our hearts from sin. To it must be added *fascination*. *Resisting* is empowered by *rejoicing*. By all means detest the ugly and revolting and destructive elements in life. But by what means? Delight!

Make no mistake: we need to be warned. But we must first be wooed. Fear drives us, but fascination draws us. The psalmist's strategy for blessedness is not mere avoidance but allurement.

I don't want you to miss this, so look again at Psalm 1:1–3. Delight, not mere duty, should characterize our study of God's Word. Reading the law of God is for the purpose of rejoicing in what is read.

This is a stretch for many Christians. They've grown up thinking and being taught that there is an inescapable tension, if not contradiction, between pleasure and principles, between rejoicing and rules. It comes as nothing short of a jolt to read of *delighting* in the *law* of God. God's law, or revealed instruction, has often been viewed as oppressive, restrictive, and burdensome, hardly the sort of thing to evoke joy or excitement.

This will always be the case until we understand the motive of the Lawgiver. What did God have in mind when he put his Word in the mouth of his prophets? To what did God *aspire* when he moved to *inspire* the biblical authors? Did he take note of what brings greatest joy to the human heart and then stir Moses, for example, to say *no*? Off limits! Out of bounds!

Would it surprise you to discover that God's primary agenda in the giving of his law is your optimal and most durable delight? God's strategy in disclosing his will and ways, whether in the form of rules, prohibitions, commandments, or exhortations isn't to muzzle human joy but to maximize it.

The precepts and principles of his Word, even those in the Pentateuch, which is probably what the psalmist had in mind with his use of the word "law," are designed to guard us from anything that might dull our spiritual senses and thus inhibit us from seeing and savoring the sweetness of God's glory. In other words, when God prohibits or prescribes, dictates or directs, it is always with a view to enhancing our highest and most satisfying enjoyment of him.

God wants nothing more than to heighten and sharpen our sensible awareness of his revelation of himself. And he knows what we don't, namely, that sin anesthetizes our souls and renders us dull and numb to his presence. Every commandment in Scripture, every precept, every prohibition or principle is lovingly designed to lead us away from what otherwise might spoil our appetite for God.

Is it unsettling for you to hear the words of the psalmist: "How sweet are your words to my taste, sweeter than honey to my mouth" (Ps. 119:103)? Sweet, not sour. God's words taste good! If there is any initial pain in embracing the dictates of God's law, do so with a view to interminable pleasure. Whatever short-term sacrifice one makes must always be with a view to the increase and intensification of long-term, indeed eternal and heavenly, reward.

Be it noted that the psalmist is far from advocating a study of the biblical text as an end in itself. We delight in the law of the Lord because *that is how we get God*. We do not worship pen or parchment. Ink on a page is not our aim but the God who inspired it. We read *it* because it tells us of *him*. We study *words* because they show us the *Word*. When we read the stories and hear the poetry and tremble at his truth, the Spirit awakens us to the beauty of their author and deepens our experience of his love and kindness and power and goodness.

But merely possessing the Word of God accomplishes nothing. We must meditate upon it, not momentarily or fitfully, but day and night. The point is, according to Jonathan Edwards, that we must "endeavor to increase spiritual appetites by meditating on spiritual objects."[4] When we surrender our minds to base and sordid things their grip on our lives is intensified. There's no way to decrease our affinity for sinful pleasure apart from a concentrated fixation on the spiritually sublime.

God's Word is a powerful and life-giving antidote to the spiritual infection caused by sin. But merely affirming that to be true heals no one. More is needed than merely defending God's Word as worthy of our affection. We must actually "think" (Phil. 4:8) about it, ponder it, pore over it, and become vulnerable to the power God has invested in his revelation to transform our values and feelings and to energize our wills.

We must "store up" or "treasure" God's Word in our hearts if it is to exert its power in keeping us from sin (Ps. 119:11). When this happens the Holy Spirit enables our souls to believe and behave in conformity with its dictates.

A passing glance at God's Word will hardly suffice. Day-and-night meditation is called for. We meditate when we slowly read, prayerfully imbibe, and humbly rely upon what God has revealed to us in the Scriptures. Meditation, then, is being attentive to God through conscious, continuous engagement of the mind with his revealed Word.

The psalmist has narrowed our options to two. Either we find satisfaction in the truth of God's law, trusting the power of his Word to make known his person, or we heed the counsel of the wicked and walk in their ways. The former yields a fruitful, enduring, and prosperous life (vv. 2–3). The latter suffers the fate of chaff that is blown in the wind (vv. 4–6).

3

The Lifter of My Head

Psalm 3:3

> But you, O Lᴏʀᴅ, are a shield about me,
> my glory, and the lifter of my head.
> —Psalm 3:3

Absalom was David's third son. His second son, Chileab, is never mentioned after reference to his birth, and the assumption is that he died early on. David's firstborn son was Amnon. The story of how Amnon died is a sordid one.

Amnon raped his half-sister, Tamar, and Absalom, Tamar's brother, swore revenge. It took two years but finally Absalom arranged for Amnon to be killed. Fearing punishment, Absalom went into exile for three years. When he finally returned to Jerusalem, David refused to see him. Two more years passed before David and his son were reunited, although even then they weren't reconciled.

Absalom's plot to take the throne from his father probably emerged gradually. He began by currying favor with the people (2 Sam. 15:1–6). He portrayed himself as one who was interested in people by telling them he was far more capable of helping them with their troubles and securing justice for their complaints than was David. According to 2 Samuel 15:6, "Absalom stole the hearts of the men of Israel."

Once Absalom felt secure in his position, he made his move. He went to Hebron, assembled his followers, and had himself anointed king (2 Sam. 15:7–12). With a considerable army behind him, he marched against his father in Jerusalem and forced David to flee (2 Sam. 15:13–17). Following a shameful period of absence from his throne, the armies of David eventually prevailed. Absalom was killed, contrary to his father's express wishes, serving only to intensify the latter's pain.

What an amazing scene: David, driven from his throne, subjected to indescribable humiliation, not by a pagan Gentile king but *by his own son!* Absalom's treachery and rebellion must have crushed David's heart. Here is the important point: it was while David was fleeing the armies of Absalom, broken by the spiteful betrayal of his own child, that he sat down and wrote the words of Psalm 3.

It wasn't while he sat on a golden throne with servants at his beck and call. It wasn't while lying on satin sheets and a soft pillow knowing that all was well with his family and among his people. Rather, it was in the midst of his most devastating and desperate hour that he penned these remarkable words:

> O Lord, how many are my foes!
>   Many are rising against me;
> many are saying of my soul,
>   there is no salvation for him in God. *Selah.*
>
> But you, O Lord, are a shield about me,
>   my glory, and the lifter of my head. (Ps. 3:1–3)

David's anguish was no doubt magnified by the fact that his adversaries were primarily from among his own people. Those once closest to him, those in whom he had once placed his confidence and trust, are now among those whose accusations are most bitter and hateful.

One of the primary tactics of such enemies is to undermine our faith in God to help us. David may well have been taunted with statements like: "If God is so good and so great, how come *we've* got the upper hand? How come *you're* on the run, David? Where is your God now, when you need him most?"

Perhaps they began to throw David's sin back in his face: his relationship with Bathsheba, the murder of Uriah, and his failure as a father to Amnon and Absalom. "God's not going to put up with that sort of thing, David. He's abandoned you for sure!" Charles Spurgeon was right:

> If all the trials which come from heaven, all the temptations which ascend from hell, and all the crosses which arise from earth, could be mixed and pressed together, they would not make a trial so terrible as that which is contained in this verse (v. 2). It is the most bitter of all afflictions *to be led to fear that there is no help for us in God.*[5]

Yet, in the midst of such affliction, accusation, and abandonment, David's cry is for the "LORD," YHWH, the covenant-keeping God (v. 1). David obviously knew that the hypnotic and paralyzing power of the enemy is broken only by turning one's gaze back to God (Deut. 1:28–30). So he encourages himself by recalling three things about God.

First, God is a *shield* about him (see Pss. 18:2, 30; 28:7; 33:20; 84:11; 91:4; 115:9–11). But the fact that God is a shield does not prevent one's enemies from continuing to shoot their arrows. Yet such an attack is fruitless in cutting us off from the security of God's love. Said Tozer:

> What we need very badly these days is a company of Christians who are prepared to trust God as completely now as they know they must do at the last day. For each of us the time is coming when we shall have nothing but God. Health and wealth and friends and hiding places will be swept away and we shall have only God. To the man of pseudo faith that is a terrifying thought, but to real faith it is one of the most comforting thoughts the heart can entertain.[6]

Second, God is his *glory*. This could mean that David awaits God's vindication. He has been driven away in shame, humiliation, and weakness, his pride broken and his reputation slandered. Still, though, he's confident that God will restore his dignity and honor as king. Or it could be his way of saying, "I have no glory of my own. I put no trust in my fame or fortune. You alone, O God, are the joy, boast, and glory of my life."

Third, God is the one who *lifts his head*. David left Jerusalem not only defeated but dejected, despondent, depressed. He hung his head in shame (see 2 Sam. 15:30). But he is confident that God will elevate his face and restore his hope.

When people are shy or unsure of themselves, perhaps due to some insecurity or recent failure, they rarely look up or make eye contact with you. Their aim is to pass by without being noticed. They hug the wall lest a personal encounter expose their shame. Their deep feelings of inadequacy lead to withdrawal and silence. The last thing they want is to see or be seen. Fixing their eyes on the floor is safety for their soul. Embarrassment always expresses itself in a physical posture that is guarded and cautious.

David was probably having doubts about himself—about the validity of his calling, about his capacity to rule, about his worth as a man. Absalom's treachery inflicted a depth of humiliation the human soul was never built to endure. It was emotionally crippling and threatened to destroy David's credibility and his confidence as a man after God's own heart.

Some of you know exactly how David felt. In your case it may have been a stinging defeat, an embarrassing failure, or perhaps a public humiliation that you fear has forever destroyed your usefulness or your value to God or a place in his purposes. It's a devastating feeling. The enemy will often exploit the opportunity by reminding you of virtually every sin you've committed, reinforcing the painful conviction that you are now beyond recovery, hopelessly helpless, a stain on the public face of the church.

It might even be the rebellion of a child, as in the case of David. For some it's the demise of a business venture into which you poured every ounce of energy and income. Or it might be something less catastrophic, but no less painful, such as a failed attempt at public ministry or an embarrassing misstep that left you feeling exposed and unprotected.

In David's case, despite this crushing blow at the hands of his son, his faith in God never wavered, or at least not so as to throw him into utter despair. There was always and only One who was able to restore his strength and straighten his body and give him reason to hold his head high.

This isn't arrogance or presumption or fleshly defiance but humble, wholehearted assurance that God can do for us what we can't do for ourselves. People often say, "I just can't bear to look anyone in the face after this." But God will make you able! He is the Lord who "makes poor and makes rich; he brings low and he exalts. He raises up the poor from the dust; he lifts the needy from the ash heap to make them sit with princes and inherit a seat of honor" (1 Sam. 2:7–8).

Yes, indeed, said David, "he will hide me in his shelter in the day of trouble; he will conceal me under the cover of his tent; he will lift me high upon a rock. *And now my head shall be lifted up above my enemies all around me*, and I will offer in his tent sacrifices with shouts of joy; I will sing and make melody to the Lord" (Ps. 27:5–6).

Finally, it's important to remember that, notwithstanding David's faith, Absalom died rebellious and estranged from his father. "O my son Absalom, my son, my son Absalom! Would I had died instead of you, O Absalom, my son, my son" (2 Sam. 18:33). Sometimes our circumstances don't turn out for the better. But no matter what transpires, of this you may be sure: God is a shield about you. He is your glory. He is the one who will lift your head.

4

More Joy

Psalm 4:7

You have put more joy in my heart
than they have when their grain and wine abound.

—Psalm 4:7

The message trumpeted by the world, the flesh, and the devil is relatively simple. It's often packaged in different shapes and sounds, but the underlying theme is monotonously the same. Like a reverberating echo in an empty cave, the refrain is incessant, unending, and unchanging: "There is more joy in illicit sex than in Jesus. There is more joy in goodies and gold than in Jesus. There is more joy in power, pride, and a drug-induced high than in Jesus. There is more joy in looking fit and feeling good and in the latest fashion than in Jesus."

I fear for my grandchildren. Not because I lack faith in God or suffer from paranoia. I'll briefly explain. When my two grandsons, Joseph and John, were three-and-a-half years old and two years old, respectively, my wife and I took them to the mall to ride the train. Directly across from it, next to the merry-go-round, was Victoria's Secret, the display case filled with near-naked mannequins clothed only in sexually seductive lingerie.

I commented to Ann that it wasn't until high school that I was confronted with images like that, and even then one had to buy a magazine in a seedy shop or sneak under-aged into an R-rated movie. The sixties weren't especially spiritual, but at least television, billboards, and the shopping mall were relatively safe. Yet here were my two precious grandsons, already exposed to the underbelly of human depravity.

As we somberly walked out, store after store, sign after sign, song after song perpetuated the refrain: "Buy me. Taste mine. Eat this. Drink ours. Smell like us. Wear these clothes. Wear *no* clothes. Drive this car. Bet on that. Look like her." I fear for my grandchildren.

I suppose the next time we could tell them the train is broken. Or we could shield their eyes, or look for another playground with less seductive surroundings. Maybe we will. But I'm not sure that's going to work. It may not even be possible—do places like that still exist? So what's the solution? Is there one?

I do have a strategy, and it's as relatively simple and straightforward as the destructive message it's designed to counter. It doesn't call for isolation, withdrawal, or the wearing of blinders. I plan on challenging the claim. I intend to confront it and confute it. Contrary to what the world may say, there is more joy in Jesus than all fleshly pleasures combined!

My aim as a father, preacher, teacher, author, and now grandfather is to hammer home with unrelenting zeal that the joys of knowing Jesus are simply incomparable. His capacity to please knows no rival. We must preach from our pulpits and model in our lives and fill our prayers and labor and suffer and sacrifice greatly to make this truth known: in the presence of our great God and Savior there is joy that is full, not partial, half-baked, measured, or parceled out; at his right hand there are eternal pleasures, not the fleeting, transient, toxic sort that promise so much and deliver so little (Ps. 16:11).

David, king of Israel and inspired psalmist, was unapologetically relentless in his effort to drive home this truth. Surrounded by those who loved "vain words" and sought "after lies" (Ps. 4:2b), he uttered one prayer for himself and his people: "Lift up the light of your face upon us, O LORD!" (Ps. 4:6). Again, "May God be gracious to us and bless us and make his face to shine upon us" (Ps. 67:1; cf. Num. 6:24–26).

On the other hand, when "you hid your face; I was dismayed" (Ps. 30:7). Even the animals of the earth know this devastation: "When you hide your face, they are dismayed; when you take away their breath, they die and return to their dust" (Ps. 104:29).

When the crowd clamored for satisfaction and demanded to know, "Who will show us some good?" (Ps. 4:6a), David fixed his gaze on the precious presence of Yahweh, whose glorious visage *alone* he longed to behold, whose life-changing power and sin-forgiving grace and covenant-keeping love *alone* can satisfy the human soul. The single, simple driving force in his battle with unbelief, temptation, and the magnetic allure of the world, the flesh, and the devil was this: "You have put *more joy* in my heart than they have when their grain and wine abound" (Ps. 4:7).

Grain and wine are good gifts of God, not to be belittled. Be grateful for them. But don't trust them! We must never despise the blessings God bestows, whether financial, physical, or political. We must guard against believing the marketing lie that more grain and increased profits and sweet wine and your neighbor's car and a computer with more memory can deliver *more joy* than Jesus can.

David envisions a time when the harvest is bountiful. Crops are abundant and the future looks good. The wine is flowing and the supply is endless. Bellies are full. Our enemies are at bay. The bank account is expanding. Our mouths savor the sweetness of the fruit of the vine. Life feels good! It seems to be working.

But there is *more joy* in the goodness and greatness of God. There is *more joy* in the promise of eternal reward than in the presence of earthly riches. Spurgeon was right: "Christ in the heart is better than corn in the barn, or wine in the vat."[7]

Is it not the case that all temptation finds its strength in our refusal to believe that one simple truth? Is it not the case that all sin, in one way or another, consists of a refusal to trust God's promise of *more joy* than what the world, the flesh, and the devil offer us?

David wasn't the only Israelite to grasp this truth. Consider Moses. Faced with the almost irresistible offer of indescribable wealth, power, and prestige—what the author of Hebrews calls "the treasures of

Egypt" (Heb. 11:26)—he said *no*. He embraced "mistreatment" (11:25) rather than the joy that comes with "the fleeting pleasures of sin" (11:25).

Why? For heaven's sake, Moses, why? Because "he considered the reproach of Christ [to be] greater wealth [read, more joy]" than anything Egypt might offer, for "he was looking to the reward" (Heb. 11:26).

As I think about the future and the world in which my grandchildren will live, I have only one hope. *They* have only one hope: knowing and believing the promise that in God's presence, not in abundant grain, is "fullness of joy"; trusting and living in the assurance that in Christ alone, not in rivers of sweet wine, are "pleasures" that never end (Ps. 16:11).

5

What Makes God Smile?

Psalm 5

Give ear to my words, O LORD;
    consider my groaning.
Give attention to the sound of my cry,
    my King and my God,
    for to you do I pray.
                  —Psalm 5:1–2

Listen to Solomon's words in Proverbs 15:8: "The sacrifice of the wicked is an abomination to the LORD, but the prayer of the upright is acceptable to him" or "is His delight" (NASB).

Although God is spirit, if he had a face he would display one of two looks when people pray. This text suggests that God frowns in disgust when the wicked hypocritically try to manipulate him with their sacrifices. But he has a beaming, glowing smile of indescribable delight whenever his children pray.

Why? It certainly isn't because he learns something from them of which he had been previously unaware. Rather, God smiles when we pray because the God of the Bible

is the kind of God who delights most deeply not in making demands
but in meeting needs. Prayer is his delight because prayer shows the

38

reaches of our poverty and the riches of his grace. Prayer is that wonderful transaction where the wealth of God's glory is magnified and the wants of our soul are satisfied.[8]

When we pray, what do we offer God? Nothing but our need. And that is what makes him happy, because it provides him with an opportunity to demonstrate the infinite resources of the riches of his grace. God issues this invitation: "Call upon me in the day of trouble [i.e., pray to me, cry for help]; I will deliver you, and you shall glorify me" (Ps. 50:15).

Let's look at some of the characteristics of David's prayer life as found in Psalm 5. There are ten things worthy of note.

1) *He prays* (vv. 1–3). I doubt if anything was as instinctive to David as prayer. Whether in turmoil or triumph, whether in pain or prosperity, the orientation of his soul was always vertical. Nothing was off-limits or too trivial. Nothing was beyond the power of God or a matter of indifference to him. When one knows God as David did, prayer will always be the first, middle, and last thing we do.

2) *He prays aloud* (v. 1). If possible, it is always best to speak your prayers. It helps give both substance and shape to your requests and helps keep your mind from wandering.

3) *He prays silently* (v. 1). Sometimes it isn't possible to formulate your feelings into words. His "groaning" or "sighing" (NIV) reveals that David asks God to hear both his spoken requests and his silent ones. He has in mind inarticulate efforts to vocalize a situation, sadness, fears, confusion, etc. They are silent words uttered inwardly (cf. Rom. 8:26–27; 1 Sam. 1:13). These are the whispers, sighs, unuttered longings, and silent meditations of his heart. As Spurgeon said, "Words are not the essence but the garments of prayer."[9]

4) *He prays passionately* (v. 2). "Give attention to the sound of my cry" for help. Sometimes we speak, at other times we sigh, but on occasion all we can muster is a half-muted cry. Whatever the shape or sound of our appeal to the Father, he hears.

5) *He prays confidently* (v. 2). He prays to "my King and my God." David is no alien or enemy of God. Though God is transcendent and lofty, high and lifted up, infinite in every way, he is still *my* God, says David. He is the king, ruler, potentate of all, president,

premier, supreme leader, and Lord, but he is still *my* King. David is confident of a personal, intimate relation with the God and King of the universe.

6) *He prays habitually* (v. 3). "In the morning you hear my voice; in the morning I prepare a sacrifice for you and watch." Thus prayer, wrote Spurgeon, "should be the key of the day and the lock of the night."[10]

7) *He prays with a purpose* (v. 3). The NASB renders this, "I will *order* my prayer" (v. 3; cf. Pss. 23:5; 50:21). This word is used elsewhere of preparing a legal brief as well as preparing the sacrifice for the altar. In other words, he thinks about what he wants to say before he says it. He has a clear idea, a plan, a well-prepared agenda that he brings before God. He prays purposefully.

8) *He prays expectantly* (v. 3). After praying, he "eagerly watches" (NASB; cf. Ps. 4:3; Mic. 7:7; and Hab. 2:1).

Do we not forget to watch the result of our supplications? We are like the ostrich, which lays her eggs and looks not for her young. We sow the seed, and are too idle to seek harvest. How can we expect the Lord to open the windows of his grace, and pour us out a blessing, if we will not open the windows of expectation and look up for the promised favor?[11]

Too often we pray and then give up if the answer is not immediately forthcoming. Our expectancy is killed. Consider the approach of George Muller:

I am now, in 1864, waiting upon God for certain blessings, for which I have daily besought Him for 19 years and 6 months, without one day's intermission. Still the full answer is not yet given concerning the conversion of certain individuals.[12]

He refers to others for whom he has prayed anywhere from one to ten years, and says,

Yet I am daily continuing in prayer and expecting the answer. . . . Be encouraged, dear Christian friend, with fresh earnestness to give yourself to prayer, if you can only be sure that you ask for things which are for the glory of God.[13]

9) *He prays for justice* (vv. 4–6, 9–10). Many would prefer to ignore the words "you [God] hate all evildoers" (v. 5b), as well as David's plea for God to "make them bear their guilt," and that God "let them fall by their own counsels," and that they be cast out "because of the abundance of their transgressions" (v. 10). For us, *hate* is an evil desire for personal revenge that is the fruit of malice, vindictiveness, spite, bitterness, resentment, jealousy, or self-centeredness. For God, *hate* is a righteous opposition to anything that is an affront to holiness. It is God's holy displeasure for sins committed and a holy determination to punish.

Notice also that although David calls for divine justice, he does not presume to stand in God's presence because of personal merit. He acknowledges that he is equally deserving of divine wrath and that it is only God's "steadfast love" (v. 7) that accounts for his salvation.

10) *He prays with joy* (vv. 11–12). "But let all who take refuge in you rejoice; let them ever sing for joy, and spread your protection over them, that those who love your name may exult in you. For you bless the righteous, O LORD; you cover him with favor as with a shield."

Don't believe the lie that how you feel doesn't matter. We must rejoice when taking refuge in God. Singing alone won't suffice. We must sing for joy! Loving God is good, but exulting in him is even better.

It's a win-win. When we pray like this, God delivers us and we honor him (cf. Ps. 50:15).

6

Enough!

Psalm 10

In arrogance the wicked hotly pursue the poor;
    let them be caught in the schemes that they have
        devised.
For the wicked boasts of the desires of his soul,
    and the one greedy for gain curses and renounces the
        LORD.
In the pride of his face the wicked does not seek him;
    all his thoughts are, "There is no God."
His ways prosper at all times;
    your judgments are on high, out of his sight;
    as for all his foes, he puffs at them.
He says in his heart, "I shall not be moved;
    throughout all generations I shall not meet adversity."
His mouth is filled with cursing and deceit and
        oppression;
    under his tongue are mischief and iniquity.
He sits in ambush in the villages;
    in hiding places he murders the innocent.
His eyes stealthily watch for the helpless;
    he lurks in ambush like a lion in his thicket;
he lurks that he may seize the poor;
    he seizes the poor when he draws him into his net.
The helpless are crushed, sink down,
    and fall by his might.

He says in his heart, "God has forgotten,
he has hidden his face, he will never see it."
—Psalm 10:2–11

It's difficult to live in a world of corruption, abuse, and mindless cruelty and not experience a recurring spiritual nausea. When one witnesses senseless injustice and the prosperity of those responsible for it, nausea turns to indignation and righteous rage.

I know a little of what the psalmist meant when he cried out, "How long, O Lord, how long?" (see Psalm 13). Sometimes the question "How long?" doesn't spring from a speculative curiosity that says, "I want to know *when*," but from an agitated conscience and a sense of moral outrage. "People who feel this way," observes Ron Allen, "want to know when the Lord will return because they cannot abide wickedness abounding, not because they want to pinpoint a date in a chart."[14]

This is the mood of Psalm 10. "Why, O LORD, do you stand far away? Why do you hide yourself in times of trouble?" (v. 1). The psalmist's *why?* isn't because of some personal harm that has come to him. It's not "Why did this happen to me?" but rather "Why would God allow such things to occur and do nothing, if indeed he is the King of all the earth?"

The question eating away at his soul is, "Why do you seem so remote, Lord, when evil is so near? Why do you seem indifferent to the oppression of the righteous by the wicked? Why do those who hate you prosper and those who love you suffer? Why do the unrighteous and unbelieving get along so well, often at the expense of your children?"

Why does God seem absent and far off and concealed from us at those times when he is needed most? Why? The psalmist's anguish is not because there is evil and corruption and oppression but because God seems to ignore it, having withdrawn his gracious presence.

It's not a pleasant scene, but we need to take note of the ways of the wicked revealed in Psalm 10:2–11. There are wicked people, and then there are *wicked* people. Here we read of the latter, those "whose wickedness is boundless, whose conscience is seared, whose humanity is beastly."[15] This is the person who's so convinced that

43

divine judgment is a myth that he doesn't even bother to hide his desires and evil intentions. He worships his own lusts. It's one thing to be a sinner; it's another to be proud of it, and still worse to indulge your sinful desires as if to worship them. This person boasts of that which ought to be his shame.

If this individual ever thinks of God, it's with contempt and disdain (v. 4b). He doesn't deny that God exists. He's just convinced that God is either unwilling or unable to judge. In other words, to this person's way of thinking, God is simply irrelevant.

This man believes he has total immunity from divine justice. He interprets divine longsuffering as divine indifference. As far as he's concerned, judgment delayed is judgment denied. If God hasn't done anything about it by now, he never will. He says, "God is too far away, too distant, to take note of what we do here on earth. He doesn't see it. Even if he sees it, he doesn't care. Even if he cares, he can't do anything about it. There's no requital, no recompense." Or so he believes. "There's no pay-off; no bottom line." So he lives in the most morally cavalier manner imaginable.

I call this sort of person a *practical atheist*. He knows God exists, but he lives as if he doesn't. True atheists, if there are any, aren't necessarily morally dangerous. Often they live civil, decent lives. Practical atheists, on the other hand, are a real threat. It isn't the absence of God that drives them but the absence of any sense or recognition of justice and morality. Anything goes. There are no rules because there is no retribution.

The problem is that often such people seem to have the upper hand. It seems at times as if they are right: justice doesn't exist, morality doesn't matter. This creates a strong temptation to jettison our faith and join them. After all, "what good [are] a belief and a moral life which appear to be so out of place in the harsh realities of an evil world? Indeed, would there not be a certain wisdom in the oppressed joining ranks with the oppressors?"[16] The temptation is to say: "If there is so much evil, it must mean there is no God."

But note well: if there is no God, there is no such thing as evil. If there is no God, there is no criterion or standard by which anything can be morally evaluated. You might have preferences, opinions, likes, and dislikes, but without an eternal and absolute God you have no basis for saying, "This is good and that is bad." Evil is evil for only one reason: it is the antithesis of God who is good. Without God, evil may well be good. Carson explains:

> The dimensions of evil are thus established by the dimensions of God; the ugliness of evil is established by the beauty of God; the filth of evil is established by the purity of God; the selfishness of evil is established by the love of God.[17]

Another temptation that is stirred by the evil around us is: "Okay, there is a God and he is good, but he's just too weak to help," contrary to the consistent witness of Scripture that testifies repeatedly of his omnipotence. Also, if it were true, we would have no assurance how the world will turn out. Odds are that evil might just as easily triumph as good.

Finally, if true, we would have no assurance that this God can help us or comfort us. "He may be able to give us quite a bit of sympathy, and even groan along with us; but he clearly cannot *help* us—not now, and not in the future. There is no point praying to such a god and asking for his help. He is already doing the best he can, poor chap, but he has reached the end of his resources."[18]

The psalmist has had enough. He's tired of hiding in his foxhole. So he emerges in verses 12 to 18 with an ancient battle cry on his lips: "Arise O God!" (cf. Num. 10:35). Read it with me:

> Arise, O LORD; O God, lift up your hand;
>   forget not the afflicted.
> Why does the wicked renounce God
>   and say in his heart, "You will not call to account"?
> But you do see, for you note mischief and vexation,
>   that you may take it into your hands;
> to you the helpless commits himself;
>   you have been the helper of the fatherless.
> Break the arm of the wicked and evildoer;
>   call his wickedness to account till you find none.
>
> The LORD is king forever and ever;
>   the nations perish from his land.

O LORD, you hear the desire of the afflicted;
>   you will strengthen their heart; you will incline your ear
> to do justice to the fatherless and the oppressed,
>   so that man who is of the earth may strike terror no
>   more.

Contrary to the presumptuous conclusion of the wicked, the psalmist knows that God does see all (v. 14a); he is not distant; eventually he will act. He prays that justice would be exacted until not a single deed of wrong remains undetected and unpunished (v. 15). Ultimately, nothing will be concealed from God.

With confidence he declares that, notwithstanding what we see and hear, God *is* King. The day is coming when the wicked will be no more, when evil men will terrify the righteous no longer. It may not be today but certainly some day. If we are not prepared to take the long view of things and evaluate the present in the light of God's promise concerning the future, we will succumb to the temptation and give in to the ways of the wicked.

So why *does* God wait? Why is justice delayed? In the first place, and as strange as it may sound, God's delay is not a sign of indifference, but kindness. His reluctance to judge quickly provides an extended opportunity for the wicked to repent (see Rom. 2:4).

Furthermore, God is delaying judgment so that the cup of the wicked might be filled to overflowing, so that there might be no question about the justice of their punishment when it finally does come (see Rom. 2:5–6).

Finally, God's judgment is delayed until the fullness of God's family comes in. God delays the return of his Son not because he has overlooked the wicked but because he still has his elect to save (2 Pet. 3:9). When the chosen of God have all come in, justice will prevail.

In the meantime, we live with injustice, cruelty, oppression, the prosperity of the wicked, and the suffering of the righteous. But one day "the Lord himself will descend from heaven with a cry of command, with the voice of an archangel" (1 Thess. 4:16a). What will he shout? What will he say? "Enough!" Enough sin, enough abuse, enough injustice, enough oppression, enough of the wicked. Enough!

7

How Long, O Lord? Part 1

Psalm 13

How long, O LORD? Will you forget me forever?
　　How long will you hide your face from me?
How long must I take counsel in my soul
　　and have sorrow in my heart all the day?
How long shall my enemy be exalted over me?

Consider and answer me, O LORD my God;
　　light up my eyes, lest I sleep the sleep of death,
lest my enemy say, "I have prevailed over him,"
　　lest my foes rejoice because I am shaken.
　　　　　　　　　　　　　　　　—Psalm 13:1–4

Depression is an ugly word and difficult to define. We've all
faced it, some worse than others. Even if we don't understand it, we know what it feels like. The confidence that
God is behind you has vanished. The courage to face anything life
might throw in your path has given way to the horrifying suspicion
that God has forgotten who and where you are.

Where is he now when you need him most? Where is he when your
life is enveloped in darkness and you can't find the light switch?

David was no stranger to depression. Listen to his anguished cry. Perhaps you may find in him a soulmate.

Although it's painful to read of someone suffering like this, I'm also encouraged by it. It tells me that the Bible is going to deal with me where I live, that I don't have to pretend everything is okay when it's not. I find hope in the fact that "there is no attempt in Scripture to whitewash the anguish of God's people when they undergo suffering. They argue with God, they complain to God, they weep before God. Theirs is not a faith that leads to dry-eyed stoicism, but a faith so robust it wrestles with God."[19]

Is life a bother for you right now? Is it a burden? Is there an ache in your soul that won't go away? When you look up do you see hovering overhead that same depressing dark cloud that dogged your every step yesterday, and the day before, and the day before that? Has it gotten to the point that when someone like me comes along and says, "God loves you," your first instinct is to punch 'em right in the nose?

"God loves me? You've got to be kidding! If he loves me so much, why won't this pain go away? If he loves me like you say, why am I all alone? He couldn't care less! And here I am, trying to believe, and all my enemies make fun of my faith in a God who seems to have forgotten where he left me!"

Sound familiar, perhaps painfully familiar? What are we supposed to do when God and his love seem hidden and we're left all alone? David has some words of insight and encouragement.

Four times he cries out, "How long, O LORD?" *Four times!* Don't just read the words; listen to the confusion behind them: "O Lord, will it *ever* end?"

It's important to note that David's feeling of abandonment is not related to some sin he's committed. We read of no confession, no contrition, no acknowledgment of personal guilt, no repentance that might shed some light on why God's blessings are missing. This isn't to say David was perfect. But at least in this case the cause for his turmoil must be traced to something other than overt transgression.

As with David, there are going to be down times in your life that are unrelated to specific acts of sin. Unfortunately, this makes it even more difficult to handle. If you had sinned you could understand and live with God's absence, knowing you deserved to be chastised. But when God seems to disappear for no apparent reason, the perplexity is unbearable.

David feels as if God has forgotten him. Has he? "Can the God of knowledge have a memory block? Can the only wise God be absent-minded? Is it possible that the Omniscient can forget, even for a moment, one of His children?"[20]

David is convinced he can. David is convinced he has! And he's frightened that God's forgetfulness might last forever.

But this was David's mistake. We must never permit our feelings to be the standard by which we measure biblical fact. God had most certainly *not* forgotten him, nor has he forgotten you.

Can God misplace one of his own children? Can God get so busy running the world and keeping the stars in space that he fails to remember our pain and our need? In all the complexities of life and the bustle of each day, can a Christian slip God's mind?

David sure thought so. He felt as though God had hidden his face from him. Since the "shining" or "showing" of God's face signifies blessing and favor (cf. Num. 6:24–26; Pss. 4:6; 31:16; 67:1; 80:3), for it to be "hidden" is to suffer his withdrawal.

A few years back a friend of mine had been rudely and unjustly dismissed from the pastorate of his church. Several families left the church with him and began a new ministry in the same town. He was describing to me how badly it hurt when so many of his former flock went out of their way to avoid contact with him. "For months," he said, "they wouldn't even look me in the face."

That's exactly how David feels. But in his case, it's worse. Here it is *God* who David believes has turned his face away. "You have said, 'Seek my face.' My heart says to you, 'Your face, LORD, do I seek.' Hide not your face from me. Turn not your servant away in anger, O you who have been my help. Cast me not off; forsake me not, O God of my salvation!" (Ps. 27:8–9).

He lies awake at night wrestling with his thoughts, searching his mind for some explanation of God's absence. But to no avail. "All the while, like slow, circling vultures, his enemies hover above, waiting for his fall—and their meal!"[21]

David wasn't the only one of God's people to feel forgotten and abandoned. Consider Moses. The first forty years of his life were anything but boring. He had been raised and educated in the palace of Pharaoh. He had access to all the power and prestige and wealth and entertainment and education that the greatest monarch on earth could provide. But it didn't last.

The next forty years were of a different order. After killing an Egyptian, he fled to Midian to save his skin (Ex. 2:11–14). For the next four decades he toiled in utter obscurity, tending the sheep and goats of Jethro, his father-in-law. Day after day, week after week, month after month, year after year, sheep and goats, goats and sheep, for forty long, tedious, quiet, boring years.

Gone? Yes. Forgotten? No. Simply because one of God's own is, for the moment, unused, does not mean he is unloved. J. I. Packer tells us that "one of the disciplines to which the Lord calls us is the willingness, from time to time, *not* to be used in significant ministry."[22] It may seem as if God has forgotten us. It may seem as if we've been interminably shelved (no doubt Moses thought this of himself). But not so. Packer gives us an example to consider:

> Imagine, now, a devoted and gifted Christian woman, whose ministry has been precious to her, finding that for quite a long period the Lord sidelines her so that her potential is not being used. What is going on? Is this spiritual failure? It is probably not spiritual failure at all, but a lesson in Christ's school of holiness. The Lord is reminding her that her life does not depend on finding that people need her. *The prime source of her joy must always be the knowledge of God's love for her*—the knowledge that though he did not need her, he has chosen to love her freely and gloriously so that she may have the eternal joy of fellowship with him. Regarding her ministry, what matters is that she should be available to him. Then he will decide when and how to put her to service again, and she should leave that with him.[23]

God hadn't forgotten this lady. He hadn't abandoned Moses or David. Nor has he forsaken you. So what can be done in the meantime?

8

How Long, O Lord? Part 2

Psalm 13

Consider and answer me, O LORD my God;
  light up my eyes, lest I sleep the sleep of death.
                                                —Psalm 13:3

The psalms come to us in a variety of spiritual colors. Some are glorious, green, glad-hearted hymns of praise. Others are filled with bright blue, unrelenting gratitude. There are psalms of confidence, psalms of remembrance, wisdom psalms, kingship psalms, and even the crimson of imprecatory psalms that call for God's judgment against the wicked.

But nothing can compare with the dismal grey of the psalms of lament. These psalms are "the polar opposite of the hymn on the emotional spectrum."[24] Their mood is unmistakable (see Psalms 3, 6, 12, 13, 26, 28, 30, 42, 43, 77, and 142, just to mention a few).

Scholars have noted a distinct passion in these psalms, as the author pours out his complaint to God. It goes something like this:

"I'm hurting!"
"They're winning!"
"You don't care!"[25]

But there's also a clear progression in such psalms that reflects the struggle and growth of the psalmist. They typically move from pain to praise, from sighing to singing; though helpless, the psalmist is never hopeless.

I can't imagine a more representative psalm of lament than Psalm 13. We saw in the previous meditation David's anguished cry, his lament, his pain and sighing, his palatable sense of God's absence when he needed him most (Ps. 13:1–2).

It is, however, in the midst of his deepest anguish, when all seems lost, that David breaks forth in prayer. But why? If it is really true that God has turned away, why pray to him? If God has forgotten, why bother? Yet, David *does* pray. He can't help but cry out to the God who, deep down, he knows is still there, loving him.

I doubt that David is talking about physical death. To "sleep the sleep of death" is most likely a reference to depression or some form of spiritual anguish.

Despair can often be seen in someone's face. Their voice may sound okay, but their eyes betray them. My father was often able to discern if either I or my sister was sick, or perhaps attempting to conceal some sin, simply by looking into our eyes. If we didn't look well "in our eyes" we probably weren't. Evidently David's emotional anguish was visibly noticeable. He requests that God would restore a spiritual sparkle to his eyes. "O God, make my eyes gleam with your grace and mercy once again."

But more was at stake than just David's sense of well-being. God's reputation was on the line. David prays, "O Lord, don't give the enemy any excuse to blaspheme your name. Don't let them gloat over my condition and slander your name when they see the defeat of your servant" (see v. 4).

Sometimes the frustrations of the present threaten to undermine the trust that comes from remembering the past. We are so lost *now* that we forget what happened back *then*. "What good is yesterday when I'm hurting so badly today?"

That is where faith comes in. Faith in the God whom we've seen act in the past renews our hope for the future. David knew it. So he makes a choice, the same choice you and I must make. He decides to entrust himself to God's pledge of undying love. Make David's confession of faith your own:

> But I have trusted in your steadfast love;
>   my heart shall rejoice in your salvation.
> I will sing to the LORD,
>   because he has dealt bountifully with me. (vv. 5–6)

Yes, on occasion God does seem hidden from view. His presence feels like a fast-fading memory. His love seems to have evaporated under the hot summer sun. When that happens, do what David did. Take yourself in hand, and contrary to every fiber of your being that demands you say otherwise, declare to the heavens: "But I trust in your unfailing love!"

God's love will not fail. It has not nor will it die. Though hidden from view, though far from what you're feeling, God's love for you lives. Go ahead if you want and punch me right in the nose. I may stop loving you (for the moment), but God won't.

Observe how David resolves to rejoice in God's salvation (deliverance), even though it has not yet come. He's still depressed. It's as if he says, "O God, I'm trusting in you to create the occasion when I can again look on your acts of deliverance and rejoice in your saving power."

From what he recalls of God's faithfulness in the past, there arises in his heart the calm of anticipation: "O God, you did it once before. I am confident you will do it again, because your love is unfailing!"

Let's remember that encouragement from the Lord sometimes comes in small doses. It's always there, but not always easy to discern at first glance. When lingering storm clouds obscure the sun's rays, we begin to wonder: "Will I ever feel its warmth again?" Then we remind ourselves of the laws of nature and wait expectantly for the skies to break.

God's love for you always shines bright. But if clouds of pain and rejection and shame have for the moment blackened the sky, rest assured that gracious winds will again blow strong, and the warmth of his passionate love will renew your once cold soul.

In anticipation, go ahead and sing like David did. Who knows, you just might hear God join you with a song of his own (see Zeph. 3:17).

9

The Rewards of Integrity

Psalm 15

O LORD, who shall sojourn in your tent?
  Who shall dwell on your holy hill?

He who walks blamelessly and does what is right
  and speaks truth in his heart;
who does not slander with his tongue
  and does no evil to his neighbor,
  nor takes up a reproach against his friend;
in whose eyes a vile person is despised,
  but who honors those who fear the LORD;
who swears to his own hurt and does not change;
who does not put out his money at interest
  and does not take a bribe against the innocent.
He who does these things shall never be moved.

Psalm 15 is short, only five verses, and to the point.[26] Be assured that the psalmist is not talking about how to be forgiven of your sins and reconciled to God. David is not describing the means by which to be saved but rather what it means to be saved. These moral declarations are not conditions for acceptance with God. They are the consequence of it. Thus, David is not talking about requirements for entrance into the kingdom on the part of those outside but about enjoyment of the King on the part of those on the inside.

The question David is asking, then, is this: "Who will enjoy God's fellowship? Who will commune with God? Who will dwell with him on his holy hill?" (v. 1). God cannot and will not abide in the presence of nor bless moral corruption (see Ps. 5:4–7).

David lists ten characteristics of the person who will "abide" in God's tent and "dwell" on his holy hill.

First, this person "walks with integrity" (NASB; or "blamelessly" ESV; Ps. 15:2). The word *integrity* is something of a summary of all that follows. Integrity here does not mean sinless, but it does describe a person who by God's grace "sins less." It refers to one who is whole, complete, sound.

Second, this individual does what is right (v. 2). The emphasis here is on *doing* what is righteous, rather than merely *talking* about it. Doing what is right and lawful and good and honest is eminently pleasing to God, whether it be in private or public, in the church or in the office.

Let me get really specific about what this means. Proverbs 11:1 declares that "a false balance is an *abomination* to the LORD, but a just weight is his delight." The same thought is found in Proverbs 20:10, "Unequal weights and unequal measures are both alike an *abomination* to the LORD" (cf. 20:23). What is it that is so horrible that God would regard it as "abominable"?

The writer is referencing an ancient practice among unscrupulous merchants. If you wanted to purchase, let's say, five pounds of sugar, the merchant would place on one side of the balance scale a stone supposedly weighing five pounds. He would then pour sugar onto the other side until the scales weighed evenly. In point of fact, the stone might weigh only four pounds. The customer was thereby cheated, having paid for a pound of sugar he did not receive. If a dishonest person were himself making the purchase, he might use a six-pound stone that is labeled as five. In either case, such deceitfulness is an abomination to the Lord. One cannot easily pass it off as shrewd bargaining or rationalize it by insisting that "everyone else does it." It is, quite simply, abominable to the Lord.

God is concerned with the little things no less than with the big ones. It's stunning to think that God views everything we do or think in life as either an abomination or a delight. We must ask this question: do we regard minor misrepresentations in business or shopping or speaking as only part of the game everyone plays, or do we regard them as an abomination to God?

Third, he speaks truth in his heart (Ps. 15:2). That is to say, there is a correspondence between what he thinks on the inside and what he says on the outside. This person doesn't resort to hypocrisy, feigned praise, or flattery. This doesn't mean we are to speak everything in our hearts (cf. Eph. 4:29 and numerous proverbs). It *does* mean that when you speak, you speak the truth.

Fourth, he does not slander with his tongue (Ps. 15:3). The word *slander* literally means "to spy out," in the sense that one goes looking for things in the life of others to use against them.

The fifth and sixth characteristics are related. He does no evil to his neighbor (v. 3). Neither does he take up a reproach against his friend (v. 3). Here he refers to both initiating and rejoicing in gossip. His point is that the person of integrity will neither contribute to slander nor tolerate it. Spurgeon said, "If there were no gratified hearers of ill-reports, there would be an end of the trade of speaking them."[27]

Seventh, this person is one in whose eyes a vile person is despised but who honors those who fear the Lord (v. 4). The "reprobate" (NASB) is someone known for evil, someone hardened in perversity, someone unrepentant and proud of his or her sin. Whom do you admire? Whom do you praise? Try to envision what society (not to mention the church) would be like if we all suddenly ceased to praise, honor, reward, or show deference or grant special privileges to the reprobates of our world, particularly those in Hollywood, the sports world, and politics.

Eighth, he swears to his own hurt and does not change (v. 4). The NIV renders this, "[He] keeps his oath even when it hurts." In other words, his honor is more important than his wallet. For this person, integrity has no price tag. He's willing to make material and physical sacrifices to be honest. Often, if there is no risk of loss or painful consequences, one will never know if one has integrity.

One will never know if what motivates you is moral *conviction* or moral *convenience* until you are forced to suffer loss for standing your ground or keeping your word.

Ninth, he does not put out his money at interest (v. 5; see Ex. 22:25; Lev. 25:35–38; Deut. 23:19–20). The primary aim of this Old Testament legislation was to protect the poor. In other words, it was motivated by compassion. The purpose for making loans in today's world is to make money, to develop industry, to expand capital, etc. But for an Israelite to charge interest on loans made to a fellow Israelite would aggravate the crisis that had produced the need for obtaining the loan in the first place, driving him yet deeper into debt.

Finally, he does not take a bribe against the innocent (Ps. 15:5). Often the poor were taken to court and exploited by the rich who could easily afford to pay a bribe to thwart justice (see Deut. 16:19–20).

And what profit is there in integrity? David's answer is "He who does these things shall never be moved" (Ps. 15:5). Moved from what? Most likely, the promise is that this individual will never cease to "sojourn" in God's "tent" (v. 1) or fail to "dwell" on God's "holy hill" (v. 1). Well, what do you know . . . honesty *does* pay after all!

Of what, then, does integrity consist? I've listed below what I regard as the ten foundational characteristics of a person with integrity. There may well be more than ten, but I can't conceive of any less than ten.

1) A person of integrity fulfills his or her promises. Being true to one's word, especially when doing so is costly (in terms of money, convenience, physical welfare, etc.) is a core characteristic of integrity.

2) A person of integrity speaks the truth, is honest, and does not lie.

3) A person of integrity is a person of sincerity. That is to say, a person of integrity hates hypocrisy.

4) A person of integrity manifests a wholeness of character, including kindness, compassion, mercy, and gentleness.

5) A person of integrity is committed to the pursuit and maintenance of justice and fairness.

6) A person of integrity loves as, when, and what God loves.

7) A person of integrity is humble. He or she shuns pride and haughtiness.

8) A person of integrity is law-abiding. He or she plays by the rules, both those in the Bible and the law of the land.

9) A person of integrity is fundamentally altruistic. In other words, he or she is committed not simply to laws and rules but to people. Could a selfish person have much integrity? What about someone who is honest and law-abiding, and fulfills his or her promises, but is self-absorbed and egocentric? Does the latter eliminate the possibility of integrity?"

10) A person of integrity manifests a high degree of consistency. That is to say, he or she is not always changing the principles by which he or she lives unless compelled to do so by the Bible or rational persuasion.

10

Satisfaction

Psalm 16

Preserve me, O God, for in you I take refuge.
I say to the LORD, "You are my Lord;
   I have no good apart from you."
                   —Psalm 16:1

Rock stars rarely age well. The Rolling Stones are a case in point. Often called The Strolling Bones (and not without cause!), this once energetic and controversial sixties group was actually invited to perform during the Super Bowl halftime show only a few years ago.

Of all their many hits, the one that lingers most in my memory is the grammatically torturous, "I Can't Get No Satisfaction." As I type it, Microsoft Word faithfully reminds me of its error with that annoying green squiggly line beneath the word *No*.

What possible reason could I have for mentioning this rather pathetic attempt at musical entertainment? It came to mind as I read Psalm 16. Although the man who wrote this psalm was himself an accomplished musician and played skillfully the ancient equivalent of the modern guitar, he would never, ever have said that he couldn't get *any* satisfaction. In spite of numerous setbacks and disappointments, recurring depression and political defeats, David was a profoundly *satisfied* man. Satisfied, that is, in God.

That God was the source of his soul's satisfaction is evident from a quick perusal of several recurring statements in the psalm:

> In you [God] I take refuge. (v. 1)
> I say to the LORD . . . "I have no good apart from you." (v. 2)
> The LORD is my chosen portion and my cup. (v. 5)
> I bless the LORD who gives me counsel. (v. 7)
> I have set the LORD always before me. (v. 8)
> Because he is at my right hand, I shall not be shaken. (v. 8)
> In your presence there is fullness of joy. (v. 11)
> At your right hand are pleasures forevermore. (v. 11)

David was unashamed of his longing for the Lord and unafraid to declare his utter dependence on God and God alone for the satisfaction his soul so passionately desired.

Psalm 16:11 is my life verse. It encapsulates and expresses the glorious gospel of Christian hedonism in a way that few other texts do. But I want to focus here on two other verses in this remarkable psalm. Look closely at verse 2 and verse 8 (consider also Ps. 73:25, where Asaph declares: "Whom have I in heaven but you? And there is nothing on earth that I desire besides you"):

> I say to the LORD, "You are my Lord;
>   I have no good apart from you." (v. 2)

> I have set the LORD always before me;
>   because he is at my right hand, I shall not be shaken. (v. 8)

I was helped greatly in my understanding of these texts by something Larry Crabb recently confessed. Larry's honesty is disarming and challenging. He's not afraid to admit what the rest of us skillfully hide. I strongly encourage you to read his many books and draw deeply from his wisdom.

Several years ago Larry's brother was killed in a tragic airplane crash. In one particularly candid moment, as he wrestled with God in his effort to make sense of what seemed utterly senseless, Larry cried out to God: "I know you are all I have, but I don't know you well enough for you to be all that I need."[28]

What I hear Larry saying is that the measure of our satisfaction is the degree to which we can both trust and rejoice when all we have left is God.

Neither Larry nor the psalmist is denying that other things are good or satisfying or capable of evoking pleasure. But they are to be embraced only when acknowledged and enjoyed as gifts of God, without whom all else is ultimately meaningless.

Everything without God is pathetically inferior to God without everything. Or as C. S. Lewis put it, "He who has God and everything else has no more than he who has God only."[29]

This is why David was so diligent to avert his eyes from all lesser beauty. His resolve was to set the Lord before him, to concentrate his attention and the energies of his soul on the majesty and power of the One who alone would sustain him when all else is shaking.

David wasn't in the least inclined to dismiss his longing for satisfaction as if it were a sinful craving to be suppressed or "crucified." He embraced the passion of his soul as the gift of God. This was no remnant of the fall, but one element in God's creative design to glorify himself by being the sole, all-sufficient source of deep and unending satisfaction for his people.

This was not an infrequent or occasional choice or one to which he reverted only in times of crisis, but an orientation of life to which he was *always* committed. We would do well to follow his example.

Before closing, we should take note of two images in this psalm that reinforce David's point, both of which are rooted in vivid Old Testament truths.

First, David prays that God would "preserve" him, for "in you," he declares, "I take refuge" (v. 1; cf. Pss. 7:1; 11:1; 17:7). It's possible that the background for this language is in the familiar "cities of refuge," those designated places to which a person might flee after accidentally killing another. They were designed to provide safe haven and protection from a family member of the deceased who might seek revenge.

God is our city of refuge. He is our safe, soul-satisfying haven of rest. Like a frightened child running to her father, hiding from danger behind the imposing presence of one committed to protect her, David sought safety in God. Like the residents of central Kansas seeking shelter from an approaching tornado, or like a soldier under attack from the enemy, retreating behind the formidable walls of a king's castle, so we find our refuge in God.

Second, the language of verses 5 and 6 is clearly based on God's apportioning of the land to and among the twelve tribes upon their entrance into Canaan. The boundaries or border lines were set to determine the inheritance of each. However, God gave no land or inheritance to the Levites (the priests). "And the LORD said to Aaron, 'You shall have no inheritance in their land, neither shall you have any portion among them. *I am your portion and your inheritance* among the people of Israel'" (Num. 18:20).

Likewise, David happily embraces God alone as his "chosen portion" and his "cup" (v. 5a). You alone, O God, "hold my lot" (v. 5b). The "lines" (v. 6a) or measuring cords used to mark off the land allotted to each "have fallen for me in pleasant places; indeed, I have a beautiful inheritance" (v. 6b).

Simply put: "You, O God, are the portion allotted to me! You, O God, supremely beautiful, are my inheritance! You, O God, are the only land I need or want!"

These are the words of a profoundly satisfied man. Why is this important? Because, in the words of John Piper, God is most *glorified* in you when you are most *satisfied* in him.

11

Look Up and Listen

Psalm 19:1–6

The heavens declare the glory of God,
and the sky above proclaims his handiwork.
—Psalm 19:1

ook up and listen, for "the heavens declare the glory of God,
and the sky above proclaims his handiwork" (Ps. 19:1). What
a way to begin the psalm that C. S. Lewis called "the greatest
poem in the Psalter and one of the greatest lyrics in the world."[30]

The grand sweep of Psalm 19 is nothing short of stunning. It
begins with the skies above (vv. 1–6), then moves to the Scriptures
below (vv. 7–11), and finally to the prayerful meditation of our own
souls (vv. 12–14).

The revelation of God's glory has been written in two volumes.
There is, first, the book of *Natural Creation*, which unveils the splendor of God in space and stars and the skies above. Second, there is
the volume of *Holy Scripture*. As glorious as the highest heavens
may be, and as breathtaking as the immensity of space assuredly is,
all pales in comparison with the glory of God revealed in his Word.
"From nature we know only the hands and feet of God," said Calvin,

"but from Scripture we may know his very heart" (more on this in the next meditation).[31]

So, I'll say it again: look up and listen, for the sky and all it contains is one continuous chorus singing God's glory (Ps. 19:1–2). It "pours out" (v. 2) praise, not in mere hints or whispers but in deafening shouts of supremacy and splendor. The phrase *pours out* means "to bubble up and over like an irrepressible mountain spring."

> One day "bubbles forth" speech to the next day, and one night speaks to the next night. As a boiling pot bubbles over, so one day cannot contain its news to itself. In never-ending succession the message is relayed, as a baton is passed from one runner to the next. The message is the revelation of the glory of God.[32]

This is no momentary melody, but an ongoing, incessant, ceaseless disclosure of God's power and splendor. Every twinkle of every star, every bolt of lightning and burst of thunder echo his majesty.

To all who will look and listen, during the day God is proclaimed in cloud and sky and rain and rainbows. When day is done, the night takes over with moon and meteors and galaxies galore. Together, day and night consistently proclaim one message: "God is elegant! God is exquisite! God is enthralling!"

There is no such thing as empty space. What appears as an endless vacuum, sheer nothingness, is in fact a glorious canvas or backdrop for the celestial portrait that proclaims his power.

Jonathan Edwards wrote often in his *Personal Narrative* of what can only be called the *sacramental power* of God's handiwork, for in the creation he saw and encountered and adored the Creator. He recounts one instance of walking alone in his father's pasture for contemplation:

> And as I was walking there, and looking up on the sky and clouds, there came into my mind so sweet a sense of the glorious *majesty* and *grace* of God that I know not how to express. I seemed to see them both in a sweet conjunction; majesty and meekness joined together; it was a sweet, and gentle, and holy majesty, and also a majestic meekness; an awful sweetness; a high, and great, and holy gentleness.

After this my sense of divine things gradually increased, and became more and more lively, and had more of that inward sweetness. The appearance of every thing was altered; there seemed to be, as it were a calm sweet cast, or appearance of divine glory, in almost every thing. God's excellency, his wisdom, his purity and love, seemed to appear in every thing; in the sun, moon, and stars; in the clouds, and blue sky; in the grass, flowers, trees; in the water, and all nature; which used greatly to fix my mind. I often used to sit and view the moon for continuance; and in the day, spent much time in viewing the clouds and sky, to behold the sweet glory of God in these things; in the mean time, singing forth, with a low voice my contemplations of the Creator and Redeemer.

And scarce any thing, among all the works of nature, was so sweet to me as thunder and lightning; formerly, nothing had been so terrible to me. Before, I used to be uncommonly terrified with thunder, and to be struck with terror when I saw a thunderstorm rising; but now, on the contrary, it rejoiced me. I felt God, so to speak, at the first appearance of a thunder storm; and used to take the opportunity, at such times, to fix myself in order to view the clouds, and see the lightnings play, and hear the majestic and awful voice of God's thunder, which oftentimes was exceedingly entertaining, leading me to sweet contemplations of my great and glorious God. While thus engaged, it always seemed natural to me to sing, or chant for my meditations; or, to speak my thoughts in soliloquies with a singing voice.[33]

Edwards never viewed the natural creation as an end in itself. He would have considered it idolatry to derive delight from the complexity and design and grandeur of the physical realm were it not that such phenomena reflect, echo, and embody the greatness and glory of their Creator.

Thus, whereas the psalmist is happy to *personify* nature, *he doesn't deify* it. Nature is not God. It is God's handiwork that sings his praise. Creation doesn't exist to proclaim creation's praise but that of its Creator.

The universe is wondrous indeed, but only because it is the "work of his hands" (NIV). The Creator cannot be reduced to or contained within what he has made. God never created the world with the intent that you stop with it, but that you trace along its lines to see the face of the Sovereign Lord who shaped it. As Piper has pointed out, "The glory of creation and the glory of God are as different as the love poem and the love, the painting and the landscape, the ring and the marriage. It would be a great folly and a great tragedy if a man loved his wedding band more than he loved his bride."[34]

So, how do the heavens declare God's glory? In what ways may it be seen? Consider our own disc-shaped galaxy, the Milky Way; it is rather small when compared to what we know of other galaxies in the universe. Our sun is only one of some 200,000,000,000 (that's right, 200 billion!) stars that comprise it. It is approximately 100,000 light-years across. How big is that, you ask? Well, light can travel at 186,000 miles per second (that's per *second*), or 670,000,000 miles per hour! So, it isn't hard to calculate that in a year's time light can travel just short of 6,000,000,000,000 miles (that's 6 trillion miles).

So, if the Milky Way is 100,000 light-years in diameter, that works itself out to 600,000,000,000,000,000 miles. In case you lost count of the zeros, that's 600 quadrillion miles.

As massive as that sounds, and as small as it makes us feel (knowing that we are tiny creatures on an indescribably tiny planet in an indescribably tiny solar system within the Milky Way), there are more than 100 billion separate galaxies in just the observable or known universe. Many of these galaxies contain over a trillion stars each!

Speaking of stars, as noted, our sun is a comparatively tiny one when we take into consideration the rest of her galactic cousins. Let's recall that the earth is 93 million miles from the sun (and be glad it is, for the sun is 9,932 degrees Fahrenheit at its surface and 27 million degrees Fahrenheit at its core). If you were to replace our sun with a typical Supergiant star, the latter would fill up the solar system beyond Jupiter's orbit. Remember that Jupiter is *483 million miles* from the sun. Some star! "God is elegant! God is exquisite! God is enthralling!"

In his book *When I Don't Desire God*, John Piper assumes that the psalmist's joy in creation "is not idolatrous—that is, I assume it does not terminate on the works themselves, but in and through them, rests on the glory of God himself. The works declare the glory of God. They point. But the final ground of our joy is God himself."[35] Edwards would no doubt joyfully concur. Again, Piper writes:

> That is, we see the glory *of God*, not just the glory of the heavens. We don't just stand outside and analyze the natural world as a beam, but let the beam fall on the eyes of our heart, so that we see the source of the beauty—the original Beauty, God himself. . . . All of God's creation becomes a beam to be "looked along" or a sound to be "heard along" or a fragrance to be "smelled along" or a flavor to be "tasted along" or a touch to be "felt along." All our senses become partners with the eyes of the heart in perceiving the glory of God through the physical world.[36]

As good as that is and as great as the heavens may be, the revelation of God in Scripture is even better.

12

Drippings of the Honeycomb

Psalm 19:7–14

> More to be desired are they than gold,
>   even much fine gold;
> sweeter also than honey
>   and drippings of the honeycomb.
> > —Psalm 19:10

I have written in a variety of places, both in books and articles, on Psalm 19, so I trust you'll indulge me yet one more time as I reflect on this magnificent portrayal of the beauty and power of God's Word. The following observations are adapted from my book *Pleasures Evermore*.[37]

In Psalm 19:7–11 we find six declarations that tell us what the Bible is and does: six nouns, six adjectives, six verbs. The focus is on the identity (the nouns), the quality (the adjectives), and the function (the verbs) of Scripture.

First, "the law of the LORD is perfect, reviving the soul" (v. 7a). As for its identity, it is a *law*, or instruction, pointing us in the direction of what is right and away from what is wrong. It does this perfectly, without the slightest defect, never lacking what is needed to address our circumstances. Its function is to revive our souls, to refresh and renew us and to remind us that the pleasures of obedience to God's law are delightfully superior to all rival claims that would lead us in another direction.

Second, "the testimony of the LORD is sure, making wise the simple" (v. 7b). Scripture is the record of God's own witness to who he is and what he will provide for us in Jesus. This testimony is *sure,* which is to say it is true in principle and verifiable in life's situations. The Bible takes the undiscerning, naïve, and gullible person and makes him wise. He who is immersed in the Word is equipped to choose wisely where no explicit direction is found.

Third, "the precepts of the LORD are right, rejoicing the heart" (v. 8a). God's rules are never wrong. We can always rely on them to provide truth and accuracy. She whose heart is fixed on the precepts of the Lord is never at the whim of public opinion polls or the fickle fluctuations of human advice. In God's precepts one finds cause for joy and reason for rejoicing. This is God's remedy for a sinking, sad, broken heart. If your heart is sour and embittered and could use an injection of joy, memorize and meditate and mull over God's precepts.

Fourth, "the commandment of the LORD is pure, enlightening the eyes" (v. 8b). That word *pure* may also be rendered "radiant" (NIV). God's commandments shine and shimmer and glow and glimmer. They are brilliant and bright and dispel the darkness of human ignorance and senseless advice.

Here we see again the inseparable link God has forged between Word and Spirit. "God has ordained that the *eye-opening work of his Spirit* always be combined with the *mind-informing work of his Word.* His aim is that we see the glory of his Son (and be changed). So he opens our eyes when we are looking at the Son—not at soaps or sales. The work of the Spirit and the work of the Word always go together in God's way of true spiritual self-revelation. The Spirit's work is to show the glory and beauty and value of what the mind sees in the Word."[38]

Fifth, "the fear of the LORD is clean, enduring forever" (v. 9a). David has in mind that fear of God that the Bible produces in us. It is *clean* both in terms of its essence and its impact on our hearts. Its power and purpose never end; we can always count on God's

Word to do its work; God's Word does not change with the seasons or with fashions; it is always "in."

Finally, "the rules of the LORD are true, and righteous altogether" (v. 9b). What God says in his word is never false or off the mark. His Word is the only barometer for reality. One need never again live in doubt and hesitation concerning what is righteous. Guesswork is gone. The certainty of God's Word is our foundation.

And the best part of all? The Word of God brings us satisfaction and joy and delight so that we will not be enticed and tempted by the passing pleasures of sin. The laws and precepts and commandments of God's Word are more to be desired "than gold, even much fine gold; sweeter also than honey and drippings of the honeycomb. Moreover, by them is your servant warned; in keeping them there is great reward" (vv. 10–11).

Yes, there is great reward in the treasuring of God's Word in our hearts. For starters, there are the six things just noted: God's Word rewards you with restoration of your soul, wisdom for your walk, joy for your heart, enlightenment for your eyes, truth you can count on, and the provision of righteousness. Wow!

Psalm 19 isn't the only place we find this truth. Consider these texts:

This Book of the Law shall not depart from your mouth, but you shall meditate on it day and night, so that you may be careful to do according to all that is written in it. For then you will make your way prosperous, and then you will have good success. (Josh. 1:8)

Blessed is the man who walks not in the counsel of the wicked, nor stands in the way of sinners, nor sits in the seat of scoffers; but his delight is in the law of the LORD, and on his law he meditates day and night. (Ps. 1:1–2)

I have stored up your word in my heart, that I might not sin against you. (Ps. 119:11)

I will meditate on your precepts and fix my eyes on your ways. (Ps. 119:15)

Even though princes sit plotting against me, your servant will meditate on your statutes. (Ps. 119:23)

I will lift up my hands toward your commandments, which I love, and I will meditate on your statutes. (Ps. 119:48)

Let the insolent be put to shame, because they have wronged me with falsehood; as for me, I will meditate on your precepts. (Ps. 119:78)

O how I love your law! It is my meditation all the day. (Ps. 119:97)

I have more understanding than all my teachers, for your testimonies are my meditation. (Ps. 119:99)

How sweet are your words to my taste, sweeter than honey to my mouth! (Ps. 119:103)

My eyes are awake before the watches of the night, that I may meditate on your promise. (Ps. 119:148)

Boring? Tedious? Hardly! When the seed of the Word sinks its roots deeply into our souls, the fruit it yields is sheer gladness. The psalmist declares him "blessed" who "greatly delights" in God's commandments (Ps. 112:1).

In the hymnic celebration of God's Word, Psalm 119, we read of the psalmist finding more joy in God's testimonies than in all riches and what they might buy (v. 14). He committed himself to "delight" in God's statutes (vv. 16, 24, 35, 47, 70, 77) and to relish the joy they bring even in the midst of affliction (vv. 92, 143).

In summary, says Piper:

> The challenge before us . . . is not merely to do what God says because he is God, but to desire what God says because he is good. The challenge is not merely to *pursue* righteousness, but to *prefer* righteousness. The challenge is to get up in the morning and prayerfully meditate on the Scriptures until we experience joy and peace in believing "the precious and very great promises of God" (Rom. 15:13; 2 Peter 1:4). With this joy set before us the *commandments* of God will not be burdensome (1 John 5:3) and the compensation of sin will appear too brief and too shallow to lure us.[39]

71

Psalms 22–37

from Book 1 of the Psalter

13

The Agony and the Ecstasy

Psalm 22

> In you our fathers trusted;
> they trusted, and you delivered them.
> —Psalm 22:4

If you've never given much thought to Psalm 22, there's no better place to begin than with the following comment of Charles Spurgeon's:

> For plaintive expressions uprising from unutterable depths of woe we may say of this Psalm, there is none like it. It is the photograph of our Lord's saddest hours, the record of his dying words, the lachrymatory of his last tears, the memorial of his expiring joys. David and his afflictions may be here in a very modified sense, but, as the star is concealed by the light of the sun, he who sees Jesus will probably neither see nor care to see David. . . . We should read reverently, putting off our shoes from off our feet, as Moses did at the burning bush, for if there be holy ground anywhere in Scripture, it is in this Psalm.[1]

I agree with Spurgeon that this psalm, however much it may speak of David's personal experience, is primarily *messianic*. The

75

opening words of the psalm (v. 1) are found on the lips of Jesus as he hung on the cross (cf. Matt. 27:46). The taunt of the scorners at the crucifixion, "And those who passed by derided him, wagging their heads" (Matt. 27:39), comes from Psalm 22:7. The scorners also challenged him (Matt. 27:43) with the very words of verse 8. And Jesus cried out from the cross, "I thirst" (John 19:28), in fulfillment of verse 15. Finally, his garments were parted among those who pierced his hands and feet, even as verses 16 to 18 describe.

There is great wealth in this psalm, but I'll restrict myself to a few important observations.

In the opening section (vv. 1–10) we see an unusual wave-like movement, almost a vacillation between the utter dregs of wretchedness and the sparkle of hope and confidence.

In vv. 1–2 the wrath of God enshrouds him, and is thus absorbed, never to be borne by those for whom he died. "My God, my God, why have you forsaken me?" is a cry of utter distress, but not of distrust. It expresses the agony of grief, but not the misery of doubt. The "why" implies a conscious innocence as far as his moral life is concerned (see 2 Cor. 5:21).

Confidence is restored when the suffering one reflects upon the holiness of God (vv. 3–5). Does it strike you as odd that he would find comfort in, of all things, the *holiness* of God?

His "formal complaint" is found in verses 6 to 8. "I am a worm," literally, a grub, such as devours the dead (see Isa. 14:11). "This verse," writes Spurgeon, "is a miracle in language. How could the Lord of glory be brought to such abasement as to be not only lower than the angels, but even lower than men? *What a contrast between 'I am' and 'I am a worm.'*"[2]

This one, before whom the angels hid their faces in praise, adoration, and fear (cf. Isaiah 6), is now the target of facial mockery from those he created. They are not merely so arrogant as to look upon him, but do so with derision.

Consider this paraphrase of verse 8: "This Jesus was always telling others to trust in God. Let him now taste his own medicine. Surely the one whom he has trusted and in whom he exhorted others to put their faith will deliver him quickly!" (cf. Matt. 27:41–43). In a remarkable display of spiritual blindness and tragic irony, they taunt him with the very words that would fulfill the ancient prophecy and demonstrate that he was, indeed, the Messiah who he claimed to be.

We now move from complaint in verses 6 to 8 to remarkable confidence in verses 9 and 10, where faith and hope begin to reassert themselves. The Lutheran commentator Leupold put it best:

> At the same time the poor sufferer does exactly what his opponents have just recommended to him to do, to commit all issues to God. He recounts what God has meant to him in the past, and what He has done for him from earliest infancy. . . . "During every moment of my life till now Thou hast been my God and hast sustained me."[3]

The lament returns in verses 11 to 18. After describing his enemies (they are like unthinking beasts, wild bulls of Bashan, encircling him; vv. 11–13), he turns to a portrayal of himself in verses 14 and 15. He compares his utter lack of strength and feeling of helplessness to water poured out upon the ground. The torment of the sin he bears has reduced him to a most feeble and pitiful state. His physical frame is tortured as one distended upon a rack. His heart has been so greatly burdened as to feel like melting wax. His resistance is nil. He is as destitute of vigor as a broken piece of earthenware is of moisture.

Note well, however, that it is ultimately God's will that he suffer: "*You* lay me in the dust of death" (v. 15b; cf. Isa. 53:4, "smitten by God"; and 53:10, "It was the will of the LORD to crush him"; see also Acts 2:23). Never let the emotion stirred by the reality of the cross obscure the fact that it was no accident.

In verse 16 he again vividly describes his enemies: they are "dogs." In the ancient Near East, dogs roamed in large bands as scavengers. They were totally undomesticated, wild, filthy, objects of abhorrence. The description of his hands and feet being pierced is especially instructive when we remember that crucifixion was unknown at this time in Israel's history.

The culmination of his suffering is not so much physical as spiritual and emotional, as he bears the *shame* of sin (vv. 17–18). All four Gospels record this incident (Matt. 27:35; Mark 15:24; Luke 23:34; John 19:23–24). Calvin writes:

> The Evangelists portray the Son of God as stripped of His clothes that we may know the wealth gained for us by this nakedness, for it shall dress us in God's sight. God willed His Son to be stripped that we should appear freely, with the angels, in the garments of his righteousness and fullness of all good things, whereas formerly, foul disgrace, in torn clothes, kept us away from the approach to the heavens.[4]

The first Adam, originally created in the righteousness of God, by his sin stripped us naked. The last Adam, suffering the shame of nakedness, by his obedience clothes us in the righteousness of God.

His prayers (vv. 19–21) are answered, but in accordance with the will and timing of the Father. Was he delivered *before* death? No. Was he delivered *out of* death? Yes. Was he delivered on Good Friday? No. Was he delivered on Easter Sunday? Yes. It was a better time and a better way.

There comes a time, when one is reading certain passages of God's Word, that commentary must yield to contemplation. May God impress deeply on your heart the profound reality that the Son did this for you.

14

God's Aim Is the Fame
of His Name

Psalm 23:3

> He restores my soul.
> He leads me in paths of righteousness
> for his name's sake.
>
> —Psalm 23:5

Perhaps the most pervasive theme in all of Scripture is God's passion for *God*. No, that's not a misprint. Many would have preferred that I say, "God's passion for *you*," but if God isn't first and foremost committed to himself and the pursuit and praise of his own glory, his love for you wouldn't amount to much at all.

But let me return to this notion of *God's commitment to God*. On what biblical grounds do I dare make what appears, at first glance, to be an outrageous and disheartening statement? Would it surprise you to discover that it is explicitly made known in over two hundred biblical texts? But my concern is with what we read in Psalm 23:3.

It may come as quite a shock to discover that in this psalm so beloved by Christians everywhere, a psalm typically understood as focusing on God's commitment to us, that I would find God's commitment to God! But there it is, in verse 3: "He restores my soul. He leads me in paths of righteousness *for his name's sake.*"

Does it surprise you to learn that the driving force in God's heart in restoring your soul and providing guidance for your life and enabling you to walk in righteousness is the fame of *his* name?

Before you too quickly dismiss me as heretical, consider these other explicit declarations, both in the Old and New Testaments, in which the fame of God's name is his aim in all he does.

In Psalm 79:9, Asaph echoes this remarkable truth with this prayer:

Help us, O God of our salvation, *for the glory of your name*; deliver us, and atone for our sins, *for your name's sake.*

One of the more vivid examples of this is found in 1 Samuel 12:22. There we read:

The LORD will not forsake his people, *for his great name's sake*, because it has pleased the LORD to make you a people for himself.

Samuel says this on the heels of Israel's demand that God give them a king. He repeatedly reminds them that to demand a king is evil and wicked, and he warns them of the disastrous consequences of not being satisfied with God as their Sovereign. Nevertheless, Samuel counsels them not to be afraid that God might abandon them or cast them aside. It would have made perfectly good sense had he done so, at least to our way of thinking. But he won't, and here's why: for his great name's sake.

The underlying reason for God's commitment to his people is his prior and more fundamental commitment to himself. God's name is at stake in your destiny, says Samuel. What happens to you reflects on the glory of God's reputation. That is why he will not cast you away.

In Psalm 31:2, David prays yet again. But note especially the ground or basis of his appeal in verse 3: "For you are my rock and my fortress; and *for your name's sake* you lead me and guide me."

There are, in fact, several places in the Psalter and elsewhere in the Old Testament where the purpose or goal for God having forgiven his people and his dealing kindly with them is his glory and the praise of his own name. Note especially the italicized words:

> Remember not the sins of my youth or my transgressions; according to your steadfast love remember me, *for the sake of your goodness,* O Lord! (Ps. 25:7)

> *For your name's sake,* O Lord, pardon my guilt, for it is great. (Ps. 25:11)

> Help us, O God of our salvation, *for the glory of your name*; deliver us, and atone for our sins, *for your name's sake!* (Ps. 79:9)

> But you, O God my Lord, deal on my behalf *for your name's sake*; because your steadfast love is good, deliver me! (Ps. 109:21)

> Though our iniquities testify against us, act, O Lord, *for your name's sake*; for our backslidings are many; we have sinned against you. (Jer. 14:7)

All these texts are similar to what we read in 1 John 2:12: "I am writing to you, little children, because your sins are forgiven *for his name's sake.*"

"These things seem to show," wrote Jonathan Edwards, "that the salvation of Christ is for God's name's sake. Leading and guiding in the way of safety and happiness, restoring the soul, the forgiveness of sin, and that help, deliverance and salvation that is consequent thereon, is *for God's name.*"[5]

We know that the redemption and deliverance of Israel from bondage in Egypt, and then again from Babylon, were types or figures of our redemption and deliverance from sin. That being the case, we should take note of numerous texts in which the former is said to have occurred for the sake of God's name or glory.

> And who is like your people Israel, the one nation on earth whom God went to redeem to be his people, *making himself a name* and doing for them great and awesome things. (2 Sam. 7:23)

> Yet he saved them *for his name's sake*, that he might make known his mighty power. (Ps. 106:8)

> . . . who caused his glorious arm to go at the right hand of Moses, who divided the waters before them *to make for himself an everlasting name*. (Isa. 63:12)

> "But I [God] acted *for the sake of my name*, that it should not be profaned in the sight of the nations among whom they lived, in whose sight I *made myself known* to them in bringing them out of the land of Egypt." (Ezek. 20:9)

> "But I [God] acted *for the sake of my name*, that it should not be profaned in the sight of the nations." (Ezek. 20:14)

> "But I withheld my hand and acted for the sake of my name, that it should not be profaned in the sight of the nations." (Ezek. 20:22)

Note the unashamed, unabashed repetitive proclamation of this truth in these texts:

> "*For my name's sake* I defer my anger, *for the sake of my praise* I restrain it for you, that I may not cut you off. Behold, I have refined you, but not as silver; I have tried you in the furnace of affliction. *For my own sake, for my own sake* [I did not mistakenly double-type that phrase], I do it, for how should *my name* be profaned? *My glory* I will not give to another." (Isa. 48:9–11)

> "But *I had concern for my holy name*, which the house of Israel had profaned among the nations to which they came. Therefore say to the house of Israel, 'Thus says the Lord God: It is not for your sake, O house of Israel, that I am about to act, but *for the sake of my holy name*, which you have profaned among the nations to which you came.

And *I will vindicate the holiness of my great name*, which has been profaned among the nations, and which you have profaned among them. And *the nations will know that I am the* LORD, declares the Lord GOD, when through you I vindicate my holiness before their eyes.'" (Ezek. 36:21–23; see also Ezek. 9:16; 39:25; Dan. 9:19)

Several texts (which I lack space to cite in full) portray the motivation for human virtue and holiness as the glory and praise of God's name (Matt. 19:29; Rom. 1:5; 3 John 7; Rev. 2:3).

The question (objection?) I most often hear in response to this is that if God loves himself preeminently, how can he love me at all? How can we say that God is for *us* and that he desires *our* happiness if he is primarily for himself and the fame of his own name? I believe it is precisely because God loves himself that he loves you. Here's how.

I assume you agree that your greatest good consists of enjoying the most excellent Being in the universe. That Being, of course, is God. Therefore, the most loving and kind thing that God can do for you is to devote all his energy and effort to elicit from your heart praise of himself. Why? Because praise is the consummation of enjoyment. All enjoyment tends towards praise and adoration as its appointed end. In this way, God's seeking his own glory and God's seeking your good converge.

Listen again. Your greatest good is in the enjoyment of God. God's greatest glory is in being enjoyed. So, for God to seek his glory (the fame of his name) in your worship of him is the most loving thing he can do for you. Only by seeking his glory preeminently can God seek your good passionately.

For God to work for your enjoyment of him —his love for you— and for his glory in being enjoyed—his love for himself—are not properly distinct.

15

The Good Shepherd
and the Gracious Host

Psalm 23

Surely goodness and mercy shall follow me
    all the days of my life,
and I shall dwell in the house of the LORD
    forever.

                        —Psalm 23:6

Aside from John 3:16, Psalm 23 may well be the most famous and oft-quoted passage in all of Holy Scripture. I've seen it printed on greeting cards, embossed on plaques, written on T-shirts and sewn into quilts; and even parts of it have appeared on bumper stickers of cars. I attribute this to its remarkable and powerfully reassuring portrait of God as both the *good shepherd* who cares for and protects his sheep and the *gracious host* who provides for their every need.

God as the good shepherd who protects his flock is the focus of verses 1 to 4.

We don't know when David wrote this psalm. Perhaps it was during his youth, as he sat under the shade of a tree on some Palestinian hillside, keeping watch over the sheep entrusted to his care. Or it may have been years later during his tenure as king over Israel, perhaps at a time when his enemies were mounting against him an especially powerful threat. Whenever and wherever it was, David wrote it as a word of reminder and encouragement not only to himself but to all of God's children.

There are countless descriptions of God in the Psalms: he is a King who rules over us, a rock of immovable stability, a deliverer in times of distress, a fortress in whom we find refuge, a shield behind whom we safely retreat. But there's something special about his being a shepherd. There's a dimension of personal tenderness and intimacy in the image of God as the one who shepherds his lambs. David well remembers the attentive watch and protective love he had for his sheep. "Yes," he may well have cried out in a moment of revelatory insight; "that's what God is to me and you!"

The Lord is *my* shepherd, declares David. He's more than simply *a* shepherd, as if one might say, "Well, yes, there are a lot of shepherds out there and the Lord, well, he's certainly one of them." No! Yahweh isn't simply one among many shepherds, nor even *the* shepherd. He's *my* shepherd. If he be a shepherd to no one else or to everyone else, he is at least *my* shepherd. He cares for me, watches over me, provides for and protects me, all the while doing it for his name's sake, which is why it's truly an act of love.

What inference does David draw from this marvelous truth—the Lord is my shepherd; therefore I can do anything I want? No. The Lord is my shepherd; therefore I can wander off whenever I choose, disregarding his commandment that I stay close by his side? No.

The Lord is my shepherd, therefore I lack nothing. There is nothing I need, says David, that God has not or will not supply. I am altogether satisfied with God's management of my life. David isn't being insensitive to the pressing demands of life, as if it is unimportant whether we have money to pay our bills and adequate clothing and a roof over our heads. His point is simply that everything we have above and beyond God is a luxury. It reminds me of that story of the elderly Puritan who sat down to dinner to find one potato and a glass of water. He looked upon his meal and with profound gratitude declared: "All this, and Jesus Christ too!"

David's point is simply this: "Take everything from me except my God and I'll die the wealthiest man in the world" (cf. Ps. 16:2).

And what does he provide? "Green pastures" in which to lie down in safety (v. 2a); "still waters" from which to drink for refreshment (v. 2b); "paths of righteousness" down which I may walk with confidence (v. 3b); all of which are a source of restoration and renewal for my soul (v. 3a).

If that weren't enough, "even though I walk through the valley of the shadow of death" I need fear nothing, for God is "with me" (v. 4a). Some might prefer (and even presumptuously demand) that God insulate us from all evil and darkness and suffering. Some might even pray that he always take us around or over or in the opposite direction from all troubles and trials. But God's unfailing promise is that he will walk with us *through* the valley.

God doesn't simply send us into the valley with truths about him nor even with angels to guard our steps. He pledges his personal presence with us. Wherever we go, whatever we suffer, he's there, with a "rod" to beat off ravenous wolves that seek to consume us spiritually (v. 4b; cf. 1 Sam. 17:33–37) and a "staff" to keep us under his control and bring us back to the fold should we stray too far.

But he's more than merely a good shepherd; he's also a gracious host (vv. 5–6), quick to "prepare a table before me in the presence of my enemies" (v. 5a). In the ancient world, far more so than today, sharing a common meal was spiritually significant. To be God's guest for dinner was more than a casual encounter. To eat and drink at someone's table forged a bond of loyalty and love, and often sealed a covenant between the parties involved. And all this "in the presence of my enemies"! Though they may continue to harass and threaten me, I'm breaking bread with the King of kings and Lord of lords.

To anoint someone with oil today would generally be regarded as little more than an inconvenient mess, but in David's world it was customary to anoint an invited guest as a sign of welcome and hospitality. It was the consummate expression of joy and acceptance.

What else can he say but that his "cup overflows" (v. 5b)? Joni Eareckson Tada put it best:

When something overflows, we usually think of *waste*. Water that overflows a dam rushes out to sea. Gas that overflows a tank pollutes the ground. Coffee that overflows a cup stains the carpet. Milk that overflows a measuring cup drains down the sink. Most folk tend to equate "overflow" with "waste" or "squandered resource." But what about a *life* that overflows? What about a man or woman who brims over with the joy and grace and love of God? Is it all down the drain?[6]

Far from it! We overflow with God's blessings as an expression of his lavish and unstinting affection for us. But there's more, notes Joni: "God doesn't intend your life to overflow down the storm drain or evaporate into the air. He wants it to soak others! The spillover of His love and goodness in our lives is to benefit and encourage those around us."[7]

But for how long? Will God grow weary of his commitment to us, or might his supply of spiritual blessings dissipate and run dry? "Surely," says David, with absolute certainty and beyond all shadow of doubt, I declare to you that "goodness and mercy shall follow" you "all the days" of your life (v. 6a). All day, every day, whether they be days of despair and disappointment or days of celebration and joy; all day, every day, whether days of fasting or feasting, days of depression or deliverance, we will live in God's abiding presence, forever (v. 6b).

16

One Thing, Once More

Psalm 27:4

One thing have I asked of the LORD,
    that will I seek after:
that I may dwell in the house of the LORD
    all the days of my life,
to gaze upon the beauty of the LORD
    and to inquire in his temple.
                            —Psalm 27:4

I've always been intrigued by Psalm 27:4, if for no other reason than that it is the last thing one would expect from David, at least when looked at from a purely human perspective.[8] Given his circumstances, this single-minded, undistracted commitment to gaze on God's beauty seems out of place.

I can't believe I just wrote that! It shows how little I know of God's beauty that I should think, if only even for a moment, that anything could justify turning away one's gaze from the glory and grandeur of God!

There are probably a few (many?) reading this who think I'm being unrealistic. Finding time to meditate on God's majesty, much less making it the "one thing" to which all else is subordinated, seems almost unimaginable when one's life is falling apart. I know. Truly, I know. But let me be so bold as to suggest that it's precisely when life is at its worst that riveting our hearts on him is far and away the most reasonable thing to do.

If you think David can say what he does in verse 4 because, as king over Israel, he's out of touch with the pains and problems of everyday life, look closely at verses 1 to 3. What we discover there, in conjunction with what we know elsewhere concerning David's experience, indicates that he didn't lead an easy life. Being king of Israel wasn't all it's cracked up to be. David didn't make his life any easier with his adulterous relationship with Bathsheba and his complicity in the murder of her husband, Uriah the Hittite. The shattering consequences it brought on him and the nation as a whole can hardly be imagined. That is why his resolution in verse 4 is so stunning.

In view of David's circumstances, one might have excused him had he opted for a little peace and quiet, or perhaps a permanent and safe home away from his enemies, or at least a month's paid vacation. With all the struggles he faced and the heartache he endured, most of us would be willing to cut the king a little slack.

Look with me at verses 1 to 3 to get a sense of what David faced on a daily basis:

> The LORD is my light and my salvation;
>> whom shall I fear?
> The LORD is the stronghold of my life;
>> of whom shall I be afraid?
>
> When evildoers assail me
>> to eat up my flesh,
> my adversaries and foes,
>> it is they who stumble and fall.
>
> Though an army encamp against me,
>> my heart shall not fear;
> though war arise against me,
>> yet I will be confident. (Ps. 27:1–3)

He speaks of "evildoers" who "assail" him (v. 2). Their ravenous desire is to "eat up" his flesh (v. 2), a vivid metaphor of their murderous intent. He speaks of "adversaries and foes" (v. 2) who sought every opportunity to destroy his reputation. He envisions an "army" (v. 3) of enemies encamped around him and "war" (v. 3) rising up to undermine his achievements. This reference to an "army" and "war" need not be taken literally but is designed to convey the truth that no matter how great or threatening the danger may be, his "confidence" (v. 3) never cratered.

Notwithstanding these factors, he declares: "The LORD is my light and my salvation; whom shall I fear? The LORD is the stronghold of my life; of whom shall I be afraid?" If distress and trouble are as darkness, the Lord is his light. If trial and tribulation are as an army, the Lord is an impenetrable fortress.

Greater still is his undying aspiration to see and savor the beauty of God. "One thing have I asked of the LORD," said David; "that will I seek after: that I may dwell in the house of the LORD all the days of my life, to gaze upon the beauty of the LORD and to inquire in his temple" (v. 4).

Who or what had the capacity to elicit such dedication from a man who had every reason, humanly speaking, to look elsewhere for comfort and relief? Tempted, no doubt, to numb his aching soul with some worldly narcotic, David fixed the focus of his faith on God: his uncreated beauty, his indescribable splendor, his glorious majesty, his unfathomable, ultimately incomprehensible grandeur.

David's identity wasn't wrapped up in his calling as king. He didn't wake up each day with a political agenda on his mind or a scheme for expanding the boundaries of his empire. David thought of one thing: to find a way to break free of routine entanglements that he might dwell in the presence of God, to avoid trivial activities that might divert his eyes from beholding God, to clear his mind of extraneous details that he might meditate upon the beauty and splendor of God, to set aside less important tasks that he might bask in the invigorating light and glory of everything that makes God an object of our affection and delight and adoration.

David makes the same point in Psalm 145:5, declaring: "On the glorious splendor of your majesty, and on your wondrous works,

I will meditate." I long for this unitary, single-minded resolve. Be it noted that this is no passing glance in God's direction. This is no token acknowledgment of God's glory at eleven o'clock on Sunday morning. Note in verse 4 how the future tense ("I will seek") is combined with the past tense ("I have asked") to express an ardent longing that extends out of the past and into the future and therefore runs through his whole life.

How utterly, absolutely, and incomparably practical this is. Nothing brings greater peace to the troubled soul than meditating on the majesty of God. Nothing puts life and its competing pleasures in greater spiritual perspective than a knowledge of the surpassing greatness of God as revealed in the face of Jesus Christ. Nothing empowers the will to make hard choices, often painful choices, to forgo the passing pleasures of sin than does a view of the superior reward of knowing and savoring and relishing the splendor of God.

Oh, Father of glory, make us a people of *one thing*. Give us *one* heart, *one* mind, *one* all-consuming passion for your name. May we, with David, find you to be life-giving light in the midst of today's darkness. May we, with David, find strength in you as our impenetrable stronghold, the place of peace, where fear cannot flourish.

17

The Blessedness of Forgiveness

Psalm 32

Blessed is the one whose transgression is forgiven,
     whose sin is covered.
Blessed is the man against whom the LORD counts no
iniquity,
     and in whose spirit there is no deceit. . . .

I acknowledged my sin to you,
     and I did not cover my iniquity;
I said, "I will confess my transgressions to the LORD,"
     and you forgave the iniquity of my sin.
                              —Psalm 32:1–2, 5

He should have known better.[9] He never should have stayed at home alone while his army was fighting in the field. He never should have lingered late at night on his rooftop. He never should have set his eyes on that beautiful lady. He never should have inquired about who she was, nor should he have sent for her, nor should he have slept with her. He should have known better. But King David sinned and Bathsheba conceived.

He should have known better. He never should have tried to force Bathsheba's husband, Uriah, to sleep with her, hoping that he would think the child was his own. He never should have arranged for Uriah's death. He should have known better. But King David sinned and Uriah died.

He should have known better. Having committed adultery with Bathsheba he should have acknowledged his sin to the Lord. But he didn't. Having conspired to kill Uriah, her husband, he should have confessed his transgression. But he didn't.

He kept quiet about his sin. He suppressed it. He shoved it deep down inside, thinking it gone for good. He ignored the tug on his heart. He denied the pain in his conscience. He numbed his soul to the persistent pangs of conviction.

Then one day the prophet Nathan told David a story. It was all about a rich man who stole the one little ewe lamb of a poor man rather than taking a sheep from his own huge flock. "Surely this man deserves to die!" shouted an enraged David.

With a bony finger pointed at David's nose, Nathan calmly declared, "You are the man! . . . Why have you despised the word of the LORD, to do what is evil in his sight? You have struck down Uriah the Hittite with the sword and have taken his wife to be your wife" (2 Sam. 12:7–9).

David should have known better.

Adultery and murder make for a sensational story. Many a TV miniseries have rocketed to the top of the Nielsen ratings on the wings of those two sins. Rarely, though, does Hollywood portray the anguish and turmoil they inflict. Listen to what David says in Psalm 32 about the impact of his sin as it festered unconfessed and unforgiven in his heart. Then listen more closely still to the song of God's forgiving love.

> For when I kept silent, my bones wasted away
>> through my groaning all day long.
> For day and night your hand was heavy upon me;
>> my strength was dried up as by the heat of summer.
>> (vv. 3–4)

Someone described David's anguish as "the inner misery of the lacerated heart." David "kept silent" about his sin. He ignored the voice of the Holy Spirit and suppressed the piercing conviction that stabbed repeatedly at his conscience. He refused to deal openly and honestly and forthrightly with God. He would not face his sin. He was living under the delusion that if *he* could somehow forget about it, God would too.

David portrays the impact of his sin in physical terms. Some think this is metaphorical language, that David is using physical symptoms to describe his spiritual anguish. Whereas that's possible, I suspect that David was feeling the brunt of his sin in his body as well.

What we see here is a law of life in God's world. If you bottle up sin in your soul, it will eventually leak out like acid and eat away at your bones. Unconfessed sin is like a festering sore. You can ignore it for a while, but not forever.

The physical effects of his spiritual choices are agonizingly explicit. There was dissipation: "my bones wasted away" (cf. Ps. 6:2). There was distress: "my groaning all day long." And David was drained: "my strength was dried up as by the heat of summer." Like a plant withering under the torrid desert sun, so too was David dried up and drained out from suppressing his sin.

In other words, he was quite literally sick because of his refusal to come clean with God. His body ached because his soul was in rebellion. Spiritual decisions always have physical consequences. "The Spanish Inquisition," wrote Charles Spurgeon, "with all its tortures was nothing to the inquest which conscience holds within the heart."[10]

God simply will not let his children sin with impunity. It was in fact *God's* hand that lay heavily on David's heart. To sin without feeling the sting of God's disciplinary hand is the sign of illegitimacy.

All of us can identify with David's reluctance. No one likes to admit being wrong. No one relishes the thought of confession, far less something as serious as adultery and murder. Facing our faults, whether intellectual or moral, is terribly discomforting.

But here is the good news: this psalm is not primarily about the agony of denial and the pain of repression. It is about the joy and blessedness of forgiving love.

David ransacks the dictionary to describe the full extent of his failure. He calls what he did a "transgression" (v. 1), a word that refers to the rebellious and disloyal nature of his actions. He refers to it as a "sin" (v. 1), a word that points to any act that misses the mark of God's revealed will. And he calls it "iniquity" (v. 5), that is to say, a crooked deed, a conscious intent to deviate from what is right.

Why do you think David goes to such verbal lengths to portray his sin? My sense is that he does so to emphasize that *every* sin, *any* sin, whatever its cause or character, no matter how small or big, secret or public, intentional or inadvertent, *all* sin can be forgiven.

David also uses three different words to describe his confession (v. 5). He "acknowledged" his sin to the Lord. He refused to "cover" his iniquity. He was determined to "confess" his transgressions.

Nothing is held back. There is no cutting of corners. No compromise. He comes totally clean. All the cupboards of his soul are emptied. All little black books are opened and read aloud. His confession is like opening the floodgates of a dam. It may be messy at first, but the release of ever-increasing pressure is life to his burdened heart.

Three different words for sin. Three different words for confession. But better still, three different words for forgiveness!

Blessed is the man whose transgressions are "forgiven" (v. 1). The word literally means "to carry away." David's sin, my sin, *your* sin, is like an oppressive weight from which we long to be relieved. Forgiveness lifts the burden from our shoulders.

Blessed is he whose sin is "covered" (v. 1). It's as if David says, "Oh, dear Father, what joy to know that if I will 'uncover' [v. 5] my sin and not hide it, you will!" David doesn't mean to suggest that his sin is merely concealed from view but somehow still present to condemn and defeat him. The point is that God sees it no more. He has covered it from all view.

Blessed is that man or woman, young or old, whose sin the Lord does not "impute" or "count" against them (v. 2). No record is kept. God isn't a spiritual scorekeeper to those who seek his pardoning favor.

I don't know how all this affects you, but I agree with David when he says (shouts?), "Blessed is the one whose transgression is forgiven. . . . Blessed is the man against whom the LORD counts no iniquity" (vv. 1–2).

Having experienced for himself the joy of forgiving love, David encourages others to seek God's pardoning favor:

> Therefore let everyone who is godly
>> offer prayer to you at a time when you may be found;
>> surely in the rush of great waters,
>>> they shall not reach him.
> You are a hiding place for me;
>> you preserve me from trouble;
>> you surround me with shouts of deliverance. (vv. 6–7)

God is like a high rock on which we stand when the flood waters of adversity begin to rise. God is a hiding place, a shelter in whom we find safety and protection from all that threatens the soul. And remember: all this for men and women like David who have spurned his ways and transgressed his will.

What accounts for this willingness in God to forgive? To what do we attribute the peace and release and joy that flood the pardoned soul? David puts his finger on it in verse 10: "Many are the sorrows of the wicked, but *steadfast love* surrounds the one who trusts in the LORD" (v. 10). God's love is the bulwark of our lives, the bodyguard of our souls, the atmosphere of immutable affection in which we move and live and breathe.

Perhaps you haven't sinned as David did. Adultery and murder may not be on your list. Perhaps your sins are more subtle and less public, whether fewer or greater in number. Whatever the case, your only hope, David's only hope, is the unfailing love of God.

18

The Stability of His Steadfast Love

Psalm 33

Shout for joy in the LORD, O you righteous!
  Praise befits the upright.
Give thanks to the LORD with the lyre;
  make melody to him with the harp of ten strings!
Sing to him a new song;
  play skillfully on the strings, with loud shouts.
  —Psalm 33:1–3

Friends fail us. Stocks plummet. Health is unreliable. A promise is broken. Need I say more?[11] The fact is, there is nothing, no one, anywhere, in which or in whom we can place our unqualified trust and be assured it or they will not let us down.

So what's a person to do? If no one is infallibly worthy of our unquestioning trust, where do we turn? To whom do we ultimately look? In what do we put our hope?

For anyone who reads the Psalms, the answer is obvious. The only thing in life or death that merits our trust is *God's love*. The dollar may rise or fall, nations may totter on the brink of destruction, a spouse may prove unfaithful, but through it all the confidence of the child of God ought to remain constant and unaffected, because God's love never fails.

Three times in Psalm 33 we are told about God's "steadfast" or "unfailing" (NIV) love or "lovingkindness" (NASB). When everything and everyone else bottoms out, the psalmist assures us, "the earth is full of the steadfast love of the LORD" (v. 5). The eyes of the Lord, he tells us, are "on those who hope in his steadfast love" (v. 18). His prayer gets right to the point: "Let your steadfast love, O LORD, be upon us, even as we hope in you" (v. 22).

Whatever else may happen in this world, whoever else may turn their back on you when the chips are down, of this you may be sure: he whose trust and hope and confidence are in the unfailing love of God will never be put to shame.

That's what Psalm 33 is all about. It was written to remind you and me that there is one refuge that is impenetrable to disappointment and betrayal. You may think you're all out of confidence, but what little you've got left, invest in the unfailing love of an undying God.

There are good reasons for that exhortation. The psalmist isn't just making noise or writing pretty poetry. There are some things he tells us about God that make this act of trust eminently reasonable. Let's look at them. He begins by pointing us to God's *unstained principles*:

> For the word of the LORD is upright,
> > and all his work is done in faithfulness.
> He loves righteousness and justice;
> > the earth is full of the steadfast love of the LORD.
> (vv. 4–5)

Whatever God does is righteous because God does it. God doesn't do righteous things because that is what righteousness requires. Righteousness is defined by who God is and what he does. Not only that, but he *loves* righteousness. He doesn't just do it, he *delights* to do it.

When I hear God say, "Sam, I love you," I take refuge in the fact that "the word of the LORD is upright." Others may loudly proclaim their affection for me. They may swear to their ultimate demise that nothing will diminish their commitment to my cause. I hope they're right. But I *know* God is, for "all his work is done in faithfulness" (v. 4b).

The psalmist also points us to God's *unlimited power*:

> By the word of the LORD the heavens were made,
>   and by the breath of his mouth all their host.
> He gathers the waters of the sea as a heap;
>   he puts the deeps in storehouses.
>
> Let all the earth fear the LORD;
>   let all the inhabitants of the world stand in awe of him!
> For he spoke, and it came to be;
>   he commanded, and it stood firm. (vv. 6–9)

When God speaks, it is done. It's as easy (easier) for God to create everything out of nothing as it is for you to utter a word. Now that's the kind of God who inspires confidence! God says "Be!" and it is. God said "Light!" and light was; "Land!" and land was; "Flowers!" and flowers were; "Cows!" and the first moo was heard. This God of power is the one in whose love we find refuge.

Our God is also one of *unstoppable purpose*:

> The LORD brings the counsel of the nations to nothing;
>   he frustrates the plans of the peoples.
> The counsel of the LORD stands forever,
>   the plans of his heart to all generations.
> Blessed is the nation whose God is the LORD,
>   the people whom he has chosen as his heritage!
>   (vv. 10–12)

Superpowers convene summit meetings and vast, multinational corporations formulate their strategies, but it is the purpose of God that shall stand. Even your weekly "to-do" list is incorporated into the accomplishment of God's purpose. Human plans and schemes are always subject to divine restraint.

Nothing is more futile than for people to oppose the purpose of God. Said Spurgeon, "Their persecutions, slanders, falsehoods, are like puff-balls flung against a granite wall."[12] The cause of God is never in danger.

When Joni Eareckson Tada visited Oklahoma City, Oklahoma, to speak at a conference on disability and the church, she explained how her initial perspective on the diving "accident" which left her a quadriplegic had changed. At first she envisioned God turning his back momentarily to attend to some problem in a faraway land. Satan, seizing the moment, placed his foot in the small of her back and shoved her into the shallow waters of the Chesapeake Bay. God, startled by her cry, whirls around . . . too late. He is left to piece back together the shattered remains of her life. No! And again she said, No!

Joni doesn't profess to understand all the intricacies of God's sovereignty, but neither is she free to dismiss him from any role in her accident. His ultimate purpose for her was not sidetracked by Satan's devices. He *can* be trusted, even when his purpose for us is not identical with ours.

The psalmist also takes comfort in what can only be called God's *universal prescience*:

> The LORD looks down from heaven;
> > he sees all the children of man;
> > from where he sits enthroned he looks out
> > on all the inhabitants of the earth,
> > he who fashions the hearts of them all
> > and observes all their deeds. (vv. 13–15)

For several years I was a season-ticket holder for all University of Oklahoma football games. I rarely missed one. The players at OU are often heard referring to "the eye in the sky," a camera strategically placed to record everything on the field. "The eye in the sky doesn't lie," so they say. But sometimes it does. Occasionally, a player can get away with a missed tackle or a penalty. Every now and then he can hide.

But there is another "Eye in the Sky" that never misses so much as a heartbeat. Even your unspoken opinions about what you've been reading in this meditation are known by God before they are thought.

As David said elsewhere, "The LORD is in his holy temple; the LORD's throne is in heaven; his eyes see, his eyelids test the children of man" (Ps. 11:4). God sees it all, instantaneously, simultaneously, and wholly, from the North Pole to the South, whether in Russia or the Rio Grande Valley, on hilltops and in riverbeds, in caves and in palaces.

If that weren't enough, he concludes by pointing us to God's *unchanging passion*:

> The king is not saved by his great army;
>> a warrior is not delivered by his great strength.
> The war horse is a false hope for salvation,
>> and by its great might it cannot rescue.
>
> Behold, the eye of the LORD is on those who fear him,
>> on those who hope in his steadfast love,
> that he may deliver their soul from death
>> and keep them alive in famine.
>
> Our soul waits for the LORD;
>> he is our help and our shield.
> For our heart is glad in him,
>> because we trust in his holy name.
> Let your steadfast love, O LORD, be upon us,
>> even as we hope in you. (vv. 16–22)

Why do our hearts fail from fear? Why is there a crisis in confidence? Because most are tempted to trust in human strength and to rely on earthly strategies. Human power and human promises are notoriously tenuous. It isn't the army that ultimately saves the king or the warrior that brings him victory.

So where must our confidence be placed? In whom or what must we place our hope? In God's steadfast love. And why does God not take pleasure in horses and chariots and the strength of men? Did he not make them all? Yes, but what displeases the Lord is those who *hope* in such earthly props. John Piper explains:

> He is displeased with people who put their hope, for example, in missiles or in make-up, in tanks or tanning parlors, in bombs or

body-building. God takes no pleasure in corporate efficiency or balanced budgets or welfare systems or new vaccines or education or eloquence or artistic excellence or legal processes, when these things are the treasure in which we hope, or the achievement in which we boast. Why? Because when we put our hope in horses and legs, then horses and legs get the glory, not God.[13]

What is the anticipated response to all this? We return to the beginning of this psalm to find it. Quite simply: our uninhibited praise. What we now know about God and his unfailing love calls for loud and jubilant exultation, not because God is hard of hearing, but because the psalmist knows it is natural for people to rejoice loudly in that which they find most delightful.

We are to sing to God a "new song." Why? Because every time we gather as the body of Christ to worship, we have new and fresh reasons to sing. "You'll never believe what God did for me yesterday!" "Oh yes I will. But first let me tell you what I learned about God's character from Romans!"

With God there's always a fresh display of goodness and grace. Each day brings a new and more powerful manifestation of his greatness and mercy. God himself creates the need for new songs by granting new insight into his works and ways. He is constantly doing new and fresh things for which we need new and fresh declarations in song. Praise God for his steadfast love!

19

Pursuing God

Psalm 34

I will bless the LORD at all times;
   his praise shall continually be in my mouth.
My soul makes its boast in the LORD;
   let the humble hear and be glad.
Oh, magnify the LORD with me,
   and let us exalt his name together!
               —Psalm 34:1–3

What does it mean to seek after God? How does one pursue the Almighty? Let's explore Psalm 34 and take note of how David did it. There are six things I want you to consider as essential in pursuing God.

First, *celebrate* God (vv. 1–3). Observe the passion and intensity of David's worship.

David's worship was *voluntary*—"I will bless the LORD." It was a choice, a decision of his soul irrespective of what others may do. "I've determined to celebrate God. I'm resolved. My mind and spirit are fixed. My heart is riveted on him!"

David's worship was *constant*—"at all times." Not just on Sunday (or Saturday, in his case). In all situations and circumstances, at every possible moment of every possible day. Not just when one feels like it, but even when life's a mess. Said Spurgeon: "Happy is he whose fingers are wedded to his harp."[14]

David's worship is *verbal*—"in my mouth." Whether in speech or song, David articulates his adoration of the Lord. If God's praise were at all times in our mouths, what place would be left for slander, gossip, complaint, or criticism?

David's worship was *boastful*—"my soul makes its boast in the LORD." Bragging comes easily to us. No one has to teach us how to boast. So let's just replace ourselves and what we've done with God and what he's done. God is our boast. Brag on the Lord. Make much of him.

David's worship is *contagious*—"let the humble hear and be glad." Only humble people will enjoy hearing others brag on God because the proud want only to hear about themselves.

David's worship is *corporate*—"magnify the LORD with me, and let us exalt his name *together*." As much as one might enjoy private praise, there is something special and empowering and encouraging in joining with others in the adoration of God. Jointly and corporately celebrating God in the community of faith is nonnegotiable.

Second, *pray* to God (vv. 4–7). David "sought" (v. 4a) the Lord by crying out to him in need and trusting him alone for both deliverance from fear (v. 4b) and salvation from trouble (v. 6). How does one know if a person is pursuing God in prayer? They glow: "Those who look to him are radiant, and their faces shall never be ashamed" (v. 5). The one who passionately seeks God's face will reflect the glory of the original. His joy will ignite theirs.

Note well: they look to "him," not just ideas or propositions or speculative theories about what he's like. They settle for nothing less than the intimacy of spiritual eye contact. The result is that they are never ashamed (v. 5b). When we seek God this way he promises never to shame us or humiliate us or mock our feeble efforts. God will never belittle or demean you for coming to him. Just think of it: no shame for those who seek God.

Third, *enjoy* God (v. 8). "Oh, taste and see that the LORD is good! Blessed is the man who takes refuge in him."

Why "taste"? Why didn't David exhort us to "think" or "remember" or some other purely cognitive exercise? Because, as John Piper says, God is most glorified in us when we are most satisfied in him. The imagery of *tasting* makes the point that experiencing God is pleasant and enriching to the soul. There's a spiritual sweetness to the knowledge of God. God is delicious. Jesus is delectable. It's as we savor the flavor of his glory and splendor that he is most honored and exalted in us. Here's how Jonathan Edwards put it:

> God is glorified not only by his glory's being seen, but *by its being rejoiced in*. When those that see it *delight* in it, God is more glorified than if they only see it. God made the world that he might communicate, and the creature receive, his glory . . . both [with] the mind and the heart. *He that testifies his having an idea of God's glory [doesn't] glorify God so much as he that testifies also his approbation [i.e., his heartfelt commendation or praise] of it and his delight in it.*"[15]

This isn't to say that those who "taste and see that the LORD is good" will be insulated from pain and persecution. Far from it. Their determination to seek ultimate satisfaction in God above all else may in fact expose them to even greater oppression and opprobrium. But it matters little, for abiding in his presence awakens spiritual joys that are incomparably full and spiritual pleasures that never lose their capacity to enthrall and satisfy (cf. Ps. 16:11).

Fourth, *fear* God (vv. 9–14). Wait a minute. First David tells us to "taste" God and savor his goodness, then turns around in the next verse and commands us to "fear" him. Are you kidding? Not at all. We must both enjoy God and tremble at his greatness. We must rejoice and revere. We must both adore him and fall on our knees in awe of his power and authority and holiness.

Fifth, *obey* God (vv. 15–18). "The eyes of the LORD," said David, "are toward the righteous," whereas the Lord "is against those who do evil" (vv. 15–16).

One of Frankie Valli's greatest hits declared: "Can't take my eyes off of you!" Well, God can't take his eyes off those who love obedience and are passionate about purity. He gazes on them with tenderness and warmth and loving affection, watching every move they make. No less so his ears: he listens to every prayer, takes note of every groan, is pleased with every song of praise, is moved by every cry of anguish. Others may slight you. Others may ignore your plea. But not God!

Don't overlook the remarkable statement in verse 18. Contrary to all our instincts, David declares that "the LORD is near to the brokenhearted and saves the crushed in spirit." The brokenhearted, more than others, are convinced God is distant and remote and uninvolved. It's the crushed in spirit who more quickly despair of all hope. Yet God is near to them in their misery, quick and able to save and comfort and console.

The weak and broken and most helpless of God's children should never think that for those reasons they are off-limits to their heavenly Father. It is to those, in fact, that he especially draws near.

Sixth, and finally, *trust* God (vv. 19–22). The key statement in this closing paragraph is David's promise that none are condemned "who take refuge in him" (v. 22).

Taking refuge in God is simply another way of saying: trust him! But for what? Many are dismayed because God didn't seem to come through for them when they needed him most. They laid hold of him in their need and came up empty.

May I suggest that God appears not to deliver the goods only because we trust him for things he never promised. You can't trust God to do things your way, according to your timetable, for your praise. You can't trust him to manipulate circumstances to bring you worldly success or to insulate you from the hatred and ill will of his enemies. This isn't because God isn't trustworthy, but simply because these are things he never guaranteed.

For what, then, may I trust him? You can trust him to provide you with eternal security for your soul, guidance and wisdom, forgiveness, spiritual satisfaction, joys that are full and abundant, pleasures that never end. You can trust him never to leave you or forsake you. You can trust him to be good and gracious and tenderhearted and kind. You can trust him to orchestrate every event, even the evil ones, to work together for your ultimate spiritual conformity to the image of his Son. You can trust him for a place in his purpose and undying peace in your soul.

In view of David's exhortations, does it not appear that the passionate pursuit of God is the most sane and sensible, and yes, the most satisfying thing anyone can do?

20

Those Troubling Psalms of Imprecation: Part 1

Psalm 35, etc.

Let them be put to shame and dishonor
    who seek after my life!
Let them be turned back and disappointed
    who devise evil against me!
Let them be like chaff before the wind,
    with the angel of the LORD driving them away!
Let their way be dark and slippery,
    with the angel of the LORD pursuing them!
                —Psalm 35:4–6

How is one supposed to respond to verses in the Psalms like the ones above from Psalm 35? Consider likewise the passages following:

Make them bear their guilt, O God;
    let them fall by their own counsels;

108

because of the abundance of their transgressions cast them out,
for they have rebelled against you. (Ps. 5:10)

Let those be put to shame and disappointed altogether
who seek to snatch away my life;
let those be turned back and brought to dishonor
who delight in my hurt!
Let those be appalled because of their shame
who say to me, "Aha, Aha!" (Ps. 40:14–15)

For their crime will they escape?
In wrath cast down the peoples, O God! (Ps. 56:7)

Pour out your anger on the nations
that do not know you,
and on the kingdoms
that do not call upon your name! (Ps. 79:6)

Appoint a wicked man against him;
let an accuser stand at his right hand.
When he is tried, let him come forth guilty;
let his prayer be counted as sin!
May his days be few;
may another take his office!
May his children be fatherless
and his wife a widow! (Ps. 109:6–9; see also vv. 10–15)

Oh that you would slay the wicked, O God!
O men of blood, depart from me!
They speak against you with malicious intent;
your enemies take your name in vain!
Do I not hate those who hate you, O LORD?
And do I not loathe those who rise up against you?
I hate them with complete hatred;
I count them my enemies. (Ps. 139:19–22)

Had enough? Get the picture? Honestly, that's only a fraction
of the psalms in which prayers for the judgment of God's enemies
are found.[16]

Many believe these "prayers," if it is even legitimate to call them "prayers," are beneath the dignity of the Christian and are not to be viewed as examples for us to follow. They are, rather, the expressions of man's sinful desire for vengeance on his enemies.

These psalms, so some have said, are not God's precepts but man's "defective prayers." They are cold-blooded expressions of malignant cruelty and must never be regarded as inspired of God.

No one struggled more with these imprecations than did C. S. Lewis: "The hatred is there—festering, gloating, undisguised—and also we should be wicked if we in any way condoned or approved it, or (worse still) used it to justify similar passions in ourselves."[17] These prayers of the psalmists, said Lewis, "are indeed devilish."[18]

Lewis and others are bothered most by what appears to be the untroubled conscience of the psalmists. They express no qualms, scruples, reservations, or shame for their desires. Indeed, they move easily from the most horrific of maledictions to petitions for deliverance according to God's "steadfast love" (Ps. 109:21).

Peter C. Craigie, one of the more highly respected commentators on the Psalms, has argued that these passages are "the real and natural reactions to the experience of evil and pain, and though the sentiments are in themselves evil, they are a part of the life of the soul which is bared before God in worship and prayer."[19] The psalmist "may hate his oppressor; God hates the oppression. Thus the words of the psalmist are often natural and spontaneous, not always pure and good."[20] In sum, Craigie states bluntly that "these Psalms are not the oracles of God."[21]

Don't try to dismiss the problem by insisting such prayers are found only in the Old Testament or that they reflect a substandard morality inappropriate to the New Testament Christian. Both Testaments present the same perfect and exalted standard for life. God's moral law is immutable and is everywhere the same. We must be careful never to pit Scripture against Scripture, as if to suggest that the Old Testament calls for a different, perhaps inferior, ethical response to one's enemies than does the New Testament.

Furthermore, one must address the fact that in the New Testament similar "imprecations" on the enemies of God are found (see esp.

Luke 10:10–16; Gal. 1:8; 5:12; 1 Cor. 16:21–22; 2 Thess. 1:6–10; 2 Tim. 4:14; Rev. 6:10; 19:1–2).

Have you considered that to pray "Your kingdom come" (Matt. 6:10) is to invoke divine judgment on all other kingdoms and all those who oppose the reign of God? "When we pray as Jesus taught us, we cry out to God for His blessings upon His church *and for His curses upon the kingdom of the evil one.*"[22]

Even Jesus used imprecatory language in Matthew 23:13, 15–16, 23–24, 27, 29, and especially 23:33. See also his use of Psalm 41:8–10 in Matthew 26:23–24 as a pronouncement of God's judgment on Judas. Henry Mennega has pointed out:

> The New Testament appears not in the least embarrassed with the Old Testament imprecations; on the contrary, it quotes freely from them as authoritative statements with which to support an argument. The New Testament not only quotes passages which, though themselves not imprecations, are found in a Psalm with an imprecatory section; but also, and this is more remarkable, it quotes with approval the imprecations themselves.[23]

One example of the latter is Peter's citation of the imprecatory section in Psalms 69 and 109 in reference to Judas Iscariot: "For it is written in the Book of Psalms, 'May his camp become desolate, and let there be no one to dwell in it'; and 'Let another take his office'" (Acts 1:20). Peter is here citing an invocation of judgment and a curse against the one who betrayed God's Messiah.

What we read in these Old Testament psalms are not emotionally uncontrolled outbursts by otherwise sane and compassionate people. Imprecations such as those listed above are found in high poetry and are the product of reasoned meditation (not to mention divine inspiration). They are calculated petitions, not spontaneous explosions of a bad temper. Certainly there are examples in Old Testament history and prose narrative of actions and attitudes that are sinful and not to be emulated. But the Psalms are expressions of public worship to be modeled.

How, then, do we explain them? And how do we reconcile them with the command of Jesus to love our enemies (Matt. 5:44)? I'll try to answer this in the next meditation.

21

Those Troubling Psalms of Imprecation: Part 2

Psalm 35, etc.

Let them be put to shame and dishonor
    who seek after my life!
Let them be turned back and disappointed
    who devise evil against me!
Let them be like chaff before the wind,
    with the angel of the LORD driving them away!
Let their way be dark and slippery,
    with the angel of the LORD pursuing them!
                  —Psalm 35:4–8

I love the Psalms. No book in all of Scripture has ministered to me as powerfully as this collection of inspired prayers and praise. Any suggestion that they are less than the inspired Word of God is deeply troubling to me. So how are we to make sense of these imprecatory outbursts in which the psalmist pleads for God's wrath and destruction of the wicked? Let me make several suggestions that might help.

1) We should remember that in Deuteronomy 27–28 the Levites pronounce imprecations against Israel if she proves unfaithful to

the covenant. Israel, in accepting the law, brought herself under its sanctions. She in essence pronounced curses upon herself should she break the covenant, and God looked on their response with favor. In other words, God's people were commanded to pray for God's curses upon themselves if they forsook him! We must never think that God is any less severe on his own covenant people than he is on the unbelieving nations who are regularly given to idolatry.

2) These prayers are not expressions of personal vengeance. In fact, most imprecations are in psalms written by David, perhaps the least vengeful man in the Old Testament (consider his dealings with Saul, Nabal, Absalom, and Shimei; see esp. 2 Sam. 24:12). David never asks that he be allowed to "get even with" or "pay back" his enemies. His prayer is that *God* would act justly in dealing with transgressors. There is a vast difference between *vindication* and *vindictiveness*. David's passion was for the triumph of divine justice, not the satisfaction of personal malice. The Old Testament is as much opposed to seeking personal vengeance against one's personal enemies as is the New Testament (see Ex. 23:4–5; Lev. 19:17–18).

3) We also must remember that imprecations are nothing more than human prayers based on divine promises. One is simply asking God to do what he has already said he will do, often repeatedly throughout the Psalms. For example, in Matthew 7:23 Jesus declares that on the day of judgment he will say to hypocrites, "I never knew you; depart from me, you workers of lawlessness." Is it wrong for us to pray that Jesus do precisely that? Is it wrong for us to build a prayer on a promise? "Oh, Lord, cause those to depart from you who do evil," appears to be a perfectly legitimate petition. (In this regard, compare Ps. 35:5 with 1:4; 58:6 with 3:7; 35:8 with 9:15; and 35:26 with 6:10.)

4) Imprecations are expressions provoked by the horror of sin. David prayed this way because of his deep sensitivity to the ugliness of evil. Perhaps the chief reason why he wasn't bothered by prayers of imprecation, and we are, is that he was bothered by sin, and we aren't! It is frightening to think that we can stand in the presence of evil and *not* be moved to pray as David did.

5) The motivation behind such prayers is zeal for *God's* righteousness, *God's* honor, *God's* reputation, and the triumph of *God's*

kingdom. Is our willingness to ignore blasphemy and overlook evil due to a deficiency in our love for God and his name? Could our reaction to the imprecatory psalms be traced to the fact that we love men and their favor more than we love God and his?

6) Another factor to keep in mind is that David, being king, was God's representative on earth. Thus, an attack on David was, in effect, an attack on God. David's enemies were not his private opponents but adversaries of God. David's ire is aroused because they "speak against *you* [God] with malicious intent; *your* enemies take *your* name in vain! Do I not hate those who hate *you*, O Lord? And do I not loathe those who rise up against *you*?" (Ps. 139:20–21; cf. Ps. 5:10).

7) The prayers of imprecation are rarely, if ever, for the destruction of a specific individual but almost always of a class or group, namely, "the wicked" or "those who oppose you."

8) We must keep in mind that in most instances these prayers for divine judgment come only after extended efforts on the part of the psalmist to call the enemies of God to repentance. These are not cases of a momentary resistance to God but of unrepentant, recalcitrant, incessant, hardened, and haughty defiance of him.

In other words, the psalmist calls for divine judgment against them *so long as* they persist in their rebellion. We love our enemies by praying for their repentance. But if they callously and consistently refuse, our only recourse is to pray that God's judgment be full and fair.

It's important to remember that there often comes a time in human sin when God withdraws his merciful hand and gives over the human heart to its chosen path. Paul described this in Romans 1. Jesus envisioned a pattern of sin so persistent and calloused that he declared it unforgivable (see Matt. 12:32; see also 1 Cor. 16:22).

9) It has also been argued that it is in fact the Lord Jesus Christ himself who is praying these psalms of imprecation. One can't help but notice in reading these psalms that whereas David surely speaks of himself, he also speaks beyond himself and his experience in anticipation of the life and sufferings of the Lord Jesus Christ. But what about Christ's prayer from the cross: "Father, forgive them,

for they know not what they do" (Luke 23:34)? James Dick offers this explanation:

> There would indeed be a great inconsistency if Christ had prayed in the same circumstances and concerning the same persons, "Destroy them," and "Forgive them." . . . It was fitting that when he was executing His great commission to give His life a ransom for sinners He should offer a prayer that would reveal His goodwill toward men, and would prove incontestably that He was long-suffering, slow to anger, willing to forgive iniquity, transgression, and sin. This, doubtless, and much more that cannot be dwelt on now may be found in the prayer for forgiveness. But there comes a time, and there come circumstances, when His long-suffering has an end, and when those who refuse to kiss the Son must perish from the way when His wrath is kindled but a little. It is equally fitting, then, that in His mediatorial character He should pray for their destruction. The Psalms themselves present both sides of His mediatorial character and work in these respects.[24]

10) John Piper makes the following important observation:

> The apostle Paul quoted the very imprecatory words of Psalm 69:22–23 in Romans 11:9–10 as having Old Testament authority. This means Paul regarded the very words of imprecation as inspired and not sinful, personal words of vengeance. . . .
>
> Paul read the imprecatory Psalms as the words of Christ, spoken prophetically by David, the type of Christ. We can see this from the fact that David's words in one imprecatory psalm (69:9) are quoted by Paul as the words of Christ in Romans 15:3, "The reproaches of those who reproached you fell on me." The implication, then, is that David spoke in these Psalms as God's inspired anointed king, prefiguring the coming King and Messiah, who has the right to pronounce final judgment on his enemies and will do so, as the whole Bible teaches.[25]

David knows that he needs spiritual protection lest he "hate" God's enemies for personal reasons. That is why he concludes Psalm 139 with the prayer that God purify his motives and protect his heart:

Search me, O God, and know my heart!
  Try me and know my thoughts!
And see if there be any grievous way in me,
  and lead me in the way everlasting! (vv. 23–24)

Therefore, when David speaks of "hatred" for those who oppose God's kingdom he is neither malicious nor bitter nor vindictive nor moved by self-centered resentment. But he most certainly *is* jealous for God's name and firmly at odds with those who blaspheme.

22

Those Troubling Psalms of Imprecation: Part 3

Psalm 35, etc.

Malicious witnesses rise up;
    they ask me of things that I do not know.
They repay me evil for good;
    my soul is bereft.
                   —Psalm 35:11–12

Let me conclude our study of these unsettling psalms with a few words of practical application taken from my book *The Singing God*.[26]

Although it may sound contradictory, we are to "love" those whom we "hate." We love our enemies by doing good to them (Luke 6:27). We love them by providing food when they hunger and water when they thirst (Rom. 12:20). We love our enemies by blessing them when they persecute and oppress us (Rom. 12:14). We love them by responding to their mistreatment with prayers for their salvation (Luke 6:28).

And yes, we are to "hate" those whom we "love." When they persistently oppose the kingdom of Christ and will not repent, our jealousy for the name of Jesus should prompt us to pray: "O, Lord, wilt Thou not slay the wicked? Vindicate your name, O Lord, and may justice prevail in the destruction of those who have hardened their hearts in showing spite to your glory."

Our love is to be the sort that cannot be explained in purely human terms. It isn't enough simply to refrain from retaliating. We are to bless and pray for those who do us harm. I don't know who said it, but I agree: to return evil for evil is demonic. To return good for good is human. But to return good for evil is divine.

That sentiment is certainly Pauline. The apostle said as much when he told us not to seek vengeance on those who do us dirty. However, many have misunderstood Paul, as if he's saying all vengeance is evil. But he says no such thing. The reason we are not to seek vengeance is because God has said *he* will (Rom. 12:19), and he can do a much better job of it than we!

Enemy-love means that instead of responding to evil with evil of our own we are to do good. "In many cases," says Dan Allender, "'doing good' is simply being thoughtful and kind. It boils down to nothing more glamorous than pouring a cup of coffee for someone or warmly greeting them at church and asking about their weekend. Kindness is the gift of thoughtfulness ('Let me look for ways I can serve you') and compassion ('Let me know how I can enter your heart')."[27]

Paul tells us that in loving our enemies we shall "overcome evil." Allender points out that when your enemy receives good for evil it both *surprises* and *shames* him, both of which have the potential to transform his heart.

The enemy spews out his venom expecting you to respond in kind. Part of the wicked pleasure he derives from being an enemy comes from provoking you to act just as wickedly as he does. "Goodness," though, "trips up the enemy by foiling his battle plans. The enemy anticipates compliance or defensive coldness, harshness, or withdrawal. The last thing he expects is sustained kindness and steadfast strength. Therefore, when evil is met with goodness, it is apt to respond with either exasperated fury or stunned incredulity. Goodness breaks the spell the enemy tries to cast and renders him powerless."[28]

Goodness, empowered by God's grace, might even open a crack in his hard-shelled heart. Powerless to explain your response in terms of what he knows about human behavior, he is led to acknowledge the life-changing presence of divine love in and through you and your response to his malicious intent. Allender explains the impact of this "turning the other cheek":

> The enemy's real pleasure in striking out is the power he enjoys to intimidate and shame. He enjoys inflicting the harm, to some degree, because it gives him a sense of control and the fantasy of being like God. Turning one's cheek to the assault of the enemy demonstrates, without question, that the first blow was impotent and shameful. What was meant to enslave is foiled. Like a boomerang, the harm swoops around and smacks the back of the head of the one who meant harm. A sorehead may, with the working of the Spirit of God, ask, "Why did I strike that man?" and eventually ask of the one hit, "Why didn't you retaliate?" Again, a measure of astonishment and curiosity is stirred, and the path toward repentance becomes slightly less dim.[29]

Furthermore, goodness shames the enemy. It forces him to look at himself rather than at you. When the light of kindness shines back in the face of darkness, the latter is exposed for what it really is. Attention is diverted from the abused to the abuser. The shame he feels upon being "found out" will either harden or soften his heart.

In the very early days of my ministry, I was interim pastor of a small church with a history of internal problems. The tiny congregation stood on the brink of yet another split. A congregational meeting was convened at which everyone was given an opportunity to speak his or her mind.

I was young and a bit uncertain of myself, but when the time came I rose to my feet and tried to speak words of encouragement and unity. Suddenly, quite literally in midsentence, I was loudly interrupted by a lady who proceeded to accuse me of trying to "steal" the church for my own selfish gain. Unknown to her, or to anyone else present, I had previously accepted an invitation to join the pastoral staff at another church in the same city.

Her words were sharp and cut deeply into my heart. I distinctly remember formulating in my mind a plan of attack, to be launched as soon as she quit speaking. Were it not for the grace of God I would have destroyed her (and perhaps, unwittingly, myself as well). But the Spirit silenced my youthful impetuosity. As soon as her verbal barrage ceased, I resumed my comments at precisely the point where I left off. I did not respond to her accusations. I made no attempt at self-defense. It was as if she had never said a word.

The outcome was stunning. My refusal to engage her in the verbal gutter (a decision I attribute wholly to God's grace) served to both silence and shame her. By declining to respond in kind, her baseless attack was exposed for what it was. Goodness acted like a shield that caused her venom to ricochet back upon her own head. My intent was not to humiliate or harm her in any way but to lovingly compel her to own up to the motivation of her heart. For the first time I understood what Paul meant when he said, "If your enemy is hungry, feed him; if he is thirsty, give him something to drink; for by doing so, you will heap burning coals on his head" (Rom. 12:20).

"But, Sam, you don't know who *my* enemies are. You have no idea how vile and vengeful and irritating they can be. They take advantage of my goodness; they are unfair; they exploit the fact that I'm a Christian; they constantly embarrass me in front of others and lie about me behind my back."

I don't doubt for a moment that what you say is true. I've still got a few enemies like that myself. But if Stephen could love those who viciously stoned him, what excuse do we have for not loving people whose attack on us is admittedly far less grievous?

And what of Jesus himself? Did he not lovingly pray for his executioners even as they drove iron spikes through his hands and feet? John Stott is surely on the mark: "If the cruel torture of crucifixion could not silence our Lord's prayer for his enemies, what pain, pride, prejudice or sloth could justify the silencing of ours?"[30]

So, the next time someone starts throwing stones in your direction, remember the words of Peter:

For this is a gracious thing, when, mindful of God, one endures sorrows while suffering unjustly. For what credit is it if, when you sin and are beaten for it, you endure? But if when you do good and suffer for it you endure, this is a gracious thing in the sight of God. For to this you have been called, because Christ also suffered for you, leaving you an example, so that you might follow in his steps. He committed no sin, neither was deceit found in his mouth. When he was reviled, he did not revile in return; when he suffered, he did not threaten, but continued entrusting himself to him who judges justly. (1 Pet. 2:19–23)

23

Delight Yourself in the Lord

Psalm 37:4

Delight yourself in the LORD,
  and he will give you the desires of your heart.
                                    —Psalm 37:4

I am an unashamed, passionate advocate of Christian hedonism.
I'm sure there are some who think that's akin to saying that I
enjoy eating fried ice or drawing round squares. After all, aren't
Christianity and hedonism mutually exclusive? This isn't the place
to explain why they aren't. I've done that elsewhere at some length
(see my books *Pleasures Evermore* and *One Thing* and, of course,
John Piper's classic defense in his book *Desiring God*).

I'll simply say that I'm a *hedonist* because I believe it is impossible
to desire pleasure too much. But I'm a *Christian* hedonist because I
believe the pleasure we cannot desire too much is pleasure in God
and all that he is for us in Jesus.

Of the many biblical texts I could cite to defend this concept, none
is more explicit than what David says in Psalm 37:4.

David doesn't stop with the words "delight yourself." Such would
be an endorsement of secular, self-indulgent hedonism. Hedonism as
it is found in the world at large is a philosophy of life and decision

making which says that choices should be made based solely on their capacity to bring us the greatest degree of personal pleasure. Hedonism, then, is the pursuit of pleasure as an end in itself. But David's counsel is that we delight ourselves in God.

I once asked John Piper how we avoid reading this text as an endorsement of the prosperity gospel or a gospel that uses God to get goodies, so to speak. In other words, what prevents us from seeking our joy and satisfaction in God as a pathway to laying hold of other desires of the heart?

He responded by saying that the desires of the heart must be desires that are satisfied in *more of God* in more and more ways. If that were not the case, we would not truly be delighting in God as an end in itself but only using God to get what we enjoy more than what may be found in him alone. He wrote to me:

> I often say that the desire of the heart that we get is God himself. True. But the text implies plurality, and so I am willing to say that we get more of God in more ways when we delight in him. It does not promise that all we can conceive of enjoying will come to us, but that our desires to taste more of God in many ways will be arranged according to God's wise and loving plan.

We should also note that if your delight is wholly in God, then your desires will not be for anything that would diminish his centrality in your soul. You won't want anything that has the potential of turning your heart to trust in anyone but him. If your "desires" are for the stuff of this world that would detract from your complete satisfaction in God, then you aren't truly delighting yourself in him.

That said, let's notice two things about this statement.

First, it is a *command*. This isn't something we are to "pray about" or "consider," as if it were an option or choice. This is a moral obligation binding on all. You can't respond to this statement by saying: "Thanks, God, but no thanks. I think I'll pass on this one. It's just not my style. It's not in keeping with my personality or temperament or spiritual gifts. But thanks anyway." No. Such would be sin! In a word: delight is a duty.

Second, delight or joy is also a *feeling*—an emotion, an affection, a subjective experience that is ultimately not under our control. It isn't something we can produce by an act of will. God has to awaken and stir and evoke such affections in our souls. He uses a variety of means to do this, including Scripture, creation, the sacraments, obedience, prayer, worship, and meditation. Our responsibility, as Jonathan Edwards put it, is "to lay ourselves in the way of allurement." God's responsibility is to allure.

How, then, are we to fulfill this command? Or, better still, in what ways does this delight manifest itself in our lives? I delight myself in my wife by spending time with her. I delight myself in baseball by watching the game and reading the box scores. I delight myself in ice cream by eating it. I delight myself in my grandsons by playing with them. I delight myself in a book by reading it. But *how do we delight ourselves in God?* Let me suggest four ways.

1) *Intellectual fascination.* We must make use of the mind to set ourselves to know him. I have in view intellectual enthrallment with God in which our understanding of him is expanded and intensified. Know him. Learn of him. Study him. Explore his ways. Investigate his will. Become a student of the personality and character of God and he will most surely captivate your mind. In sum, trust God to be sufficiently intriguing that you will be ruined for anything else.

2) *Aesthetic adoration.* We are fundamentally, and by God's design, aesthetic creatures. Being fashioned in the image of God means, at least in part, that we are instinctively drawn to beauty and repelled by ugliness. We have an innate capacity to recognize and rejoice in beauty (unless, of course, we pervert and diminish that capacity by hardening our souls in unrepentant sin). God is ultimate Beauty. To delight in him is to behold his beauty in all its vast array: the symmetry of his attributes, the intricacies of his handiwork, the splendor of his power, the majesty of his mercy, and the list could go on quite literally, infinitely. We must therefore labor to cultivate our aesthetic sensibility and refine our taste for the sweetness of his glory. In sum, trust God to be sufficiently beautiful that all idols become ugly in comparison.

3) *Emotional exhilaration.* Our affections are also designed to find their focus and fulfillment in God. He is worthy of our zeal, love,

devotion, delight, fear, joy, passion, gratitude, and hope. Although we do not see him now, we "love him," and "believe in him and rejoice with joy that is inexpressible and filled with glory" (1 Pet. 1:8). With the Spirit's help we must learn to cultivate and redirect all affections so that they are rooted in him and riveted on him. In sum, trust God to be sufficiently enjoyable that all else pales in comparison.

4) *Volitional dedication.* Delighting in the Lord also entails the engagement of our wills and the choices we make. We must do two things. First, we must choose to obey his commands and, second, we must choose to avoid all that he has prohibited. Obedience nourishes delight and joy. God's commands are his prescription for happiness and spiritual health. We must therefore trust God when he says that sin will corrupt and destroy. We must trust God when he says obedience will bless and enrich.

Disobedience dulls and anesthetizes our spirits to God's presence and activity. It's like injecting Novocain into our spiritual nerves. Disobedience diminishes our capacity to delight in him; it drains our spiritual energy; it lays waste to our ability to focus on God and trust him confidently. It unleashes in our spiritual system a toxin that will progressively cause our spiritual eyes to go blind and our spiritual ears to go deaf. To the extent that we insist on eating the appealing, but ultimately toxic, delicacies of this world, our spiritual taste buds will lose their sensitivity to enjoy the sweet savor of Jesus. In sum, trust God's commandments to be sufficiently good that the ways of the world are exposed as noxious and fatal.

Don't treat delight or joy as merely an aftereffect of obedience, a mere by-product of duty. Make your joy in Jesus central in all you do and say and think, for in your gladness in him is his glory in you most vividly seen.

Psalms 42–63

from Book 2 of the Psalter

24

Preaching to Your Soul

Psalms 42–43

Why are you cast down, O my soul,
and why are you in turmoil within me?
Hope in God; for I shall again praise him,
my salvation and my God.

—Psalm 42:5

What are you to do when all you've had for breakfast is tears, followed by a late-night snack of sorrow? The answer of the psalmist sounds as strange as the question: *preach to your soul!* Take yourself in hand, look yourself in the eyes, and preach to yourself the message of these two psalms.

If the sentiment of Psalms 42 and 43 sounds familiar, it's because here we once again encounter the psalms of lament, those mournful prayers birthed in desperation and affliction. These two psalms should probably be read as one. A number of Hebrew manuscripts join them together; also, Psalm 43 has no heading of its own and concludes with the same refrain found in Psalm 42:5, 11. Although probably written by the sons of Korah (note the superscription), they likely describe David's experience, perhaps during his time of exile when Absalom had rebelled (see Psalm 3).

In spite of the disconsolate spirit of the psalmist, there is an undeniable poetic structure to his anguish. In fact, within Psalms 42–43 we have three smaller psalms, each self-contained, each with three parts. There is, first, an expression or declaration of anguish in which the psalmist, in a manner of speaking, lets himself go (42:1–3, 6–7; 43:1–2). Second, he forces himself to think, by way of remembrance, of what God has done in the past (42:4, 8; 43:3–4). Third, and finally, in the refrain or chorus he composes himself, pulls himself together, as it were, and preaches to his soul (42:5, 11; 43:5).

No simple words will suffice to account for the depth and intensity of his longing for God: "I'm like a deer panting for flowing streams of life-giving water. O God, I thirst for you!" (Ps. 42:1–2, my paraphrase). No one has explained this more vividly than Spurgeon:

> Debarred from public worship, David was heartsick. Ease he did not seek, honour he did not covet, but the enjoyment of communion with God was an urgent need of his soul; he viewed it not merely as the sweetest of all luxuries, but as an absolute necessity, like water to a stag. Like the parched traveler in the wilderness, whose skin bottle is empty, and who finds the wells dry, he must drink or die—he must have his God or faint. His soul, his very self, his deepest life, was insatiable for a sense of the divine presence. . . . Give him his God and he is as content as the poor deer which at length slakes its thirst and is perfectly happy; but deny him his Lord, and his heart heaves, his bosom palpitates, his whole frame is convulsed, like one who gasps for breath, or pants with long running. Dear friend, dost thou know what this is, by personally having felt the same? It is a sweet bitterness. The next best thing to living in the light of the Lord's love is to be unhappy till we have it, and to pant hourly after it—hourly, did I say? Thirst is a perpetual appetite, and not to be forgotten, and even thus continually is the heart's longing after God. When it is as natural for us to long for God as for an animal to thirst, it is well with our souls, however painful our feelings.[1]

It would be enough had all he faced was the sense of God's absence, but his grief was heightened by the taunts of others: "They say to me all the day long, 'Where is your God?'" (Ps. 42:3). David was no doubt asking himself the same question. "O my God, where *are* you indeed?"

The lament continues in 42:6–7 and 9–10. "My soul is cast down within me" might more literally be rendered, "my soul prostrates itself upon me," the picture being of the soul bent double upon itself, a vivid portrayal of a downcast and disconsolate person.

"Deep calls to deep at the roar of your waterfalls; all your breakers and your waves have gone over me" (42:7). This vivid imagery calls to mind an ancient Near Eastern symbol of the powers of chaos and evil crashing in upon him. "His woes were incessant and overwhelming. Billow followed billow, one sea echoed the roaring of another; bodily pain aroused mental fear, Satanic suggestions chimed in with mistrustful forebodings, outward tribulation thundered in awful harmony with inward anguish: his soul seemed drowned as in a universal deluge of trouble."[2]

Goldingay points out that "as the stanzas develop the screw gets tighter, the agony deeper. At first it was 'I can't get to God' (42:1–2); then 'God has forgotten me' (42:9); now 'God has abandoned me' (43:2). . . . I came to you as my refuge, my hiding-place; and you shut the door and left me at the mercy of my pursuers. *Why?* (42:9a). *Why?* (42:9b). *Why?* (43:2a). *Why?* (43:2b)."[3]

What possible hope is there? The psalmist, though in lament, is not in despair. He turns his mind from the disease to the cure, from anguish to remembrance, deliberately recalling to mind God's grace and faithfulness and covenant vow. He forces himself to think of realities other than his own troubles. It is here that we come to the second element in these two psalms: remembrance (42:4, 8; 43:3–4).

He begins by calling to mind those glorious seasons of corporate celebration at the temple of God (42:4). This was, no doubt, a bittersweet experience, for it both aggravates his distress—in that he is at present far from it—and alleviates it, confident that in the future he will return. Although sensibly bereft of God's love, he reminds himself of God's steadfast affection for him (42:8). What he needs most is a personal experience of the exodus itself. His desire is for the light of God's presence that guided Israel by day (cloud) and night (pillar of fire) (43:3–4). He longs to recapitulate in himself that national liberation from bondage and deliverance into the place of God's presence (43:3).

Thus far we've seen in each stanza how the psalmist first expresses his grief and frustration and then forces himself to think of past victories God brought to his children. The third element in each stanza is his determination to resolve the tension between these two. He argues with himself; he pulls himself together and regains his composure, preaching to his soul. "As though he were two men," says Spurgeon, "the Psalmist talks to himself. His faith reasons with his fears, his hope argues with his sorrows."[4] David chides David out of the dumps!

What does he say to himself? Hope in God! Wait for God! This is no mindless meditation, a closing of the eyes or a passive twiddling of the thumbs. Rather we are to envision an expectant, straining anticipation for God's deliverance. This is a *spiritually aggressive confidence* that God will act and show himself faithful based on past performance.

In fact, David begins to praise God and thank him for his gracious deliverance while yet mired in his grief and affliction! "Hope in God; for *I shall* again praise him" (42:5b; 42:11b; 43:5b). Faith makes it possible to say "thank you" before one receives the answer. "Given what I know of God's record in dealing with his people," says David, "my confidence triumphs over my despair. I don't have to wait until he acts to thank him for doing so!"

There are countless lessons to learn from these two psalms, but I'll note only three. First, the psalmist grieves, remembers, and composes himself with a sermon to his soul, not once, or even twice, but three times! David never felt as if he were being needlessly repetitive or that his pleadings were akin to nagging. Rather, he was spiritually relentless, refusing to concede the battle to his enemies, knowing that his God was the kind of God who quenches the thirst of those who faithfully seek him for the water of renewal and hope.

Second, we learn much of the nature of prayer in these psalms. David gives vent to his fears and confusion, not merely in emotional catharsis but in a focused expression of faith that the God who acted graciously on his behalf in the past would do so yet again in the future. He is up front with God, telling it to him straight away on the assumption that God is sufficiently big and merciful to embrace it and absorb it.

Finally, the troubles that David endured (and dare I say, the troubles that you likewise often face), hardly catch God by surprise. They are not the result of some inadvertent oversight or weakness on his part. Look again at 42:7 where David refers to "the roar of *your* waterfalls; all *your* breakers and *your* waves have gone over me." The powers of chaos, trouble, and evil that threaten David's life are not beyond God's sovereign control. They all must submit to his overarching lordship.

"At first sight," says Goldingay, "the belief that God is behind the trouble that comes to us is a frightening doctrine: what kind of a God is this, whose purpose includes so much distress? But the alternative—a God whose purpose is continually being frustrated by evil—is even more frightening. Better a God whose mystery we cannot understand (but who has given us grounds for trusting when we cannot understand) than one whose adequacy we cannot rely on, or whose interest we cannot be sure of."[5]

So, perhaps the time has come for you to take hold of yourself and preach a sermon, not to others, but to your own soul. Remember God's ways. Recall his faithfulness. Compose and calm yourself with the reminder that he who acted powerfully in the past will do so yet again in the present and future.

25

A Mighty Fortress Is Our God

Psalm 46

The LORD of hosts is with us;
the God of Jacob is our fortress.
—Psalm 46:7

*E*in feste burg ist unser Gott! Say what? Well, that's how Martin Luther would have written it in his famous hymn:

A *mighty fortress is our God,*
A bulwark never failing;
Our helper he, amid the flood
Of mortal ills prevailing.

There can be no doubt but that Luther's sturdy, unshakable, un-flappable confidence in God as his refuge, his strength, his mighty, impenetrable fortress is what ultimately accounted for what he was able to accomplish in bringing about what we know as the Protestant Reformation.

The same could easily be said of Elijah as he faced the treachery of Ahab and Jezebel and the prophets of Baal.

The same could be said of Daniel as he fearlessly confronted the power and pressures that came from Nebuchadnezzar and Belshazzar.

And what was it that empowered the apostle Paul as he stood in the presence of his Jewish persecutors or his Roman captors? The same God, who for all of these folk proved himself to be a mighty fortress, a bulwark never failing.

Don't let the fame of these people suggest that God is any less a mighty fortress for you in the midst of your daily struggles or in the minor trials that come your way. Psalm 46 is a powerful word of encouragement for the Christian troubled by the lingering memory of a moral lapse or the parent in agony over the rebellion of a teenage son or daughter. This is a message of hope for the believer who lost his job because he refused to compromise his integrity, as well as the woman who lost her husband to cancer. This is a psalm for you, no less than for the Old Testament Israelite, such that you can confidently declare: "The Lord of hosts is with me; the God of Jacob is my fortress."

The structure of the psalm is simple but important to note. It begins with a declaration of God as our refuge and protection in the midst of natural upheaval (vv. 1–3) and then turns to God as our security in the midst of national uproar (vv. 4–7). The psalmist concludes, appropriately, with a call to worship (vv. 8–11).

Note carefully the language of verse 2: "We will not fear though the earth gives way, though the mountains be moved into the heart of the sea." There's little doubt that the psalmist is describing, as best he can, an earthquake, a phenomenon which more than any other conveys a sense of instability and uncertainty. It's one thing to feel the force of a destructive tornado or the raging waters of a flood. It's another thing entirely when the ground under your feet begins to shake and convulse. Suddenly, all man-made props, all structures of support, crumble and leave you helpless. There's something psychologically unsettling about an earthquake that isn't necessarily the case with other natural phenomena. All one's moorings, one's sense of balance, one's physical and emotional stability are swept away. There's nothing left to grab hold of. Or is there?

In spite of the worst possible scenarios, "God is our refuge and strength, a very present help in trouble" (v. 1). Though the basis of all things visible should convulse, though the most solid and stable of all things created should shake or fall headlong into the sea, our God remains steadfast and faithful. There is no earthquake of any sort, whether natural, moral, physical, financial, or spiritual, that can shake us out of his loving arms.

It's hard to read this passage and not think back to Psalm 18 where David described God in similar language:

> I love you, O LORD, my *strength*.
>> The LORD is my *rock* and my *fortress* and my *deliverer*,
>>> my God, my *rock*, in whom I take refuge,
>>> my *shield*, and the *horn* of my salvation, my *stronghold*.
>> (vv. 1–2)

From the upheavals of nature (46:1–3) to the uproar of nations (vv. 4–7), God is an ever present help and a source of safety for his people. Whether the roar of the waters in verse 3 or the roar of the nations in verse 6, God is greater. Whether the collapse of the mountains in verses 2–3 or the tottering of the kingdoms in verse 6, God is greater. In all cases and scenarios, "the LORD of hosts is with us; the God of Jacob is our fortress" (v. 7).

I suspect it is the rage and terror of the nations even more than the devastation of natural disasters that threaten the serenity of our souls. In the days of the psalmist it may have been the onslaught of Sennacherib or the attack of the Assyrians. In our day it is the threat of international terrorism, the lingering potential of a nuclear bomb, or the vicious release of a lethal nerve gas.

Whatever the circumstances, the city of God rests secure (vv. 4–5). Certainly in its original context this referred to historical Jerusalem, "made glad" by the "streams" that brought refreshment and provision. Today it must also encompass the heavenly Jerusalem (see Heb. 11:10; 12:22). In those days "the gentle Siloam ran from the Gihon spring and, at least from the time of Hezekiah's tunneling work (2 Ki. 20:20; 2 Ch. 32:30), filled a pool inside the city walls."[6]

Don't miss the contrast here between "the destructive, roaring, seething waters of the sea, with its arrogant self-assertiveness, and the refreshment of *a river with its streams*, which remind us of the ones which watered the garden that God planted at the beginning of the human story (Gn. 2:10–13). They point us on also to the water flowing from the temple mount in Ezekiel's vision (Ezk. 47) and the river of the water of life flowing from God's throne in the New Jerusalem (Rev. 22:1–2)."[7]

Whatever deprivation nature and nations may inflict, God will lavishly provide and gently refresh his people who are his eternal dwelling (46:5). Whenever he speaks, the earth simply melts (v. 6).

And what is our response? "Come," says the psalmist, "behold the works of the LORD" (v. 8) and worship! Behold his deliverance of his people from Egypt. Behold his defeat of Pharaoh at the Red Sea. Behold his humbling of the once powerful Nebuchadnezzar. Behold his salvation of your soul and his triumph over all your enemies.

The "nations" that formerly raged (v. 6) and the "earth" that once gave way (v. 2) are now together a platform on which God makes known his glory and power: "Be still, and know that I am God. *I will be exalted* among the nations, *I will be exalted* in the earth" (v. 10). Whatever threat they once posed, they are now harnessed and subdued and brought into service of the God who is Lord over all.

This God, dear friend, "is with us [*you*]" (v. 11a). This God "is our [*your*] fortress" (v. 11b).

Not even Martin Luther was immune to depression and frustration and fear. When he came face-to-face with his enemies, he would often turn to his young friend and coworker Philip Melancthon and say: "Philip, let us sing forth the forty-sixth Psalm." And this is how it sounded:

> A sure stronghold our God is He,
> A timely shield and weapon;
> Our help he'll be, and set us free
> From every ill can happen.

> And were the world with devils filled,
> All eager to devour us,
> Our souls to fear shall little yield,
> They cannot overpower us.

26

When Mercy Scrubs Clean
the Soul: Part 1

Psalm 51

Have mercy on me, O God,
according to your steadfast love;
according to your abundant mercy
blot out my transgressions.
—Psalm 51:1

This psalm has a special message for several groups of
people.

First, Psalm 51 is for those who have never come to grips
with the horror of human sin and the magnitude of divine grace.
Often grace becomes meaningless, and certainly less than "amazing,"
because we lose sight of the depths of our depravity. David helps us
on both counts by describing in graphic detail the reality of his sin
and the breathtaking glory of forgiving grace.

Second, this psalm is for those who think some people are too
high or too holy to fall. Let us never forget that this psalm describes
the experience of David, King of Israel, the "man after God's own
heart" (1 Sam. 13:14).

Third, this psalm is also for those who think that once they have fallen, they can never get back up again. It is for those who think it's possible to fall beyond the reach of God's grace and forgiveness or that there is a quantifiable limit to divine mercy. But no one is so holy that he or she can't fall, or so fallen that he or she can't be forgiven.

Fourth, Psalm 51 is for those who think that if they have fallen and have actually gotten back up, perhaps even forgiven, they are still useless from that point on, both to God and the church. David's experience will prove otherwise.

The historical setting for this psalm is stated in the superscription: "To the choirmaster. A Psalm of David, when Nathan the prophet went to him, after he had gone in to Bathsheba" (see 2 Sam. 11:1–18, 26–27; 12:1–18). None of us likes to have our struggles and problems broadcast publicly, much less our sins of the flesh. Yet here we are told that this psalm was written "to the choirmaster." How would you like your worst sins to be projected on the screen at church and set to music for the corporate worship of God's people?

This psalm is a remarkable, and in many ways unparalleled, description of the nature of conviction, confession, and forgiveness. But at the same time we celebrate, with David, the joy of having one's sins washed clean, we dare not forget that his transgressions yielded significant and far-reaching consequences: (1) his denunciation by Nathan and the public shame it brought (2 Sam. 12:1–14); (2) the death of David's son (12:15–23); (3) trouble with Amnon, who raped Tamar, Absalom's sister (13:1–22); (4) the rebellion of Absalom (13:23–18:33); (5) trouble with affairs of state (e.g., the revolt of Sheba in 19:41–20:26). The lesson is that whereas sin is certainly personal, in many cases it is anything but private.

On what basis does David ask for acquittal (vv. 1–2)? Does he appeal to his track record as king over Israel? Does he remind God of how many psalms he has written and how much of a blessing they've been to God's children? Does he cite his faithful service or marshal forth a long list of character witnesses? Not in the least.

He doesn't expect to be forgiven based on his sincerity or spiritual intensity or deep pain for having sinned or fervor of heart or promise not to sin again or his depth of determination to somehow "make it up" to God. That's not to say sincerity and zeal and conviction aren't important. But David's appeal is based on what he knows of God's mercy and compassion and steadfast love.

Note the three words David uses in verses 1–2 to describe his sin. If nothing else, it indicates on his part an acknowledgment that it *is* sin and not just some trivial mistake. He calls it a "transgression," a willful, self-assertive defiance of God; an "iniquity," a deviation from the right path; and a "sin," a missing of the divine mark.

Equally vivid are the three words he uses in his plea for forgiveness. He asks God to "blot out" his transgressions, to erase it from the record (Ex. 32:32; Num. 5:23) or wipe it away (2 Kings 21:13; Isa. 44:22).

He beseeches the Lord to "wash" him from his sin (vv. 2, 7b). This word was often used of a woman first saturating a garment with lye soap and then treading it under foot on a rock, beating and pummeling it as the rushing waters poured over it. One can almost hear David tearfully praying: "Gracious Lord, do that to my spirit! My sin is like a deep-dyed stain that has soiled the fabric of my soul, and no ordinary soap or detergent, far less any good works I might perform, can remove it. My transgressions are like ground-in dirt. Lord, scrub me clean by your mercy and grace!" Finally, the word *cleanse* (v. 2) was one used for ceremonial purification in the Old Testament.

When David turns, in verses 3–4, to confess the magnitude of his sin, his language is no less graphic. Edward Dalglish writes:

> The sin is not vaguely expressed and in a neutral context but intensely personal—MINE—and is so described five successive times in the first three verses. True penitence is not a dead knowledge of sin committed, but a vivid, ever-present consciousness of it. Thus poignantly affected by this fixation of sin and dominated by a feeling of complete submission, the psalmist opens the hidden world of his soul, exposing his guilt-stricken conscience.[8]

David makes no excuses, offers no rationalizations, and refuses to shift blame. He doesn't say, "Well, now wait a minute, God. Yes, I sinned. But it takes two to tango. What about Bathsheba's complicity in all this? She's so beautiful and seductive. And my wife wasn't meeting my needs. Besides, the pressures of being king over your people are enormous. Given what I faced on a daily basis, I'd expect you to cut me a little slack." No!

There's no insanity plea or appeal to diminished capacity. Do you recall the infamous "Twinkie defense" used by Dan White when he killed San Francisco Mayor George Moscone and supervisor Harvey Milk in 1985? He pleaded innocent based on his alleged "diminished capacity" brought on by certain biochemical reactions to junk food. "I'm innocent, Your Honor. I overdosed on Twinkies!" None of that here.

"My sin," he says, "is ever before me" (v. 3b). It is no intermittent flash but a perpetual obsession, a sight from which I can never turn away. It is, as it were, seared on the inside of my eyelids: I see it all the time. Worse still, it is a sin ultimately against God alone (v. 4a).

But how can it be against God only if he committed adultery with Bathsheba, conspired to kill her husband, Uriah, disgraced his own family, and betrayed the trust of the nation Israel? Perhaps David would argue that whereas one commits *crimes* against people, one *sins* only against God. More likely still, "face to face with God, he sees nothing else, no one else, can think of nothing else, but His presence forgotten, His holiness outraged, His love scorned."[9] David is so broken that he has treated God with such disregard that he is blinded to all other aspects or objects of his behavior.

David's confession is not simply to "get things off his chest," as if confession were merely a therapeutic release of sorts. His confession is designed to tell everyone that God was in the right all along, that God's judgment was true and just, and that the Almighty is blameless (v. 4b).

How long has David had this problem with sin? Did it start with puberty? Was he turned to the dark side by some childhood or teen-aged trauma? "The problem," says David, "isn't so much that I sin. The problem is that I'm *sinful*, and *always have been*. These deeds of the flesh are symptomatic of a much deeper problem. The fact is, 'I was brought forth in iniquity, and in sin did my mother conceive me' (v. 5). My transgressions are not of recent vintage. This was no freak, one-off event. I've been a sinner from my mother's womb!"

Thus David confesses his hereditary sin (v. 5) as the root cause of his actual sin (v. 4), but makes no effort to exculpate himself on that basis. In explaining his sinfulness by reference to the natural propagation of the species, David moves beyond his birth (v. 5a) to the very genesis of his being in the womb of his mother, indeed, to the very moment of conception (v. 5b). However, "David is not trying to accuse his mother in order to excuse himself!"[10] The focus of the entire psalm is the personal accountability of David. No one is to blame but him alone. His point is simply that "his very being is shot through and through with the tendencies that produced the fruits of adultery and murder. As far back as he can go, he sees his life as sinful."[11]

David's intent isn't to impugn the sex act itself but rather to confess the native corruption of that which is its product. Dalglish contends that the words *in sin* "ought not to be conceived as qualifying the coitus which resulted in the conception of the psalmist's being. It should properly be taken either to describe the status of the generating mother or else be referred generally to the embryological development resulting in transplanting the predicate of sinfulness to the child. It would be utterly opposed to the thought of the Old Testament [cf. Gen. 1:28; 9:1, 7; Ps. 127:3, 5; Gen. 29:31; 30:22, 33; Ruth 4:13; Ps. 139:13; Job 10:8ff.] to imagine that conception or parturition was sinful."[12]

In other words, David's problem (yours and mine too) isn't that we commit individual acts of sin. The problem is that we have a constitutional propensity to sin. What we need most isn't a new lifestyle, but new life; not new habits, but a new heart. And what hope is there for this? The answer comes in the next meditation.

27

When Mercy Scrubs Clean the Soul: Part 2

Psalm 51

The sacrifices of God are a broken spirit;
a broken and contrite heart, O God, you will not
despise.

—Psalm 51:17

Countless Christians feel spiritually paralyzed by the lingering stain of sin. Neither therapy nor religious formulas nor good intentions nor good deeds can erase the vivid memory of their transgression(s) or bring cleansing to the defiling sense of guilt. The oppressive weight of their failure(s) is virtually suffocating.

Thank God for Psalm 51! It is a refreshing and heartwarming reminder of the hope of forgiveness. But it's even more than that. David not only prays for *pardon* from past sin but also for the *power* to walk in future purity.

He begins with an impassioned plea for ceremonial cleansing, cast in the form of what Hebrew scholars call *synonymous parallelism*: "Purge me with hyssop, and I shall be clean; wash me, and I shall be whiter than snow" (v. 7). David's choice of words is instructive.

"Hyssop," an aromatic herb with a straight stalk and a bushy head (it looked a lot like broccoli), was dipped in the blood of the sacrifice and then sprinkled seven times on the person who was defiled (cf. Lev. 14:1–9; Num. 19). The word translated "purge" might more literally be rendered "de-sin," as in "de-sin me." Only then will David be "clean" and "whiter than snow." Can this actually happen for sinners like you and me?

But David longs for more. He asks that God would enable him to "hear joy and gladness" (v. 8a; cf. Isa. 35:10; 51:11). David employs a common figure of speech called *metonomy of effect for cause*, according to which he means: "Make me to experience the joy and gladness that come from hearing the announcement of forgiveness." He may even have in mind a priestly or prophetic oracle in which another loudly declares that his sins are forgiven (cf. 2 Sam. 12:13; Ps. 143:7–8).

Sin can be as spiritually devastating and painful to the soul as broken bones are to the body; thus his cry: "Let the bones that you have broken rejoice" (v. 8b). David's desire is that his entire being, body, soul, and spirit might once again revel and rejoice in the blessedness of communion with God.

Once more he prays: "Hide your face from my sins, and blot out all my iniquities" (v. 9). Don't look any longer on my failures! Let not your eyes gaze on my wickedness! Blot it from view, erase it from memory (cf. Ps. 103:12; Isa. 27:9; Jer. 1:20; 18:23; Mic. 7:19; Zech. 3:4, 9)!

With verses 10–12 David's prayer gets even more specific. He petitions the Lord for spiritual power (v. 10), spiritual presence (v. 11), and spiritual pleasure (v. 12).

Simply asking for pardon isn't enough. One must also have the power by which not to commit the same sin again. Dalglish explains:

> The prayer for forgiveness is complete, but pardon, boon though it be, cannot suffice. Its reference is to the past and to excision of iniquity erstwhile accumulated. But what of the future? Unless something different, something new, is done within the personal life of the psalmist, the future will but repeat the past. The forgiveness of iniquity may

grant to the suppliant a clean record, but it is the perpetuation of that purity that deeply troubles the psalmist. This problem forms the burden of the prayer for renewal.[13]

No mere makeover will do, no matter how "extreme." David refuses to settle for a glossing over of his faults but pleads for a replacement of the old with the new. A "clean heart" (v. 10a) and a "right spirit" (v. 10b; or steadfast, firm, reliable spirit), his way of describing the inner core and center of his life, are essential for a life of holiness.

David can't bear the thought of the loss of intimacy of fellowship and its attendant joys, and thus prays that he not be cast from God's "presence" (see Pss. 16:11; 21:6; 73:27–28) or suffer the loss of God's Spirit (v. 11).

What does David mean when he prays that God would not take his Spirit from him? Does he envision the possible loss of his salvation? Does he envision the withdrawal of divine grace? No.

Aside from the saving activity of the Holy Spirit in the Old Testament and the empowering ministry by which believers are sanctified and enabled to live holy lives, the Holy Spirit was poured out on select individuals to equip them to perform important tasks in the covenant community of Israel:

1) Craftsmen who worked on the tabernacle/temple (Ex. 31:1–6);
2) Civil administrators such as Moses and the seventy elders (Num. 11:16–17, 25–26);
3) Military commanders such as Joshua (Num. 27:18);
4) Judges appointed and empowered to rule over Israel (Judg. 3:10; 6:34);
5) Samson (Judg. 14:5–6, 19; 15:14; 16:20);
6) Prophets (1 Chron. 12:18; Mic. 3:8);
7) Kings over Israel such as Saul (1 Sam. 10:1, 6, 10; 16:14) and David (1 Sam. 16:12–13).

Thus, there was a ministry of the Holy Spirit in the Old Testament, unrelated to personal salvation or character, designed solely to empower, enable, and equip someone for a task to which God had appointed him or her. Such, I believe, is what David has in mind in Psalm 51:11. His prayer is that God would not withdraw the enabling anointing of the Spirit that empowers and equips him to lead Israel as king. Indeed, he may well have had in mind that disturbing scene where "the Spirit of the LORD departed from Saul" (1 Sam. 16:14) and prays that such would never befall him.

God's power, God's presence, and yes, even God's pleasure is at the heart of David's prayer: "Restore to me the *joy* of your salvation" (v. 12a). Sin suppressed is delight destroyed. David was saved, but his soul had soured. He longs once again for the enjoyment of God that comes with intimacy.

David concludes with a vow of commitment in verses 13–19.

It is possible for the fallen to be forgiven and used of God in ministry to others. David anticipates that after his restoration he will again "teach transgressors [like himself] your ways" (v. 13). David anticipates once again singing "aloud" of the "righteousness" of God (v. 14b). With pardon and power comes the opportunity to once more "declare" God's "praise" aloud (v. 15).

Note also the relationship between testimony and praise in verses 13–15. "When God answers our prayers, we respond by telling him how great he is; but we do so in public, and this is of the essence of the matter."[14] Often guilt acts like glue: it seals shut the mouth of praise. It's as if David says, "My conscience has shamed me into silence. Right now my lips are sealed because of my sin. Forgive me and open my mouth and I will surrender my voice to you!"

People have often misunderstood the concluding verses of Psalm 51, particularly verses 16–17, thinking that God has rejected his own appointed sacrifices. But in the Old Testament, "not that, but this," is merely an emphatic way of saying "not that, without this" (cf. 1 Sam. 15:22; Hos. 6:6). David is simply telling us that what matters most to God is the inner spiritual reality of a truly contrite and broken heart. Without it, sacrifices are worthless. With it, they are a sweet-smelling aroma to God (see vv. 18–19).

Gordon MacDonald tells the story of how as a child he once knocked over a lamp, cracking the ceramic shaft on one side. He quickly placed it back on the table, turning the lamp so the crack was not visible. He lived in fear each day that his misdeed would be discovered. "The longer the confrontation was delayed," he writes, "the worse the consequences promised to be in my mind." When the day finally arrived, his mother asked him, "Did you do this?" He confessed. What happened next is instructive for us all:

> But Mother never said a word. She took it to the kitchen, glued the pieces so that they once more fit tightly together, and within a few hours returned the lamp to the table. The crack was always there, but the lamp was rebuilt. And it served its purpose for years. Broken worlds may always have cracks to remind us of the past; that's reality. But sometimes the grace of God is like the glue my mother used on her lamp. The bonded edges can become stronger than the original surface.[15]

Some of you have cracked lamps in your past and live in constant fear, devoid of joy, paralyzed in life, relationships, and ministry. You wonder whether you will ever again experience the joy of intimacy with God, much less a fruitful ministry to others.

But God is in the business of rebuilding cracked lives and shattered dreams. His "steadfast love" is a soul-cleansing power, his "abundant mercy" a force for restoring long lost hope (v. 1). All he asks of you is a "broken spirit" and a "contrite heart"; these, says David, he will "not despise" (v. 17).

28

I Will Lift Up My Hands

Psalm 63:4

So I will bless you as long as I live;
   in your name I will lift up my hands.
           —Psalm 63:4

On more than one occasion I've been asked: "Sam, why do you lift your hands when you worship?" My answer is twofold.

First, I raise my hands when I pray and praise because I have explicit biblical precedent for doing so. I don't know if I've found all biblical instances of it, but consider this smattering of texts along with Psalm 63:4:

To you, O LORD, I call;
   my rock, be not deaf to me,
lest, if you be silent to me,
   I become like those who go down to the pit.
Hear the voice of my pleas for mercy,
   when I cry to you for help,
when I lift up my hands
   toward your most holy sanctuary. (Ps. 28:1–2)

My eye grows dim through sorrow.
Every day I call upon you, O LORD;
　　I spread out my hands to you. (Ps. 88:9)

I will lift up my hands toward your commandments, which I
　　love,
　　and I will meditate on your statutes. (Ps. 119:48)

Lift up your hands to the holy place
　　and bless the LORD! (Ps. 134:2).

O LORD, I call upon you; hasten to me!
　　Give ear to my voice when I call to you!
Let my prayer be counted as incense before you,
　　and the lifting up of my hands as the evening sacrifice!
　　　　(Ps. 141:1–2)

I stretch out my hands to you;
　　my soul thirsts for you like a parched land. (Ps. 143:6)

Then Solomon stood before the altar of the LORD in the presence
of all the assembly of Israel and spread out his hands. Solomon had
made a bronze platform five cubits long, five cubits wide, and three
cubits high, and had set it in the court, and he stood on it. Then he
knelt on his knees in the presence of all the assembly of Israel, and
spread out his hands toward heaven. (2 Chron. 6:12–13)

And at the evening sacrifice I rose from my fasting, with my garment
and my cloak torn, and fell upon my knees and spread out my hands
to the LORD my God. (Ezra 9:5)

And Ezra blessed the LORD, the great God, and all the people answered, "Amen, Amen," lifting up their hands. And they bowed
their heads and worshiped the LORD with their faces to the ground.
(Neh. 8:6)

Let us lift up our hearts and hands to God in heaven. (Lam. 3:41)

I desire then that in every place the men should pray, lifting holy
hands without anger or quarreling. (1 Tim. 2:8)

If someone should object and say that few of these texts speak of worship (see Pss. 63:4; 134:2), but only of prayer (as if a rigid distinction can even be made between the two—indeed, I can't recall ever worshiping God without praying to him), my question is simply this: Why do you *assume* that the appropriate place for your hands is at your side and you need an explicit biblical warrant for raising them? Wouldn't it be just as reasonable to assume that the appropriate place for one's hands is raised toward heaven, calling for an explicit biblical warrant, other than gravity or physical exhaustion, to keep them low?

The second answer I give to the question, "Why do you lift your hands when you worship?" is: "Because I'm not a gnostic." Gnosticism, both in its ancient and modern forms, disparages the body. Among other things, it endorses a hyper-spirituality that minimizes the goodness of physical reality. Gnostics focus almost exclusively on the nonmaterial or spiritual dimensions of human existence and experience. The body is evil and corrupt, little more than a temporary prison for the soul that longs to escape into a pure, ethereal, altogether spiritual mode of being.

But biblical Christianity celebrates God's creation of physical reality; after all, he did pronounce it "good" in Genesis 1. We are more than immaterial creatures. We are embodied souls, and we are to worship God with our whole being. Paul couldn't have been more to the point when he exhorted us to present our "bodies as a living sacrifice, holy and acceptable to God," which is our "spiritual worship" (Rom. 12:1).

By all means, we must worship with understanding. We must think rightly of God and love him with our heart and soul and mind (see Matt. 22:37). But we are not, for that reason, any less physical beings. We will have glorified bodies forever in which to honor and adore our great God. If we are commanded to dance, kneel, sing, and speak when we worship, what possible reason could there be for not engaging our hands as well?

Ronald Allen is spot on in his portrayal of the significance of the human hand:

It is the human hand which beautifully typifies the human spirit. It is distinct from the hands of the lower animals in appearance and dexterity. Observe the hands of a skilled person; no matter the field, it is an amazing exhibition of the genius of our creative Lord. Think of the fingers of the typist, the seamstress, the potter, the painter, the violinist, the mechanic, the builder; the list could be endless. The hand allows the creative to be expressive; it can do so much good or evil. The hand can be firm, as a parent's spank or firm grasp; it can be gentle, stroking the hair or face of a child or lover.[16]

In addition, the human hand gives visible expression to so many of our beliefs, feelings, and intentions. When I taught homiletics, one of the most difficult tasks was getting young preachers to use their hands properly. Either from embarrassment or fear, they would keep them stuffed in their pockets or hidden from sight behind their backs or nervously twiddle them in a variety of annoying ways.

Our hands speak loudly. When angry, we clench our fists, threatening harm to others. When guilty, we hide our hands or hold incriminating evidence from view. When uneasy, we sit on our hands to obscure our inner selves. When worried, we wring them. When afraid, we use them to cover our face or hold tightly to someone for protection. When desperate or frustrated, we throw them wildly in the air, perhaps also in resignation or dismay. When confused, we extend them in bewilderment, as if asking for advice and direction. When hospitable, we use them to warmly receive those in our presence. When suspicious, we use them to keep someone at bay, or perhaps point an accusing finger in their direction.

Does it not seem wholly appropriate, therefore, to raise them to God when we seek him in prayer or celebrate him with praise? So again, why do I worship with hands raised?

Because like one who *surrenders* to a higher authority, I yield to God's will and ways and submit to his guidance and power and purpose in my life. It is my way of saying, "God, I am yours to do with as you please."

Because like one who expresses utter *vulnerability*, I say to the Lord: "I have nothing to hide. I come to you openhanded, concealing nothing. My life is yours to search and sanctify. I'm holding nothing back. My heart, soul, spirit, body, and will are an open book to you."

Because like one who needs help, I confess my utter *dependency* on God for everything. I cry out: "O God, I entrust my life to you. If you don't take hold and uplift me, I will surely sink into the abyss of sin and death. I rely on your strength alone. Preserve me. Sustain me. Deliver me."

Because like one who happily and expectantly *receives* a gift from another, I declare to the Lord: "Father, I gratefully embrace all you want to give. I'm a spiritual beggar. I have nothing to offer other than my need of all that you are for me in Jesus. So glorify yourself by satisfying me wholly with you alone."

Because like one who aspires to direct *attention* away from self to the Savior, I say: "O God, yours is the glory; yours is the power; yours is the majesty alone!"

Because as the *beloved* of God, I say tenderly and intimately to the Lover of my soul: "Abba, hold me. Protect me. Reveal your heart to me. I am yours. You are mine. Draw near and enable me to know and feel the affection in your heart for this one sinful soul."

For those many years when I kept my hands rigidly at my side or safely tucked away in the pockets of my pants, I knew that none would take notice of my praise of God or my prayers of desperation. No one would dare mistake me for a fanatic! I felt in control, dignified, sophisticated, and above all else, safe. These matter no more to me.

Please understand: these are not words of condemnation but confession. I know no one's heart but my own. I judge no one's motives but mine. I'm not telling you how to worship but simply sharing how I do and why. I'm at that point in life where I honestly couldn't care less what the immovable evangelical is thinking or the crazy charismatic is feeling. What matters to me is that God have my all: my mind, will, feet, eyes, ears, tongue, heart, affections, and yes, my hands.

No, you need not raise your hands to worship God. But why wouldn't you want to?

Psalms 73–88

from Book 3 of the Psalter

29

It's All a Matter of Perspective

Psalm 73

Truly God is good to Israel,
   to those who are pure in heart.
But as for me, my feet had almost stumbled,
   my steps had nearly slipped.
                              —Psalm 73:1–2

S ome Christians would like us to believe that their faith in God
is invulnerable to challenges from without. They act and talk as
if their faith has never suffered a crisis of any sort, never been
stretched or strained almost to the point of breaking. My opinion
of such folk is that they are either pathetically naïve, dangerously
dishonest, or perfect.

You simply can't live long in this world and not experience crises
in spiritual confidence every once in a while. Even the most mature
believers will tell you that occasionally they have their doubts about
God and his ability to run things the way the Bible says he does.

Challenges to faith come in all shapes and sizes: the devastation of
a hurricane, the death of a child, genocide in Darfur, an unexpected
bankruptcy . . . Need I go on?

Yet another challenge to faith is when good things happen to bad people. Are you ever bothered when the wicked become even more wealthy, when perverts prosper, or when atheists live long and fruitful lives? Is it unsettling to your faith when those who hate Jesus triumph and those who love him endure unspeakable tragedy?

It bothered Asaph. It got under his skin and was a thorn in his side and threatened to turn his soul sour. In fact, it got so bad that he was tempted to jump ship, to abandon his faith in God, to chuck it all in and join the other side.

Asaph, author of Psalm 73, was deeply disturbed and perturbed by the prosperity of the wicked and the oppression of the righteous. It led him to question God's goodness and greatness. It stirred him to wonder if the pursuit of godliness was really the wisest path to follow.

His problem wasn't with the traditional problem of evil; Asaph's struggle was with why it so often seems that those who do deserve to suffer don't, and those who don't deserve to suffer do. His problem wasn't whether God exists but whether God is just.

Asaph is brutally honest about his struggle. "As for me," he confessed, "my feet had almost stumbled, my steps had nearly slipped. For I was envious of the arrogant when I saw the prosperity of the wicked" (vv. 2–3). "I'm the one who obeys God. I'm the one who worships. So why are the wicked the ones who get all the rewards?" Of course, when one gets in that frame of mind one tends to generalize to the point of exaggeration and distortion. As far as Asaph was concerned, no wicked person ever suffered; all wicked people are prosperous. It's a classic case of self-pity gone to seed.

As he reflects on the wicked, he is tormented by their power and seemingly care-free existence (vv. 4–12). They appear utterly unconcerned about the consequences for their actions. They don't seem to suffer from the same frailties of life as do the righteous. Adversity, toil, disease, and typical frustrations escape them. It all seems so unfair.

When it does come time for them to die, they seem to do so painlessly (v. 4a). Routine troubles are foreign to them, and daily distresses are absent (v. 5). They appear to live above the trials

156

that plague the righteous. They seem immune to ordinary domestic disappointments.

This doesn't lead to gratitude or joy but to presumption and arrogance, vices they proudly wear like a woman who was just given a new necklace or an expensive dress (v. 6). They feel no inclination to put a check on their thoughts or fantasies (v. 7). Far from being grieved when the righteous suffer, they threaten them with even greater oppression (v. 8). Nothing is sacred to them as they curse men and blaspheme God (v. 9).

The power and wealth of the wicked perverts others as well. People are drawn to the rich, as those who long for a piece of the action are seduced into following their ways (v. 10). They justify it by arguing that *if* God exists, he probably doesn't even take notice, and if he is aware of what's happening, he simply doesn't care (v. 11).

Asaph has let these thoughts fester in his soul until he draws this dangerous conclusion: "All in vain have I kept my heart clean and washed my hands in innocence" (v. 13). The bottom line is this: piety doesn't pay. Moral earnestness is a waste of time. "Poor Asaph! He questions the value of holiness when its wages are paid in the coin of affliction. . . . There were crowns for the reprobates and crosses for the elect. Strange that the saints should sigh and the sinners sing."[1]

But let's not be too quick to judge, for this is what Asaph *might* have said had he allowed his thoughts to run rampant and unchecked (cf. v. 15a). Perhaps the shocking nature of such a conclusion jolted him back to reality. In any case, he stopped short of blasphemy. While tempted to abandon his faith, something held him in check. What was it? He mentions three things.

First, he reflects on how his decision might impact others in the community of faith (v. 15). He was evidently a man highly esteemed by others and whose opinions carried considerable weight. He knows if he were to go public with his doubts and fears it would adversely affect the faith of others. His love for them keeps his tongue in check.

Second, Asaph had a powerful and transforming experience while in the sanctuary (temple) of God (vv. 16–20). We don't know what it was, but perhaps he had a vision like that of Isaiah's (Isa. 6:1ff.)

or some other revelatory encounter. In any case, he was suddenly gripped by the reality of ultimate and inescapable judgment for those who defy God (v. 17). He looked away from their present prosperity to their future judgment ("their end," v. 17b). He is reminded that justice delayed is not necessarily justice denied. God has arranged it all! He is in control of both their prosperity and their consummate demise. God has temporarily lifted them up and God will eternally bring them down.

He came to realize that the prosperity of the wicked is like a dream: it seems so real until one awakens to see it was all a fleeting fantasy (v. 20). "As a dream vanishes so soon as a man awakes, so the instant the Lord begins to exercise his justice and call men before him, the pomp and prosperity of proud transgressors shall melt away."[2]

But there is a third and more important reason why Asaph does not permit himself to be swept away by the apparent injustice of wicked people prospering. He describes it in verses 21–28. His point is simple, yet profound: *God is with him*. I should let Asaph say it for himself:

> Nevertheless, I am continually with you;
>> you hold my right hand.
> You guide me with your counsel,
>> and afterward you will receive me to glory.
> Whom have I in heaven but you?
>> And there is nothing on earth that I desire besides you [not even the opulence and apparent success of the wicked!].
> My flesh and my heart may fail,
>> but God is the strength of my heart and my portion forever.
> (vv. 23–26)

What is all the wealth of the world compared with the spiritual riches of God's presence? Can the power and prestige of earthly fame trump the assurance and peace of God's grip on our lives? Our having him and his having us is simply unparalleled, unsurpassed, and unfathomable. Intimacy with the Almighty transcends all earthly pleasure.

What it all comes down to, then, is a matter of perspective. So I close with these insightful words of D. A. Carson. Carson says:

> [Everything] depends on where you start. If you begin by envying the prosperity of the wicked, the human mind can "interpret" the data so as to rule God out, to charge him with unfairness, to make piety and purity look silly. But if you begin with genuine delight in God, both in this world and in the world to come, you can put up with "flesh and heart failing," and be absolutely confident that, far from being the victim of injustice, you are in the best possible position: near to the good (v. 1) and sovereign (v. 28) God.[3]

30

Our Lack, His Supply

Psalm 84

My soul longs, yes, faints
    for the courts of the LORD;
my heart and flesh sing for joy
    to the living God.
            —Psalm 84:2

Some people are terrified of appearing needy. Obsessed with their public image and how they are perceived, they put on a false front of self-sufficiency and self-reliance.

Not David! That's one of the things I admire most in the author of so many of these psalms. He is utterly unashamed to acknowledge before others his weakness and dependency on God. Typical is this cry of desperation in Psalm 63:1:

O God, you are my God; earnestly I seek you;
    my soul thirsts for you;
my flesh faints for you,
    as in a dry and weary land where there is no water.

The psalmists recognized that nothing serves to glorify God more than our honest and heartfelt acknowledgment that, apart from what he supplies, we die. Again, we read:

> As a deer pants for flowing streams,
>   so pants my soul for you, O God.
> My soul thirsts for God,
>   for the living God. (Ps. 42:1–2a)

Try to imagine the following conversation between the thirsty deer and the oasis of refreshing waters:

OASIS: "Well, what is it that you bring me today that I might be glorified and honored in you?"

DEER: "Only one thing: my thirst! All that I have to offer is my confession that if I don't drink from the waters that you alone supply, I'm going to die!"

Need, per se, is not sin. Neither is spiritual hunger and thirst. Your heart's desire for joy is not a result of the fall or bad breeding or a deficient education. Your passion for pleasure is not a demonically induced deviation from true godliness.

Sin is simply the refusal to believe that Psalm 16:11 is true. Sin is the selfish determination to find "fullness of joy" somewhere other than in God's presence and "pleasures forevermore" somewhere other than at God's right hand.

That is why the one thing God will gladly receive from you and me is whatever reveals our lack and his supply, our dependence and his support, our poverty and his abundant generosity in overflowing goodness to weak and needy people.

Let's pause here in Psalm 63 for just a moment. David unapologetically declares his need: he speaks of seeking, thirsting, even fainting for God (v. 1). Not only is he needy, he is *earnestly* needy, *desperately* needy. As noted above, there's no hint of anything sinful in this; nothing worthy of rebuke; nothing that calls for repentance. He continues:

So I have looked upon you in the sanctuary,
    beholding your power and glory.
Because your steadfast love is better than life,
    my lips will praise you. (vv. 2–3)

Here again, David makes no apologies for his enjoyment of God's enjoyment of him. He would rather experience the steadfast love of God than revel in all the riches this life affords. There's something in the lovingkindness of God that fills the emptiness of his soul immeasurably beyond any and every earthly promise. God's steadfast love reassures and satisfies the desperate ache and longing in his heart. Is that wrong? Is David off-base in focusing so firmly on the passion of his soul? Not in the least.

This same point is made in Psalm 84. The soul of the psalmist "longs" for the courts of the Lord (v. 2a). The intensity of his desperation for God has brought him to the brink of fainting (v. 2a). People today faint for all sorts of reasons: a brief glimpse of their favorite celebrity, the news of a financial windfall, or possibly a game-winning touchdown in the final seconds of the Super Bowl. The psalmist, on the other hand, faints for lack of God's presence, or perhaps from the prospect of that breathtaking vision of divine and transcendent beauty.

His singular, all-consuming passion was that he might be found in "the courts of the Lord." There alone his "heart and flesh sing for joy to the living God" (v. 2b).

Why? Because he found it altogether "lovely" (84:1). The beauty and sweetness of God's courts transcend the most sublime of earthly locales. Of course, it has nothing to do with its physical composition or aesthetic features. The dwelling place of God is lovely because *God* is there.

The author of Psalm 84 undertook a comparative study as he prepared to worship. He investigated the best and the most and the sweetest and the highest and the happiest this world could offer and drew this profound conclusion: "A day in your courts [O God] is better than a thousand elsewhere. I would rather be a doorkeeper in the house of my God than dwell in the tents of wickedness" (v. 10).

All of life is inescapably competitive. Every choice we make is a decision between competing pleasures. Even if we are not immediately conscious of what is happening, such choices demand of us a comparative evaluation of rival claims.

These crossroad decisions in life don't spring up *ex nihilo*. They aren't causeless. The psalmist declares, "I choose God and the pleasures of life in his courts" *because* "the LORD God is a sun and shield" (v. 11a). The world, on the other hand, leaves me scorched and defenseless. "The LORD bestows favor and honor" (v. 11b). The passing pleasures of sin, on the other hand, lead only to misery and despair.

"No good thing does he withhold from those who walk uprightly" (v. 11c). People, on the other hand, demand their pound of flesh. This is precisely what we see yet again in Psalm 63.

> So I will bless you as long as I live;
> in your name I will lift up my hands.
> My soul will be satisfied as with fat and rich food,
> and my mouth will praise you with joyful lips. (vv. 4–5)

But what does worship have to do with my soul or your soul being satisfied? Doesn't that detract from the glory of God? How can God be honored as he deserves if we are concerned with the longing and passion and desire of our souls?

In the answer to that question is seen the glory of Christian hedonism, for the revelation of God's splendor is the extent to which his people find unrivaled satisfaction in who he is on their behalf. Or, to paraphrase Piper yet again, God is most glorified in you when you are most satisfied in him. Your passion for gladness competes with God's glory only when you seek it in something other than him.

So, don't apologize for that relentless and chronic ache for joy. Rather, like the thirsty deer that you are, come to him who alone is life-giving water and drink to your soul's everlasting delight.

31

Reaching God's Ear

Psalm 86

Incline your ear, O LORD, and answer me,
for I am poor and needy.
                                                   —Psalm 86:1

My book on prayer, *Reaching God's Ear*,[4] has been out of print for nearly two decades. When the few who purchased a copy took a look at the cover, they immediately asked me, "Is that you in the picture?" No, but I have to admit, the man sitting in the chair did bear a striking resemblance to what I looked like in 1988.

Those of you who've seen the cover also know that there is a young boy standing on tiptoes, whispering into his father's ear. It's a powerful picture and beautifully illustrates the point of the book.

You can imagine my surprise, then, when I met that young boy while teaching at Wheaton College. His name is Taylor Clausen. Although I didn't have him in class, he became a close friend of my daughter Joanna who was a classmate of his at Wheaton. Taylor told us that in order to induce him to pose for the camera in this way, his mother said, "If you'll go whisper in Daddy's ear, he'll take you to McDonald's for a treat later today." It worked.

It made me wonder, is that why we pray? Are we disinclined to bring our petitions to our Heavenly Father and prompted to do so only on the promise of a goody or some other earthly reward? Taylor was only around four years old at the time the picture was taken, and can therefore be excused for yielding to such a carnal motivation.

So why do you pray? What motivates you to whisper in your Father's ear? Is it even worthwhile to do so? Let's explore this for a moment by asking five questions and seeking the answers in Psalm 86.

1) Why did David, the psalmist, pray so fervently in Psalm 86? (I encourage you to pause, if you haven't already, and read the entire psalm.) Why should we do the same?

David gives one powerfully persuasive reason in verse 5 when he says, "For you, O Lord, are good and forgiving, abounding in steadfast love to all who call upon you." We are repeatedly exhorted in Scripture to "call" upon the Lord "in the day of trouble" (Ps. 50:15), and to "offer prayer" to him at a time when he may be found (Ps. 33:6), and to pour out our hearts before him.

It is stunning, is it not, that we have to be commanded to pray? The sick hardly need an exhortation to visit a doctor or the hungry a soup kitchen, yet we must be told repeatedly to avail ourselves of a God who stands ready to richly supply our need and draw near when we call.

David was also quick to pray because he was confident that God did not command him to do so in vain. In other words, he was assured that God commands prayer because he takes indescribable delight in giving answers. "In the day of my trouble," said David, "I call upon you, *for you answer me*" (Ps. 86:7). "Call to me," said God to Jeremiah, "and *I will answer* you, and tell you great and hidden things that you have not known" (Jer. 33:3). "When he [the believer] calls to me [God], *I will answer him*" (Ps. 91:15).

This isn't to say the answer he gives is always the one we want (cf. 2 Cor. 12:7–10). But it is to say that it is always the answer we need.

2) What is required of those who pray? In the first place, they must be "poor and needy" (Ps. 86:1b). People who pray must be

keenly aware of their spiritually destitute condition and their utter dependence on God for all things good. It's another way of saying that humility is required of all who seek God. I've often heard the excuse: "I can't pray to God. I'm not good enough." This is actually pride masquerading as humility and robs God of his glory. It is prideful because it is based on the assumption that it's actually possible for people to become good enough by their own efforts and thus worthy of receiving God's answer. Of course you're not good enough, but that's precisely why you must pray!

To be "poor and needy," to use David's terms, is to recognize one's spiritual distress, lingering doubts, anxiety, physical weakness, emotional struggles, and lack of wisdom—the very things God delights to heal and overcome as a way of magnifying his strength and mercy.

David mentions yet another prerequisite in verse 11: "Teach me your way, O LORD, that I may walk in your truth; *unite my heart* to fear your name." We are by nature divided within, at one moment trusting the Lord and at another defying his will. This disingenuous and disintegrated state of soul must be overcome by a unified commitment to seek fervently after God and to tremble at his Word.

3) How often ought we to pray? According to David, "all the day" (Ps. 86:3)! There are no fewer than fifteen petitions in this psalm alone. We, on the other hand, are quick to quit. We must train ourselves to distrust the certainties of discouragement, the "nevers" and the "alwayses" and the "impossibles" that creep into our heads when heaven seems silent.

4) What reason do we have for confidence that our prayers will be heard? Answer: the character of God. Look at how David put it. He prays:

> because "you, O Lord, are good" (v. 5a);
> because "you, O Lord, are . . . forgiving" (v. 5b);
> because "you, O Lord, are . . . abounding in steadfast love" (v. 5c);
> because "there is none like you among the gods, O Lord, nor are there any works like yours" (v. 8);
> because "you are great and do wondrous things" (v. 10a);
> because "you alone are God" (v. 10b).

5) Finally, are not my sins too many, too evil, and too frequent that God should hear my prayer and answer it?

There is no greater obstacle to prayer than the burden of sin and guilt that weighs heavily on the human heart. Add to this the accusations of the enemy, who says: "Why should *you*, of all people, pray? How could *you* ever hope to prevail upon God? Your sins have caused him to turn away his face. You're a traitor to his cause, a thankless rebel. You, pray? Ha!"

What makes these words of Satan so powerful is that they seem so reasonable, so true. After all, we are often precisely what he says. We have done precisely what he claims.

This is why David is so relentless in his affirmation that "you, O Lord, are a God merciful and gracious, slow to anger and abounding in steadfast love and faithfulness" (v. 15; see Ps. 106:6, 13–15, 19–21, 24–25, 37–39, 40–43 and compare these with vv. 44–46. See also Psalm 107 and the fourfold refrain in vv. 4–6, 10–13, 17–19, 23–28). For every accusation of the enemy, there is a corresponding remedy from the throne of grace.

In the final analysis, how do we overcome the lethargy of heart and discouragement of mind and spirit and pray as we ought? David's solution was simple: pray for strength. "Turn to me and be gracious to me," said David; "give your strength to your servant" (v. 16a).

We must not act as if we were four-year-old children who need to be cajoled and manipulated into prayer. God is ever ready to stoop and "incline" his "ear" (Ps. 86:1) to hear those why cry to him for help. What excuse do we still have not to obey?

32

Darkness, My Only Companion

Psalm 88

O LORD, God of my salvation;
   I cry out day and night before you.
           —Psalm 88:1

I was greatly tempted to quietly skip over Psalm 88. But then I realized that there are many reading these meditations who can identify with the palpable sadness of Heman, its author, and wonder if anybody else has ever experienced the depths of despondency it expresses.[5]

This has been called the darkest, most depressing, and saddest of all psalms. Unlike the other psalms of lament, this one does not conclude with praise or a declaration of joy or hope for renewed confidence in what God will do. It ends as it began: in grief and despair. This disturbing fact has led some to suggest that Psalm 89 is really a continuation of 88. But aside from the natural desire to consummate Heman's experience on a higher and happier note, there is little evidence to support this theory.

Few Christians have ever heard the name of Heman. He was the father of seventeen children and one of the choir directors appointed by David to lead the congregation of Israel in praise and worship (see 1 Chron. 6:31–33; 15:16–17; 16:41–42; 25:5–7). He was both a singer and a musician. Some suggest this may have been the source of his struggles, as it has often been noted that musicians are especially prone to radical mood swings. That may not be altogether fair, but it certainly applies in the case of this man who wrote such a woeful psalm.

Heman's anguish is unrelenting. His distress is unrelieved. In spite of the dark language of the psalm, he does at least acknowledge God as the source of his "salvation" (v. 1) and is persistent in his petitions both day and night: "Let my prayer come before you; incline your ear to my cry!" (vv. 1–2). But aside from this there is no word of hope, no confidence or consolation for his soul.

His prayers go unanswered, or so it seems. His cry for help falls on deaf ears. Here's how he put it:

> For my soul is full of troubles,
>   and my life draws near to Sheol.
> I am counted among those who go down to the pit;
>   I am a man who has no strength,
> like one set loose among the dead,
>   like the slain that lie in the grave,
> like those whom you remember no more,
>   for they are cut off from your hand.
> You have put me in the depths of the pit,
>   in the regions dark and deep.
> Your wrath lies heavy upon me,
>   and you overwhelm me with all your waves. (vv. 3–7)

Like a jar brimfull of water, Heman's soul overflows with trouble. He might as well be dead, for his life seems hardly worth living. Again, he laments:

> You have caused my companions to shun me;
>   you have made me a horror to them. (v. 8a)

Perhaps Heman suffered from a disease or affliction that made his physical appearance loathsome to the sight (see Job 2:11–13; 17:7). Or it may simply be that his so-called friends could take it no more. Sadly, it doesn't take much of an excuse for us to justify abandoning our friends when they become an imposition on our lives. No one enjoys spending too much time with a Job. Perhaps Heman's trials finally became more than they were willing to bear, so they left him to his misery. It's not a pretty sight:

> I am shut in so that I cannot escape;
>> my eye grows dim through sorrow.
> Every day I call upon you, O Lord;
>> I spread out my hands to you.
> Do you work wonders for the dead?
>> Do the departed rise up to praise you?
> Is your steadfast love declared in the grave,
>> or your faithfulness in Abaddon?
> Are your wonders known in the darkness,
>> or your righteousness in the land of forgetfulness?
>> (vv. 8b–12)

Heman is persistent in his prayers, but his patience is wearing thin. We don't know how much Old Testament saints knew about the afterlife, but Heman sees no profit for God should he die. "I can't praise you from the grave," he cries. "What good am I to you if these troubles end my life?"

> But I, O Lord, cry to you;
>> in the morning my prayer comes before you.
> O Lord, why do you cast my soul away?
>> Why do you hide your face from me?
> Afflicted and close to death from my youth up,
>> I suffer your terrors; I am helpless.
> Your wrath has swept over me;
>> your dreadful assaults destroy me.
> They surround me like a flood all day long;
>> they close in on me together. (vv. 13–17)

Like a lot of us, Heman can't help but interpret his distress as a sign that perhaps God has abandoned him. After all, it isn't as if he has suffered only for a while. Don't we all? No, Heman has seen hardship from his youth on. His agony is lifelong. Hear his concluding words:

> You have caused my beloved and my friend to shun me;
> my companions have become darkness [or, darkness has become my only companion]. (v. 18)

Bereft of friends, cut off from the compassion and love of his family, Heman has but one companion to soothe his pains: darkness. Alone, isolated, seemingly without hope, he feels engulfed by night. How tragic! As commentator Franz Delitzsch has said, "The gloom of melancholy does not brighten up to become a hope, the Psalm dies away in Job-like lamentation."[6]

I'm not at all suggesting that Heman's experience is normative. There is joy in Jesus. There is deliverance in God's grace and hope in his mercy. Still, we should not write off Heman as some sort of demented exception to an otherwise universal rule. Heman's experience is not as uncommon as we might think. There are people all around us who know and feel all too well the sorrows of Heman. They are not surprised by Psalm 88. They read it and nod with understanding. Like Heman, darkness is their closest friend.

If Heman shares anything with other psalmists, it is brutal honesty. When I read these plaintive hymns, I see nothing of our modern fear of exposure. The psalmists candidly declare their distress (4:1), sorrow (6:7), loneliness (25:16; 142:4), affliction (25:16), grief (35:14), mourning (35:14), fear (55:5), and dismay (143:4). They don't hesitate to confess that they are consumed by anguish (31:10), weak with sorrow (31:9; 119:28), worn out from groaning (6:6), bowed down and brought low (38:6), feeble and utterly crushed (38:8), troubled by sin (38:18), downcast (42:5–6), forlorn (35:12), faint (6:2), overcome by trouble (116:3), and in desperate need (79:8).

The last thing I want anyone to think, upon reading Psalm 88, is that their situation is hopeless. Although Heman never confessed it in so many words, I trust he knew, and I pray you know, that "the eye of the LORD is on those who fear him, on those who hope in his steadfast love" (Ps. 33:18).

Psalms 91–104

from Book 4 of the Psalter

33

Hiding Place

Psalm 91

He who dwells in the shelter of the Most High
    will abide in the shadow of the Almighty.
I will say to the LORD, "My refuge and my fortress,
    my God, in whom I trust."
                         —Psalm 91:1–2

Not too far from the house in which I was raised in Shawnee, Oklahoma, there was an area called Broadway Woods. It would hardly classify as a forest, but to a nine-year-old boy it seemed as big and vast as the deepest, darkest jungles of Africa.

I loved playing in Broadway Woods. My friends and I would build little hideouts and secret meeting places there, using whatever material we could scrounge up. We'd throw together a few pieces of discarded plywood and cover it over with tree branches and make for ourselves a hidden clubhouse. All we wanted was a refuge from parents, big sisters, and older boys in the neighborhood who beat up on us. It was great.

Psalm 91 is also about secret hiding places. It's all about finding refuge. It's all about protection from enemies and dwelling in safety and security. But not in some poorly constructed shanty. Our spiritual fortress is God himself. *He* is our hiding place, as we see from the psalm's powerful opening promise in verses 1–2.

Psalm 91 is both anonymous and timeless, and I'm glad for that, because it makes it easy and natural to apply its truths to any Christian at any time in history, regardless of circumstance or situation.

David could easily have written this psalm, for he says much the same thing in another of his compositions:

> Oh, how abundant is your goodness,
>> which you have stored up for those who fear you
>> and worked for those who take refuge in you,
>>> in the sight of the children of mankind!
> In the cover of your presence you hide them
>> from the plots of men;
> you store them in your shelter
>> from the strife of tongues. (Ps. 31:19–20)

And yet again:

> For you have been my refuge,
>> a strong tower against the enemy.
> Let me dwell in your tent forever!
>> Let me take refuge under the shelter of your wings!
>> (Ps. 61:3–4)

Try to envision God's power as forging his love into a strong and impregnable fortress. God doesn't build us a shanty out of leaves and rotting wood. God's *love* is our shelter. He himself is our hiding place. His presence is our peace, our protection, our refuge.

I said that Psalm 91 applies to any Christian at any time, but that's not entirely accurate. The promise of peace and security and protection is for the one "who dwells in the shelter of the Most High" (v. 1a), the one who says to the Lord, "My refuge and my fortress, my God, in whom I trust" (v. 2). That is to say, it is for anyone who consciously and zealously embraces the Lord and consistently entrusts himself to God's loving care. The blessings of Psalm 91 are for those who seek after God as their highest and greatest good in life, their *summum bonum*, if you will.

This wording forces me to ask: Do you live in God's presence every day or do you merely visit him for an hour on Sunday? The promised blessings of this psalm are not for those who occasionally run to God for help when they're in trouble. Nor is it for the sporadic, once-in-a-while pray-er. God is a refuge to those who habitually seek their abode in him.

Let me return to Broadway Woods for a moment. Eventually, my friends and I would have to leave our fortress behind. The comfort of our tree house lasted only a short while. The time would come for us to emerge from the secrecy of our hideaway and reenter the real world.

But that never happens for those who seek shelter in the Most High. God is our permanent refuge in whom we abide while at work or at school or wherever. We never have to leave God and go home. He *is* our home. It is in him and in his love that we live and move and have our being (cf. Acts 17:28).

If there is any lingering doubt as to the focus of the psalmist's faith, take note of how he describes his God. He is the "Most High" (v. 1a), the one who is "over all the earth" (Ps. 97:9a), the one who is "exalted far above all gods" (Ps. 97:9b). What a remarkable act of grace: the Most High God stoops so very, very low to reach us with his love and affection!

He is also "the Almighty" (91:1b), "the LORD" (v. 2a; i.e., Yahweh), "my God" (v. 2b; i.e., Elohim), and thus more than capable of providing a sufficient shelter for his people who seek refuge in him.

The protection he provides is now portrayed with the most vivid of imagery.

> For he will deliver you from the snare of the fowler
>   and from the deadly pestilence.
> He will cover you with his pinions,
>   and under his wings you will find refuge;
>   his faithfulness is a shield and buckler. (vv. 3–4)

Though our adversary be like the hunter who sets a snare for his prey (cf. Pss. 119:110; 124:6–8; 141:8–10), God will deliver us. In him we are immune to the onslaught of pestilence. And what "transcendent condescension"[1] that the eternal God, who is without body or parts, should liken himself to a mother bird covering her young with her feathers, shielding them from wind and rain (cf. Deut. 32:10–11; Pss. 17:8; 36:7; 57:1; 63:7; Matt. 23:37).

What a God, that he who is tender like a mother bird is also as strong and sturdy, as immovable and unyielding as battle armor ("a shield and buckler," v. 4b).

Honestly, though, it's starting to sound a bit far-fetched. Is it realistic to think that we need never fear "the terror of the night" (v. 5a) or "the arrow that flies by day" (v. 5b)? Is it actually the case that although thousands may fall, we will never endure such an end (v. 7)? Are we supposed to conclude from this psalm that if we but make God our dwelling place and refuge (v. 9), "no evil shall be allowed to befall" us and "no plague" will come near our tent (v. 10)?

The promises of verses 11–13 appear even greater: angelic protection from stumbling as well as when trampling underfoot, with no apparent harm, both lion and adder, young lion and serpent. If that weren't enough, we read in verses 14–16 of deliverance, protection, rescue, honor, and a long life. What are we to make of this? Such declarations seem as unrealistic as they are unconditional.

I often struggled with this until I read something John Piper wrote in his devotional book *A Godward Life*.[2] There he argues that the psalmist means that "God does in fact rule the flight of arrows and the spread of disease and the length of life; and he can and does give safety and health and life to whom he pleases, so that it is always a free gift of God. But he does not mean for us to presume upon these promises as guarantees that God will not permit us to fall by an arrow, succumb to disease, or die at age thirty-eight. In other words, the promises have exceptions or qualifications."[3]

Or again, none of these plagues will befall us without God's express permission and by his sovereign design. We know this because even in the Psalms we read of God's faithful children suffering affliction and enduring martyrdom (cf. Pss. 34:19; 44:22). And let's not forget "that Satan quotes Psalm 91:11–12 to Jesus in the wilderness."[4] But Jesus rejects this abuse of the sacred text "and sets his face to prove that the psalm *does* have a qualification: He dies at a *young* age; he feels the *blow* of ripped flesh; and he is *pierced* by the nail and sword while ten thousand get off without a scratch."[5]

So what is Piper's advice? Simply this: "In your Gethsemane of suffering, pray for deliverance according to God's sovereign power and mercy . . . But then say, 'Not my will but thine be done.' And believe that what befalls will not, in the end, be evil for you, but good (Romans 8:28)."[6]

34

Worship That Pleases God

Psalms 92–98

It is good to give thanks to the LORD,
    to sing praises to your name, O Most High.
                                —Psalm 92:1

I don't know about you, but I'm weary of the worship wars that have wreaked havoc in so many churches. It's sad to look back over the past twenty-five years or so at the damage and division that have resulted from this internecine conflict. Should we use traditional hymns or contemporary songs? Which do you prefer, a robed choir or a praise team? Baldwin piano or acoustical guitar? Liberty or liturgy? Standing or sitting? Formal or free? Long or short? Hands raised or at your side? Solemnity or celebration?

As much as I may wish otherwise, I suspect the battle will continue. No, I don't have a solution for a cease-fire or a remedy that will make everyone happy. But perhaps we could start by returning to the biblical text to determine, not what makes us feel comfortable, but what it is in worship that pleases God.

As I was reading through Psalms 92–98 I couldn't help but notice the exhortations and counsel concerning how and why and to what end we are to worship. So, without further ado, look with me at ten truths or principles that we need to keep in mind when we worship, and as we try to draw near the throne of grace in a way that will honor and exalt the name of Jesus.

1) Worship that pleases God is *perpetual and constant.* It is always and ever appropriate. The psalmist resolves "to declare your steadfast love in the morning, and your faithfulness by night" (Ps. 92:2). We should never think of worship as something reserved for a Sunday morning, as if there were any hour of any day where it isn't the thing to do.

2) Worship that pleases God is *instrumental.* The psalmists speak of "the music of the lute and the harp" as well as "the melody of the lyre" (Ps. 92:3) and "trumpets and the sound of the horn" (Ps. 98:5–6). This isn't to say that singing a cappella is forbidden or unacceptable to God—far from it—but our Lord does appear to enjoy the loud and harmonious sounds that come from all sorts of instruments. Psalm 150 speaks of "trumpet sound" and "lute and harp" and "tambourine" and "strings and pipe" and "sounding cymbals" and even "loud clashing cymbals" (vv. 3–5).

3) Clearly God delights in *joyful* worship (Pss. 92:4; 98:4). "For you, O LORD, have made me glad by your work; at the works of your hands I sing for joy" (Ps. 92:4). Again, we are to "make a joyful noise to the LORD" and "break forth into joyous song" (Ps. 98:4).

So, I guess there are good grounds for the hymn writer having penned the words, "Joyful, joyful, we adore Thee" rather than "Grumpy, grumpy, we adore Thee" or "Somber, somber, we adore Thee."

4) Worship that pleases God is grounded in the recognition and celebration of his *greatness.* Listen again to the psalmist: "How great are your works, O LORD! Your thoughts are very deep!" (Ps. 92:5). Contrary to the blasphemous sentiments of Christopher Hitchens's recent book,[7] I concur with King David: "Great is the LORD, and greatly to be praised, and his greatness is unsearchable" (Ps. 145:3). A great God calls for great praise.

5) Worship that pleases God is both *loud and logical.* That may sound a bit strange, but seems reasonable in light of Psalm 95:2 (cf. also Pss. 66:1; 88:1; 98:4–6), for there we are exhorted to "make a joyful noise to him with songs of praise!" Note well that worship

here entails noisy songs. There is volume to David's praise but not random or chaotic sounds. His noise takes the form of songs, of theologically precise and well-formed articulations of God's worth and glory and majesty. It is good to know that one can be both exuberant and exact, both passionate and precise, or as I said, both loud and logical. We do not merely shout aimlessly in the air but fashion our delight into melodies of spiritual substance and theological clarity.

6) Worship that pleases God is *physical*. In an earlier meditation I focused on the raising of one's hands and its symbolic importance. Later, in our study of Psalms 149 and 150, we'll look at the place of dancing. But in Psalm 95:6 we are called to "worship and bow down" and to "kneel before the LORD, our Maker!"

I can't recall the number of weddings I've performed, but one in particular stands out in my memory. The bride was from England and asked that I use portions of the Anglican ceremony that she had heard so often growing up. At one point the bride and groom take this pledge:

> My body will adore you,
> And your body alone will I cherish.
> I will, with my body, declare your worth.

What a beautiful expression of marital affection! So I'll ask, do you adore and cherish God with your body, no less so than with your mind and heart? Do you declare his worth physically as well as spiritually? Ron Allen put it well:

> We are not simply spirit beings. We are more than hearts or souls or "inner beings." We are persons possessing an intricate complex of physical and spiritual realities. We who worship God truly with the heart, do so with our physical bodies as well.[8]

7) Worship that pleases God is *fresh and creative*. Numerous times in the Psalter we are exhorted not simply to sing a song, nor even to sing a song joyfully, but to sing a *new* song (see Pss. 96:1; 98:1; as well as 40:3; 149:1; Isa. 42:10; Rev. 5:9).

I can only surmise that we are to sing new songs because God is always doing new and creative and unprecedented and heretofore unseen and unrevealed things for his people. God is fresh in his love and his redemptive and providential dealings with us, so let our worship of him be fresh as we constantly compose new and exciting songs of praise.

8) Worship that pleases God is *public*. Now, no one enjoys private worship more than I do. Whether in my car or on my bed at night or in my study by day, I love to have a continuous flow of worship filling the air. But this should never justify the failure to corporately worship in the presence of all. "Declare his glory among the nations, his marvelous works among all the peoples!" (Ps. 96:3).

9) Worship that pleases God *ascribes glory* to his name but doesn't add to it. Take special note of Psalm 96:7–9: "Ascribe to the LORD, O families of the peoples, ascribe to the LORD glory and strength! Ascribe to the LORD the glory due his name; bring an offering, and come into his courts!"

We should never purport to give God glory as if we were capable of adding to his supply or somehow enhancing and expanding the quantity of divine splendor. God's glory and worth always have been, are now, and forever will be infinite. Our responsibility, indeed our joyful and delightful privilege, is to ascribe or predicate or declare or make known or display or pronounce what is inherently and eternally true of him.

10) God is especially honored when *the whole of creation* joins in celebrating his goodness and greatness. So, "let the heavens be glad, and let the earth rejoice; let the sea roar, and all that fills it; let the field exult, and everything in it! Then shall all the trees of the forest sing for joy before the LORD . . ." (Ps. 96:11–13a). And "let the rivers clap their hands; let the hills sing for joy together before the LORD, for he comes to judge the earth" (Ps. 98:8–9a).

I've been known to be quite exuberant at times in my worship of the Lord, both in terms of passion and physical posture. Several years ago a man approached me and said, no doubt sincerely, "Sam, I'm not comfortable with the way you worship."

I did my best to be kind and considerate but found this response in my mouth: "I'm certainly open to correction, and I'm sorry you were offended, but I'm not particularly concerned with what puts you at ease. When the day comes that *you* are the object of my praise and adoration, I'll pay a bit more attention to what makes you feel comfortable. Until then, I'm primarily concerned about what pleases God."

That may not have been the most diplomatic response, but I do hope all of us have but one preeminent concern in our souls: to worship in a way that pleases and honors our great triune God. When I'm persuaded from Scripture that my worship brings God discomfort, I'll be the first to change.

35

The Fragrance of Gratitude

Psalm 100

Make a joyful noise to the LORD, all the earth!
—Psalm 100:1

I can't see as well as I used to, especially without my glasses. There are times when I don't hear everything going on around me. And I must admit that I have a finicky sense of taste. But I'm proud to say that I have a marvelous sense of smell. And believe it or not, so too does God!

Of course, I'm speaking anthropomorphically when I say that God has a perfect sense of smell. And few things smell as good to him as *gratitude*.

In the book of Leviticus God gave specific instructions on the proper way to offer sacrifices, whether peace offerings or sin offerings or whatever. This included what the Bible calls the "thank offering," that is, sacrifices that were an expression of gratitude to God for his mercy and his many blessings. Like so many other offerings, the remains of the thank offering were to be burned.

I'm sure the priests became accustomed to it after a while, but a first-time visitor to the temple in ancient times couldn't help but notice the strong aroma that filled the air. But the fragrance wasn't

185

intended primarily for the people, but for God. We read in Leviticus that the smoke from the burning sacrifice would ascend toward heaven as a soothing, fragrant aroma to the Lord. God has a great sense of smell and nothing smells so sweet to him as the gratitude of his people.

God loves the aroma of thanksgiving. He takes special delight in the smell of his people saying, "Lord, thank you!" When we offer up to God the sacrifice of praise, giving thanks for all he has done, there is a spiritual aroma that fills the room, eminently pleasing to God. The reason for this is that gratitude always glorifies the giver. Or again, thanksgiving always glorifies the "thanked." Thanksgiving focuses the attention on the goodness and generosity of God from whom all things come.

Psalm 100 is all about gratitude. It is a call to worship, a call to give thanks, a summons to fill our hearts and homes and auditoriums with the sweet-smelling aroma of gratitude to God. The structure of the psalm consists of a call to worship in verses 1–2, the cause for worship in verse 3, another call in verse 4, and yet another cause in verse 5.

During the time of the old covenant, the so-called manifest presence of God was geographically and spatially restricted. One had to "come" to God's presence (v. 2); one had to "enter his gates" and "his courts" with praise (v. 4). In other words, the worship described here is something that took place in the temple because that is where God's manifest presence was revealed, behind the veil in the Most Holy Place.

But now each individual Christian as well as the church corporately is the temple of God, and thus we are always in God's presence because God's presence is always in us.

In the initial call to worship there are three exhortations: we are to "make a joyful noise to the LORD" (v. 1a), we are to "serve the LORD with gladness" (v. 2a), and we are commanded to "come into his presence with singing" (v. 2b). What strikes me immediately is the emphasis on mood: we make a *joyful* noise, we serve with *gladness*, and we *sing*.

I read somewhere that there are twenty-seven words in Hebrew for *joy*. In the Psalms alone these words occur 108 times. This pattern continues into the New Testament as well:

> For the kingdom of God is not a matter of eating and drinking but of righteousness and peace and *joy* in the Holy Spirit. (Rom. 14:17)

> May the God of hope fill you with all *joy* and peace in believing. (Rom. 15:13a)

> The fruit of the Spirit is . . . *joy*. (Gal. 5:22a)

> "These things I [Jesus] have spoken to you, that my *joy* may be in you, and that your *joy* may be full." (John 15:11)

> And we are writing these things so that our *joy* may be complete. (1 John 1:4)

The list could go on almost without end. There's simply no escaping the fact that the Bible exhorts us to experience clear, radiant, unpolluted delight in God. Sherwood Wirt put it thus:

> Joy is merriment without frivolity, hilarity without raucousness, and mirth without cruelty. Joy is sportive without being rakish and festive without being tasteless. Joy radiates animation, sparkle and buoyancy. It is more than fun, yet it has fun. It expresses itself in laughter and elation, yet it draws from a deep spring that keeps flowing long after the laughter has died and the tears have come. Even while it joins those who mourn, it remains cheerful in a world that has gone gray with grief and worry.[9]

Joy, says Wirt, "becomes the ecstasy of eternity in a soul that has made peace with God and is ready to do His will, here and hereafter."[10] Wirt has some strong words for those who are suspicious of joy in church life today:

> Veneration and respect are always due to our blessed heavenly Father. We are commanded to worship Him in the beauty of holiness, but for

Heaven's sake let's not lose the joy in the midst of it. Let's not worship by transposing our thoughts into an everlasting minor key.[11]

Wirt has observed the diminishing presence of joy in many of our churches and thinks he knows why:

> The problem is the pseudo-spiritual smog we spread over our church life, the unnecessary gravity with which our leadership protects its dignity, the unnatural churchly posturing that so easily passes into overbearing arrogance and conceit.[12]

To attend many church meetings today, says Wirt, "is to run the risk of humongous boredom. The 'odor of sanctity' turns into polluted air."[13] He rightly warns us of "the sludge of religious sobriety which is so often mistaken for reverence."[14]

No one is advocating flippancy or a casual, carefree triumphalism in our corporate praise. But the alternative must not be limited to a sour and depressing sobriety that fails to recognize, unlike the psalmist, that "the LORD, he is God! It is he who made us, and we are his; we are his people, and the sheep of his pasture" (Ps. 100:3). He calls for loud, joyful, grateful praise because "the LORD is good; his steadfast love endures forever, and his faithfulness to all generations" (v. 5).

"The invitation to worship here given," wrote Spurgeon, "is not a melancholy one, as though adoration were a funereal solemnity, but a cheery, gladsome exhortation, as though we were bidden to a marriage feast."[15]

Since I began with an emphasis on *gratitude* in this psalm, let me close on that theme as well. It's interesting that there is no word in Hebrew for "to give thanks." The word (*yadah*) behind our English translations means to praise or to give public acknowledgment; to tell others what God has done. If someone did you a favor or provided a blessing, instead of saying "thank you" you would respond by saying: "I'm going to declare your name to others. I'm going to praise your kindness and generosity and thoughtfulness to everyone I see." That's what thanksgiving or gratitude was in the Old Testament.

Finally, there is immense practical, sin-killing power in joyful, heartfelt gratitude. Gratitude protects us from sinful presumption or acting as if we are owed the gracious blessings God provides. Gratitude also guards our hearts from selfish pride, or living as if we are ultimately responsible for whatever good we accomplish (see 1 Cor. 4:7). But most of all, gratitude deflects all glory and praise to God alone. It turns our eyes and attention away from self to the Savior, to him from whom all good gifts ultimately come (cf. James 1:17).

So, whatever else we do in worship, whatever style we embrace, let us be careful and diligent and devoted to "enter his gates with *thanksgiving,* and his courts with praise! *Give thanks* to him; bless his name!" (Ps. 100:4). Who knows but that God responds: "Mmmmm! That smells goooood!"

36

Before the Throne
of God Above

Psalm 103:10–12

He does not deal with us according to our sins,
  nor repay us according to our iniquities.
For as high as the heavens are above the earth,
  so great is his steadfast love toward those who fear
    him;
as far as the east is from the west,
  so far does he remove our transgressions from us.
                                        —Psalm 103:10–12

W ere ever more beautiful words penned than these?
       Consider for a moment how we deal with others. We
       keep fresh in our minds their injustices toward us. We
nurture the memory of their faults and failings. We never let them
forget what they did, and we often make sure others are mindful of
it as well. We seek every opportunity, often secretly and surrepti-
tiously, to make them pay for their transgressions. We hold it in our
hearts and over their heads and persuade ourselves that it's only fair
that they be treated this way.

Now consider again this description of God in his dealings with us: "He does *not* deal with us according to our sins" (v. 10a). Our sins do not constitute the rule or standard or plumb line according to which God makes his decisions on how to treat us. He does not recall or bring to the fore or publicly announce our history of hatred and lust and blasphemy and greed and pride before he formulates his plan for our life or before responding to something we've just said or done.

Better still is the second statement in verse 10, namely, that God does *not* "repay us according to our iniquities" (v. 10b). It's certainly not because our iniquities do not deserve repayment. They are deep and many and heinous and are deserving of the most severe, indeed, eternal judgment. But those who "fear him" (v. 11b) need never fear that he will exact payment or demand suffering or insist, according to the rigors of his law and unyielding holiness, that we endure the penal consequences of violating his will and ways.

In fact, so far is it from the realm of possibility that we might ever be dealt with "according to our sins" or repaid "according to our iniquities" that David compares it to the distance between earth and the highest heavens and the distance between east and west.

The Hubble Space Telescope has given us breathtaking pictures of a galaxy some 13 billion lights-years from earth. Yes, 13 *billion* light-years! Remember, a light year is 6,000,000,000,000 (six trillion) miles. That would put this galaxy at 78,000,000,000,000,000,000,000 miles from earth. In case you were wondering, we count from million, to billion, to trillion, to quadrillion, to quintillion, to sextillion. So, this galaxy is 78 sextillion miles from earth.

If you traveled 500 mph nonstop, literally sixty minutes of every hour, twenty-four hours in every day, seven days in every week, fifty-two weeks in every year, with not a moment's pause or delay, it would take you 20,000,000,000,000,000 years (that's 20 quadrillion years) to get there. And that would only get you to the farthest point that our best telescopes have yet been able to detect. If the universe is infinite, as I believe it is, this would be the *mere fringe* of what lies beyond.

My point, the point of the psalmist, is that the magnitude of such distance is a pathetically small comparison to the likelihood that you will ever be dealt with according to your sins or repaid for your iniquities. If you were ever inclined to pursue your transgressions so that you might place yourself beneath their condemning power, 78,000,000,000,000,000,000,000,000 miles is an infinitesimally small fraction of the distance you must travel to find them.

Now, here's the question: *Why* does God not deal with us according to our sins? *Why* does he not repay us according to our iniquities? In other words, on what grounds does he take such magnanimous and marvelous action? Does he simply wave the wand of mercy and dismiss our guilt? Does he merely shrug off our rebellion and unbelief and hostility as if they were nothing and of no consequence? Does he ignore the dictates of his holiness when he forgives us? Does he pretend that justice matters little or that love trumps righteousness?

Clearly the answer is no. The reason why God does not deal with us according to our sins is that he has dealt with Jesus in accordance with what they require. The reason why God does not repay us according to our iniquities is that he has repaid his Son in accordance with what holiness demands—in perfect harmony, I might add, with the will and voluntary love of the Son himself.

David wrote these words of hope and life from within the context of the Old Testament sacrificial system. He could confidently speak of such grace and kindness because he personally knew of the Day of Atonement, of the blood sacrifice, of the scapegoat onto whose head his sins were symbolically placed and transferred (see Leviticus 16).

In our case, on this side of the cross that forever and finally fulfills these old covenant types and symbols, we can confidently rest in the freedom of forgiveness because God has "put forward [Christ Jesus] as a propitiation by his blood" (Rom. 3:25).

God did not willy-nilly cast aside our sins as if they were of no consequence. Rather, he "laid on him [the Son, our Savior] the iniquity of us all" (Isa. 53:6b). God did not casually ignore the dictates of his holiness and righteous character. Rather, he "wounded" Jesus "for our transgressions" and "crushed" him "for our iniquities" (Isa. 53:5).

This, and this alone, is why we can sing and celebrate that God does not and never will "deal with us according to our sins" or "repay us according to our iniquities." The measure of God's "steadfast love" (v. 11) is the depth of the sacrifice he endured in giving up his only Son to suffer in our stead (cf. Rom. 8:32).

I hope all can see why the current debate over penal substitutionary atonement is so eternally important, for if God did *not* deal with the Lord Jesus Christ according to your sins, he will deal with *you* in accordance with them. And if God did not repay in his Son what your iniquities deserve, he will repay you. It's just that simple.

Psalm 103 begins with the exhortation that we not forget all the many benefits that God has graciously bestowed, chief among which is that he "forgives all your iniquity" (v. 3a). Now we know how. Now we know why. So let us all sing:

> Before the throne of God above
> I have a strong and perfect plea.
> A great high Priest whose Name is Love
> Who ever lives and pleads for me.
> My name is graven on His hands,
> My name is written on His heart.
> I know that while in Heaven He stands,
> No tongue can bid me thence depart.
>
> When Satan tempts me to despair
> And tells me of the guilt within,
> Upward I look and see Him there
> Who made an end of all my sin.
> Because the sinless Savior died
> My sinful soul is counted free.
> For God the just is satisfied
> To look on Him and pardon me.
>
> Behold Him there the risen Lamb,
> My perfect spotless righteousness,
> The great unchangeable I Am,
> The King of glory and of grace.
> One in Himself I cannot die,
> My soul is purchased by His blood,
> My life is hid with Christ on high,
> With Christ my Savior and my God! (C. L. Bancroft, 1863)

37

God's Compassion for "Dust"

Psalm 103:14

For he knows our frame;
 he remembers that we are dust.
 —Psalm 103:14

One of the greatest obstacles to experiencing intimacy with God is *our knowledge of God's knowledge of us*. That may sound strange, so I suggest you read it again.

Let me explain by asking a question. Why do you hesitate to draw near to God? Why do you and I strive to keep God at arm's length, especially after we've sinned? There are, to be sure, many reasons and thus a variety of ways of answering the question. But let me suggest one that I have found to be most prevalent among Christians, one that has certainly been true, at times, of my own experience.

I think we run *from* God rather than *to* him because we know our own hearts all too well and his barely at all. Here's what I mean by that. Each of us is painfully aware of the depth of our sin and depravity. We are daily in agonizing touch with our weakness and how prone we are to repeat those sins for which we have just repented and sought forgiveness. The presence of ingratitude and presumption in our relationship with God is all too real and convicting.

In other words, the inescapable and undeniable knowledge that we have of ourselves is a persistent roadblock to the pursuit of intimacy with God. The contempt and disdain in which we hold ourselves makes it ever so difficult to seek out an infinitely holy and righteous God.

I've often spoken with sincere Christian men and women who are convinced that God is disgusted with them. After all, why shouldn't he be (so they contend), given the fact that they are so deeply disgusted with themselves? They live daily with the paralyzing conviction that God is so utterly repulsed by them that all hope of a meaningful relationship is shattered.

If you'll stop and think about it, you'll realize how this affects the way we relate to other people. Convinced that if they knew the truth about us they would be repulsed, we work to hide our true selves from sight. We live in fear that if they knew us for who and what we know ourselves to be, they'd turn and run, ending all hope of friendship or intimacy. So we create a relational style that will keep people at a safe distance from our souls. We adopt personality traits that will mask the true self and, we hope, convince others that we aren't that bad or ugly after all.

Here's my point. If we react that way to people whose knowledge of us is limited, imagine how we react to God whose knowledge of us is infinite! Biblical texts such as Psalm 139:1–4 and Hebrews 4:12–14 are frightening to many people rather than affirming. God's omniscience, according to the way they think, ends all hope for intimacy. "How could God stand to be in my presence, knowing me as he does? He is holy and I'm unholy. He is righteous and I am a sinner. He is faithful and I am fickle." End of story. End of hope.

We might be able to fool some people some of the time, but we can never fool God at any time. His knowledge of us is perfect and penetrating and pervasive. He sees every motive, he knows every impulse, he is privy to every thought before it enters our heads. People then draw this conclusion: If I am disgusting to myself, how much more must I be disgusting to God.

I don't want to be misunderstood. I'm not suggesting for a moment that God isn't displeased with our sin. King David couldn't have been clearer when he said of God, "For You are not a God who takes pleasure in wickedness; no evil dwells with You. The boastful shall not stand before Your eyes; You hate all who do iniquity" (Ps. 5:4–5; NASB). This being the case, is all hope shattered of comfort and joy in God's presence? How can I draw near to a God whose purity would seem to drive me away?

Clearly, our knowledge of God's knowledge of us appears to be an imposing obstacle. As I said at the beginning, our problem is that we know our own hearts all too well and his barely at all. That was certainly true of me, until I came across something in Psalm 103.

Psalm 103 is an amazing chapter in the Bible. Virtually nothing can rival its glorious declarations of God's saving and forgiving love for his people. "The LORD is merciful and gracious, slow to anger and abounding in steadfast love" (v. 8). Wow!

But it gets better. "He does not deal with us according to our sins, nor repay us according to our iniquities" (v. 10). Double wow! As I noted in the previous meditation, this isn't because God doesn't repay or punish people in accordance with their iniquities and sins. Rather, he doesn't deal with *us* according to our sins because he has dealt with his *Son* according to what our sins deserve. He doesn't reward us according to our iniquities because the Son "was crushed for our iniquities . . . [for] the LORD has laid on him the iniquity of us all" (Isa. 53:5–6).

Then follow in Psalm 103 several declarations of God's compassion and kindness:

> For as high as the heavens are above the earth,
>> so great is his steadfast love toward those who fear him.
> As far as the east is from the west,
>> so far does he remove our transgressions from us.
> As a father shows compassion to his children,
>> so the LORD shows compassion to those who fear him.
> (vv. 11–13)

All well and good, you say. But doesn't God's knowledge of me shatter whatever hope I might have had that this could ever be my experience? No. For the next thing we read, in Psalm 103:14, is this: "For he knows our frame; he remembers that we are dust."

Don't miss the connection between verse 14 and all that preceded in verses 8–13. God loves us and has compassion on us and forgives us *for,* or *because,* he knows us. His knowledge of us doesn't repel him. His knowledge of us doesn't forever terminate his blessings. His knowledge of us is, in some sense, the reason or explanation why he chooses to be loving and forgiving and compassionate.

This is divine logic, because it certainly isn't human. It's not how you and I would reason. Our tendency would be to say, "It's because he knows that I'm dust, that my frame is fickle and weak and prone to wander, that he will have nothing to do with me." David says, "No, no! It's precisely because he knows what you are made of and how you function and what you think and feel and how often you fail that he chooses, in sovereign grace and mercy, to shower you with a compassion and kindness and saving love that you could never hope to earn or merit on your own."

Your knowledge of God's knowledge of you is not a good reason to run from him rather than to him when you sin. God's infinite and incisive and perfect knowledge of every fiber of your frame was no obstacle to his saving intentions. It was precisely because he knew and knows you in such exhaustive detail that he determined to send his Son to endure in your place the wrath and indignation that your frame and choices and rebellious ways so richly deserve.

This done, God sees you in his Son, clothed in his righteousness. He sees in you the work of his grace and the fear and awe and reverence in which you hold him. Knowing full well what you and I are in ourselves, he has compassion on us as a father on his children. Indeed, he sings over us in joyful and jubilant celebration, with deep and passionate affection (Zeph. 3:17).

So, no matter how well we know our own hearts, if we would but know God's heart, all fear and hesitation would disappear. We would find him full of compassion and kindness and ready to receive us no matter how often or egregious our "dust" may lead us into sin, no matter how weak and fickle our "frame" may be. He is an ever-flowing, never-ending fountain of forgiveness to those who, in repentance and faith, seek him for refuge and safety.

38

Lord of the Stork
and the Rock Badger

Psalm 104

O LORD, how manifold are your works!
In wisdom have you made them all;
the earth is full of your creatures.
—Psalm 104:24

When was the last time you gave a second thought (much less a first) to a donkey slaking its thirst in a muddy stream? I doubt that you've spent much time pondering the fir trees that provide a home for the stork, or the rocks that serve as a refuge for the badger.

Many Christians picture God as distant and uninvolved in the routine, trivial, uneventful affairs of life. This especially holds true when it comes to the phenomena of nature. Surely the God of heaven and earth, the Father of our Lord Jesus Christ, would not bother himself with such things as grass, rain, cattle, lifeless rocks, and odd animals in remote regions of the world that nobody knows of or cares about.

But Scripture, and particularly the Psalms, tell a different story. God is very much present, not in some passive sense as merely a concerned spectator, but actively upholding, preserving, and guiding all things to their ultimate goal of triumph in and through Christ for the praise of his glory (see Col. 1:16–17; Heb. 1:3).

Nowhere is this better seen than in Psalm 104. There are two ways of looking at the psalm. One is to see a prologue in verse 1 and an epilogue in verse 35b, in between which is sandwiched, as it were, a picturesque portrayal of God's providential care of his creation. It is a portrayal designed to arouse in us wondering awe and devoted love. Thus there are three divisions: first, verses 2–23, a description of the beauty of God's creation; second, verses 24–32, a portrayal of the utter dependence of the creation upon the Creator; and third, verses 33–35, praise for all God's marvelous works.

One may also look at the psalm in terms of its correspondence to the initial creation as found in Genesis 1. Thus, verses 2–4 parallel the creation of the first and second days in Genesis 1:3–8; verses 5–9 parallel the creation of the first part of the third day in Genesis 1:9–10, when the earth and waters were separated; verses 10–18 parallel the second part of the third day in Genesis 1:10–13; verses 19–23 parallel the creation of the fourth day of the heavenly bodies in Genesis 1:14–18; verses 24–26 parallel the creation of the fifth day; and verse 31 parallels an allusion to the sabbath rest of the seventh day.

But rather than try to track with either of these approaches to the psalm, I simply want to make several observations relating to God's providential love for and control over all he has made.

Before I do, you may ask: "Why should I care?" The answer is: "Because God does!" More than care about the creation, God *rejoices* in all that he has made. He takes profound *delight* in beholding the work of his hands. The marvel and majesty of nature bring joy to his heart as he reflects on the wonder of what he has shaped and all that he sustains.

I say this because of what we read in verse 31. There the psalmist prays: "May the glory of the LORD endure forever; may the LORD *rejoice* in his works." These "works" in which God takes such profound pleasure are the many manifestations of his activity in creation: "things like water and clouds and wind and mountains and thunder and springs and wild asses and birds and grass and cattle and wine and bread and cedars and wild goats and badgers and rocks and young lions and sea monsters. God delights in all the work of his hands."[16]

If it is essential to Christian holiness that we love what God loves, I pray that we may learn to "rejoice in his works" throughout creation even as he does. So let's begin.

First, let's start with verses 1–2 and the focus on the creation of the heavens and the light and their utter subservience to God. Note especially verse 2, where God is portrayed as "covering" himself "with light as with a garment." Says Calvin:

> In comparing the light to a robe he signifies that though God is invisible, yet His glory is manifest. If we speak of His essential being, it is true that He dwelleth in light inaccessible; but inasmuch as He irradiates the whole world with His glory, this is a robe wherein He in some measure appears to us as visible, who in Himself had been hidden. . . . It is folly to seek God in his own naked Majesty. . . . Let us turn our eyes to that most beautiful frame of the world in which He would be seen by us, that we may not pry with idle curiosity into the mystery of His nature.[17]

Second, according to verse 4 "he makes his messengers winds, his ministers a flaming fire." This verse has been variously interpreted, but there are only two ways that make sense. Either God makes his angels or ministering spirits swift as the wind and quick as lightning in his service, or God makes the wind his messengers and the lightning his servant. In other words, it is figurative language designed to tell us that the wind and lightning, no less than the clouds and the light itself, are in his control, fulfilling his command.

Third, as noted above, verses 6–8 may be a poetic expansion of Genesis 1:9 ("Let the waters under the heavens be gathered together into one place, and let the dry land appear"). The earth as originally formed was enveloped in water. God spoke a word of rebuke that the waters might give way to land. The verb translated "fled" (104:7) means "were panic stricken." As someone said, the waters "were terrified by the despotic command of God." But the important point to note is that "none of this movement was left to blind chance: both mountains and valleys sought out the place that God had founded for them. Everything was continually under perfect divine control."[18]

Others have suggested that verses 5–9 do not describe the original creation but rather the work of God in restoring the earth after the flood of Noah. Verse 9 certainly seems to support this view. In any case, Spurgeon rightly notes that "not so much as a solitary particle of spray ever breaks rank, or violates the command of the Lord of sea and land, neither do the awful cataracts and terrific floods revolt from his sway."[19]

Fourth, in verses 10–18 we move away from the original creation and catch a glimpse of divine providence. I can do no better than quote Spurgeon yet again:

> We see here, also, that nothing is made in vain; though no human lip is moistened by the brooklet in the lone valley, yet are there other creatures which need refreshment, and these slake their thirst at the stream. Is this nothing? Must everything exist for man, or else be wasted? What but our pride and selfishness could have suggested such a notion? It is not true that flowers which blush unseen by human eye are wasting their sweetness, for the bee finds them out, and other winged wanderers live on their luscious juices. Man is but one creature of the many whom the heavenly Father feedeth and watereth.[20]

Fifth, in verses 14–18 the psalmist includes a reference to God's care for mankind in addition to what he does for the animal world. In verse 14 we see that "divine power is as truly and as worthily put forth in the feeding of beasts as in the nurturing of man; watch but a blade of grass with a devout eye and you may see God at work within it!"[21] Indeed, even the wildest and most inaccessible regions of the creation exist for a purpose, to shelter some form of God-given life.

There is no such thing, therefore, as a "God-forsaken land." Even the rocks and cliffs never seen by human eyes are monuments to divine wisdom. If nothing else, the lifeless stone exists to serve as shelter for the scorpion and spider.

Sixth, God also governs the heavenly luminaries (vv. 19–23). Even darkness exists by divine design. It serves his purposes for us by limiting the time of our labor.

Seventh, note especially in verses 29–30 that all living things, from the most ferocious of lions to the smallest field mouse, exist by the favor of his countenance. If God hides his face, they are terrified, their breath is taken away, and they die. God suspends and withdraws his life-supporting benefits no less than he supplies them. All existence is his to sustain or destroy as he wills.

Eighth, we also see in verses 31–32 that both earthquakes and volcanoes are his doing. "These are again not merely the operation of certain natural potencies that are imbedded in nature and are bound to appear by way of automatic reactions."[22] God glances at the earth and it trembles. He lays his finger on a volcano and it erupts.

In view of what has been said, the conclusion of the psalmist is eminently reasonable: "I will sing to the LORD as long as I live; I will sing praise to my God while I have being" (v. 33). "If the Lord be such a God to all his creatures, then I can do no better than expend the remainder of my life in praising him."[23]

Finally, let us never forget that all the works of creation point us beyond themselves and to the Creator himself. Yes, God wants us to be stunned and in awe of his handiwork. "But not for its own sake," says Piper. "He means for us to look at his creation and say: 'If the mere work of his fingers (just his fingers! Psalm 8:3) is so full of wisdom and power and grandeur and majesty and beauty, what must this God be like in himself!'"[24] In the end, "it will not be the seas or the mountains or the canyons or the water spiders or the clouds or the great galaxies that fill our hearts to breaking with wonder and fill our mouths with eternal praise. It will be God himself."[25]

That is why the psalm ends appropriately with this exclamation of praise: "May my meditation be pleasing to him, for I rejoice in the LORD. . . . Bless the LORD, O my soul! Praise the LORD!" (vv. 34–35).

Psalms 115–150

from Book 5 of the Psalter

39

How's Your Aim?

Psalm 115

Not to us, O LORD, not to us, but to your name give glory,
    for the sake of your steadfast love and your faithfulness!
                                                —Psalm 115:1

According to legend, an Austrian bailiff by the name of Gessler issued an order requiring all citizens of Switzerland to bow to a hat that he had set atop a pole in the main square of the town of Altdorf. When William Tell refused, he was arrested. Gessler knew of Tell's expertise with the crossbow and struck a deal with him. If Tell could shoot an apple off the top of his son's head, Gessler would set him free.

As you know, Tell's arrow was perfectly on target. Afterwards, Tell confessed that if he had harmed his son he planned to shoot another arrow through Gessler's heart. When Gessler heard of it, he once again placed Tell under arrest. But he escaped and finally managed to assassinate the Austrian leader.

Few people know these details in the story of William Tell. Most remember only one thing: the pinpoint accuracy of his skill with the crossbow. They remember that had his aim been only slightly off target, the results would have been fatal.

I would like to draw an analogy between the experience of William Tell and our worship of God. I want to suggest that, much like Tell, if the arrow of our adoration is even slightly off target, the results can be disastrous. If our worship is not fixed and focused on the Triune God of Scripture alone, what we are doing is not only foolish, but fatal, not only dumb, but deadly.

Worship can and ought to occur at any time, in any place, in a variety of ways and postures. But *whenever* and *wherever* we worship, we must not think that *whomever* we worship is of secondary importance. Nowhere is this better seen or described than in Psalm 115.

"Not to us, O LORD, not to us, but to your name give glory" (v. 1a). That's not a typographical error. The repetition is intentional, designed to highlight the centrality of our focus and the deadly danger of any and all forms of idolatry.

Beginning with verse 4, the psalmist contrasts the one true and absolutely sovereign God who does whatever he pleases (v. 3, which I'll address in the next meditation) with the impotent idols of the world.

"*Their idols are silver and gold, the work of human hands*" (v. 4). No matter how costly the substance or precious the metal, it is still only lifeless, inert matter, unlike God who is spirit, who is alive. These deities of false worship are not creators but mere creations. They do not make; they are made. And insofar as the maker is always greater than the thing that is made, these idols are worthy of even less honor than the men who fashion them. "How irrational," notes Spurgeon, "that men should adore that which is less than themselves."[1]

"*They have mouths, but do not speak*" (v. 5a). Such dead idols cannot communicate. They make no promises to comfort the troubled soul. They issue no threats to those who would wander. They are incapable of making commands or offering consolation. They give no explanation of the past or predictions of the future.

They have "*eyes, but do not see*" (v. 5b). Whether rubies or diamonds or whatever precious stone is placed in the blind sockets of these lifeless statues, they are of no use. They are unaware of the needs of people, unable to perceive an impending threat, blind to all that is around them. They cannot behold the beauty of earthly grandeur nor gaze upon the stars that the one true God has set in space.

"*They have ears, but do not hear*" (v. 6a). However fervent or passionate or loud the prayers of their followers, they cannot hear. They are utterly deaf to the pleas of their people. On reading this I'm reminded of Elijah's taunting the worshipers of Baal:

> And at noon Elijah mocked them, saying, "Cry aloud [i.e., shout louder!], for he is a god. Either he is musing, or he is relieving himself, or he is on a journey, or perhaps he is asleep and must be awakened." And they cried aloud and cut themselves after their custom with swords and lances, until the blood gushed out upon them. And as midday passed, they raved on until the time of the offering of the oblation, but there was no voice. No one answered; no one paid attention. (1 Kings 18:27–29)

They have "*noses, but do not smell*" (v. 6b). Contrast this with Yahweh, who "smelled the pleasing aroma" of Noah's sacrifice and promised never again to "curse the ground because of man" (Gen. 8:21). Contrast it with the way the apostle Paul described the monetary support of the Philippian church: "a fragrant offering, a sacrifice acceptable and pleasing to God" (Phil. 4:18). Contrast it with the way God views the evangelistic efforts of his people, through whom he "spreads the fragrance of the knowledge" of Christ. "For we are the aroma of Christ to God among those who are being saved and among those who are perishing" (2 Cor. 2:14–15).

"*They have hands, but do not feel*" (v. 7a). They can neither receive what is given to them nor give that others might receive. They lack the capacity to touch or to feel or to embrace in love. How different it is with Yahweh, who extends his mighty hand to heal and deliver and save. How different it is with him at whose "right hand are pleasures forevermore" (Ps. 16:11).

They have "*feet, but do not walk*" (v. 7b). They have to be carried wherever they go and must be fastened down where they are set lest they topple over. They cannot rush to the rescue of their friends or flee from their enemies. They are immovable, immobile, inert.

Again, on reading this I am reminded of the Philistine god Dagon. Having captured the ark of the covenant, the Philistines "brought it into the house of Dagon and set it up beside Dagon. And when the people of Ashdod rose early the next day, behold, Dagon had fallen face downward on the ground before the ark of the LORD. So they took Dagon and put him back in his place. But when they rose early on the next morning, behold, Dagon had fallen face downward on the ground before the ark of the LORD, and the head of Dagon and both his hands were lying cut off on the threshold. Only the trunk of Dagon was left to him" (1 Sam. 5:2–4).

"*They do not make a sound in their throat*" (Ps. 115:7c). As Spurgeon put it, "neither a grunt, nor a growl, nor a groan, nor so much as a mutter, can come from them."[2]

Worst of all, "those who make them become like them; so do all who trust in them" (v. 8). In the end, you will become like that which you behold.

The counsel of the psalmist is simple and to the point: Trust in the Lord, and fear him, for he is your help and shield (vv. 9–18).

If you struggle with this psalm, perhaps thinking it irrelevant insofar as you would never consider owning an idol, much less bowing in its presence, remember this: false worship begins not with a sculptor's tool but in the mind of the man.

Idolatry exists anywhere or at any time that our aim is off-target. When we lose sight of the one true God and yield our affections to money and what it can buy, to sex and how it feels, to people and what they can do, or to self and what we desire, we are as guilty as those who prostrate themselves before a marble statue or pray to a false god.

"Our God," on the other hand, "is in the heavens; he does all that he pleases" (Ps. 115:3). To this glorious truth we turn in our next meditation.

40

Now to Him Who Is Able

Psalm 115:3

Our God is in the heavens;
he does all that he pleases.
—Psalm 115:3

When was the last time you thanked God simply *for being able*? I can't imagine anything more disheartening and depressing than believing in a God who lacks the power to fulfill his purposes, whose energy wanes in the heat of battle, or whose strength diminishes in a moment of crisis. Good intentions notwithstanding, if God can't carry out his plans and can't fulfill his goals and can't keep his promises, I'm not sure I want anything to do with him.

The apostle Paul consistently celebrated the *ability* of God and his limitless power to act on behalf of his people. Typical is this doxology in his letter to the Ephesians:

Now to him who is able to do far more abundantly than all that we ask or think, according to the power at work within us, to him be glory in the church and in Christ Jesus throughout all generations, forever and ever. Amen. (Eph. 3:20–21)

Or again, in his letter to the Romans:

> *Now to him who is able* to strengthen you according to my gospel
> and the preaching of Jesus Christ. . . . To the only wise God be glory
> forevermore through Jesus Christ! Amen. (Rom. 16:25, 27)

There's one more in the book of Jude:

> *Now to him who is able* to keep you from stumbling and to present
> you blameless before the presence of his glory with great joy, to the
> only God, our Savior, through Jesus Christ our Lord, be glory, maj-
> esty, dominion, and authority, before all time and now and forever.
> Amen. (Jude 24–25)

Our God is able. Unlike the pathetic impotence of the false deities excoriated in Psalm 115:4–8, our God is limitless in strength,
unending in power, omnicompetent in all things. He is, declares
the psalmist (v. 3), "in the heavens." Indeed, "he does all that he
pleases"!

Let's unpack that statement for a moment, giving due weight to
the implications of each word and phrase.

First, our God, the only God, is *in the heavens*. In other words, he
is transcendent over all, supreme in majesty, unparalleled in splendor.
He rules over the earth, sovereign and supreme in all its affairs.

Second, our God, the only God, *does*. Again, unlike the lifeless
idols who lack life and power and energy, our God, the only God,
is active and involved in all that he has made. He is not passive or
idle. Our God is immediately and intimately engaged in all of life.
Not so much as a sparrow falls to the ground, said Jesus, apart from
the will of our heavenly Father.

Third, our God, the only God, does *all* that he pleases. He will
not fail to accomplish one thing he purposes to do. Whatever he
plans, he fulfills. If it is in the heart of God to attain a goal, he will
utilize every essential means thereto and bring it to pass. If God has
decreed, will it not come to pass? If God has purposed, will he not
pursue it to its proper consummation? Yes, indeed, he will!

Fourth, God does what *he* pleases. He is free in his sovereignty.
He is not conditioned or controlled by anyone or anything outside

himself. I'm thrilled and relieved to know that God will do what I please only when it is pleasing to him. My aim in life and in my prayers of intercession is not to bend his will to my good pleasure but to shape and fashion my will to his.

Fifth, and finally, God does what he *pleases*. You need not fear what he does, for all he does is an expression or reflection of his good pleasure, which is to say, an expression of his moral character. God's sovereignty is not casual, flippant, arbitrary, or ill-advised. God's pleasure is the fountain and standard of God's purpose.

So celebrate with me the God who is able. Let us labor to fill our minds with the revelation of a God who is both mighty and merciful, a God who is both gracious and great, a God who not only intends to do good things for his people but also is infinitely strong and capable and powerful enough to pull it off.

My prayer is that you (and I) be stunned with the majesty of this God, that you be left breathless in his presence, dazzled by his strength, trembling in your spirit because you've seen something of this God who works tirelessly and relentlessly on behalf of those who trust in him.

And why is this important? I'll mention only three reasons, although countless others could be cited.

1) Your spiritual growth is governed by the greatness of your God. If your God is small, you will be too. If his power is limited, so is yours. It's important that we know and celebrate the God who is able, because your spiritual maturity and conformity to the likeness of Jesus himself will always be in proportion to the greatness of the God you know. Those who worship a diminutive deity will forever remain spiritual pygmies.

Henry Scougal once said, "The worth and excellency of a soul is to be measured by the object of its love."[3] If you want to learn what's most important *about* a person, take note of what's most important *to* that person. What does he most admire? Whom does she most cherish? What monopolizes his time and energy? If our God, the only God, the God who is able, is the one for whom we seek, to whom we are passionately devoted, in whom we have invested our lives, the "excellency" of our souls will be known by all.

2) According to Daniel 11:32, "The people who know their God shall stand firm and take action." The knowledge of this God who is able empowers the soul, energizes the heart, strengthens the will, exalts the mind, inflames the spirit, and moves our hands in ministry and mercy to others. Ignorance, on the other hand, immobilizes.

3) Finally, and most important of all, this is what you were created for. We exist not simply to think about God or to sing about God or to obey God or to fear God but to glorify him by enjoying and rejoicing in him forever. But your delight in God will be only as deep and intense as your knowledge is accurate. You cannot enjoy someone you don't know.

So, if your doubts and fears are fueled by skepticism concerning God's ability to pull off what he has promised, I encourage you again to meditate on this glorious revelation: unlike every idol, over against the best intentions of men and women, "our God is in the heavens; he does all that he pleases."

41

Sweeter than Honey to My Mouth

Psalm 119

Open my eyes, that I may behold
wondrous things out of your law.
—Psalm 119:18

Psalm 119 has long been an enigma to many Christians, especially those who testify to boredom and confusion when they read God's Word. The attitude of the psalmist is baffling to them. He speaks repeatedly of a joy and unparalleled delight and a spiritual exhilaration when he reads and meditates on Scripture, affections that are largely foreign to their experience.

So here's what I propose. Quickly read this meditation and then slowly read the psalm in its entirety. Then read it again. And then yet again, slowly, saturating your spirit in every syllable and sentence. This is what I did on the day I composed this meditation, only to discover, as if for the first time in a long time, a progressive awakening in my heart and a quickening in my spirit of the mind-blowing beauty, sin-killing power, and breathtaking expanse of God's Word.

As I read the psalm, and then reread it, again and again, I began to see a number of issues and points of emphasis that are obviously dear to the psalmist's heart, issues for which I long to find a permanent place in mine as well. I pray that these ten observations will assist you in your reading of this stunning portrayal of God's Word and its operation in your life.

1) One of the first things that struck me was the variety of ways in which God's rules and laws and precepts are described: they are "righteous" (vv. 7, 75, 106, 164), indeed "righteous forever" (v. 144); they are "good" (v. 39); they are "sure" (v. 86); they are "firmly fixed in the heavens" (v. 89); they are "exceedingly broad" (v. 96); they are "right" (vv. 128, 137, 172); they are "wonderful" (v. 129); they are "true" (vv. 142, 151); and they endure forever (v. 160).

2) Little wonder, then, that the psalmist would go to such vivid verbal lengths to describe his attitude about, indeed his appetite for, the Word of God. Consider, for example, the following brief sampling, and ask yourself if such colorful and passionate language accurately describes your perspective toward the glory and power of God's Word:

In the way of your testimonies *I delight as much as in all riches.* (v. 14)

I will delight in your statutes. (v. 16)

My soul is consumed with longing for your rules at all times. (v. 20)

Your testimonies are my *delight.* (v. 24; cf. vv. 35, 77, 92, 143, 174)

Behold, *I long* for your precepts. (v. 40)

For I find my *delight* in your commandments, *which I love.* (v. 47)

The law of your mouth is *better to me than thousands of gold and silver pieces.* (v. 72)

Oh how I love your law! (v. 97)

How *sweet* are your words to my taste, *sweeter than honey to my mouth*! (v. 103)

Your testimonies are my heritage forever, for they are *the joy of my heart*. (v. 111)

I love your law. (v. 113b; cf. vv. 119, 159, 163)

Therefore *I love your commandments above gold, above fine gold*. (v. 127)

Your testimonies are *wonderful*. (v. 129)

I open my mouth and pant, because I *long* for your commandments. (v. 131)

I *rejoice* at your word like one who finds great spoil. (v. 162)

My soul keeps your testimonies; *I love them exceedingly*. (v. 167)

3) One of the more remarkable things in this psalm is the number of times the psalmist pleads with God to teach him and instruct him and give him insight and open his eyes that he might understand the Word. The psalmist has no illusions about his own ability to understand God's Word apart from the illumination of its ultimate author. We see this in verses 12, 18–19, 26–27, 29, 33–34, 64, 66, 68, 71, 73, 75, 108, 124–25, 135, 144, 169, 171. If God does not act to unveil and illuminate the meaning of his Word, we shall forever remain in darkness. May I suggest, then, that you take these texts and make them your first prayer each time you open God's Word for study or meditation.

4) There is great significance in the fact that the psalmist also prays that God would do more than teach him what the Law means; he prays that God would incline his heart to observe them (see vv. 10, 35–37, 88, 117; cf. 133). In other words, God is present to incite our souls to obey the insight of our minds. He is committed not simply to illumining our understanding but also to inclining our wills. Knowledge that does not lead to action serves only to breed arrogance and pride.

5) Although utterly and in all ways dependent on God for help, don't overlook the fact that the psalmist repeatedly commits himself and "promises" to take action to learn, store up, and diligently keep the Word of God. The antecedent priority of God's work in his heart does not preclude or undermine his responsibility to exercise his will in the active embrace of the Word. We see this, for example, in verses 8, 11, 15, 30, 32, 44, 57, 59–60, 101–102, 106, 112, and 145.

6) The psalmist is also determined to undertake the discipline of *meditation*. He often speaks of "fixing" his eyes on the commandments of God and laboring "never to forget" them (see vv. 6, 15, 16, 23, 27, 48, 61, 78, 83, 97, 99, 141, 148, 176). This is a healthy and much-needed reminder that God does not operate on us in an intellectual or spiritual vacuum. In other words, if he is going to illumine our minds and incline our wills, his Word must first take root in our hearts.

7) What blessings and benefits accrue to those who by God's grace and energizing presence actually ingest his Word? What may those expect who fix their faith on obedience to what he has revealed? Here's a sampling: they are declared "blessed" (vv. 1–2); they "shall not be put to shame" (vv. 6, 31, 46, 80); they will be kept from sinning against God (vv. 9, 11); they enjoy beholding wondrous things (v. 18); they are spared scorn and contempt (v. 22); they receive counsel (v. 24); they experience true life (vv. 25, 37, 93); they are strengthened (v. 28); they experience the enlargement of the heart (v. 32); they avoid selfish gain (v. 36); they find wise answers for their enemies (v. 42); they experience comfort and delight in the midst of affliction (vv. 50, 52, 92, 107, 143, 153); as well as "great peace" (v. 165). Wow!

8) I referred above to the sin-killing power of God's Word that the psalmist emphasizes throughout this psalm, the capacity of God's revealed truth to strengthen us in the face of temptation and to believe his promise of superior joy (cf. Ps. 16:11) when confronted with the passing pleasures of sin. In other words, we find in God's Word the only reliable remedy against the impulses of the flesh and the temptations of the world (see vv. 9, 11, 36–37, 104–105). Only when God's ways are sweet to the taste will sin turn sour in our souls.

9) On numerous occasions the psalmist speaks of his commitment to persevere in obedience to God's Word in spite of the evil done to him by the wicked. What he has in mind is how the Word of God satisfies his heart and keeps and preserves him from the ways and destructive tendencies of those who hate God. "The insolent smear me with lies, but with my whole heart I keep your precepts; their heart is unfeeling like fat, but I delight in your law" (vv. 69–70). Or again, "Princes persecute me without cause, but my heart stands in awe of your words" (v. 161). See also verses 78, 85–87, 95, 98, 110, 115, 150–51, and 157–58.

10) Finally, if you're still tempted to cast aside God's Word for the sake of worldly gain, consider how he compares the value of God's Word to all earthly treasures:

The law of your mouth is better to me than thousands of gold and silver pieces. (v. 72; cf. v. 14)

Therefore I love your commandments above gold, above fine gold. (v. 127)

God's Word is exquisite, sublime, splendid, and sweet. God's Word is powerful, faithful, righteous, and true. God's Word is great, glorious, grand, and good. Why? Because in it we see God. Through it, he draws near. By means of its truth, we experience the incomparable joy of knowing him and seeing him and beholding the beauty of his infinite elegance.

Hear, O Lord, our prayer: "Open my eyes, that I may behold wondrous things out of your law!" (Ps. 119:18).

42

Forgiveness:
The Foundation for Fear

Psalm 130:3–4

If you, O LORD, should mark iniquities,
O Lord, who could stand?
But with you there is forgiveness,
that you may be feared.
—Psalm 130:3–4

I f the title to this meditation strikes you as a contradiction in
terms, read on.

Let me begin by asking a simple question: what do you fear
most? As for me, the first things that come to mind, in no particular
order, are squash, wasps, and the possibility of no baseball in heaven.
Of course, I realize that I can hold my nose when I eat squash and
wait for my taste buds to recover. I assume, as well, that no matter
how painful a wasp sting may be, I won't die. And, of course, as
long as Jesus is in heaven I'll be infinitely happy in the age to come.
But it's a good question, nonetheless. So, what do *you* fear most?

A lot of people will supply the expected spiritual answer: God.
But if pressed to define what that means, many will falter and fumble

for an explanation. Needless to say, it all depends on how we define our terms. What precisely do we mean by the word *fear*?

Before we set forth an answer, let's consider how pervasive and important "fearing God" is in Scripture. Of the literally dozens of texts I could cite, there are a few that come immediately to mind. For example, as Abraham was about to slay Isaac, God said: "Do not lay your hand on the boy or do anything to him, for now I know that you *fear God*, seeing you have not withheld your son, your only son, from me" (Gen. 22:12).

When Satan stood before God, the Lord said to him: "Have you considered my servant Job, that there is none like him on the earth, a blameless and upright man, who *fears God* and turns away from evil?" (Job 1:8). We're all familiar with the declaration in Proverbs that "the *fear of the* LORD is the beginning of knowledge" (Prov. 1:7a).

The New Testament is also familiar with this truth, as Peter, for example, issues this command to his readers: "Honor everyone. Love the brotherhood. *Fear God*. Honor the emperor" (1 Pet. 2:17).

What, then, does it mean for the believer to "fear" God? The most frequently heard response is that it entails reverence and awe, and that is no doubt true. By this I understand that we must live and speak and think and act with a keen and ever-present awareness that God is holy and we are not, he is powerful and we are weak, he is self-sufficient and we are utterly dependent for every breath on his goodness and grace. This is the sort of fear that expresses itself in trembling and amazement and an overwhelming sense of personal frailty and finitude.

This sort of fear is the antithesis of presumption, pride, and self-righteousness. Yes, God is our heavenly Father and he sings over us with rapturous delight. But he is also a consuming fire (Heb. 12:28–29), in whose glorious presence both John the apostle and the twenty-four elders fall prostrate in humble adoration (Rev. 1:17; 4:9–10).

To fear God means to live conscious of his all-pervasive presence, conscious of our absolute, moment-by-moment dependence on him for light and life, conscious of our comprehensive responsibility to do all he has commanded, fearful of offending him, determined to obey him (Deut. 6:1–2, 24; 8:6; Pss. 112:1; 119:63; Mal. 3:5), and committed to loving him (Deut. 10:12, 20; 13:4).

When we look to Proverbs, we discover that to fear God is to know him (Prov. 1:29; 2:4–5) and to hate evil (Prov. 8:13; 16:6). Fearing God yields confidence (Prov. 14:26) and humility (Prov. 3:7; 22:4), and contentment (Prov. 23:17).

The fear of God, then, is many things. But we now come to what it is *not*. It is not being frightened of him in the sense that we live in uncertainty as to whether he might one day turn on us and lay upon us the condemnation that our sin deserves. It is not being afraid of him in the sense that we live in doubt about his intentions or whether he plans on fulfilling the promises of his Word. It is not being terrorized and paralyzed at the prospect of having our transgressions visited yet again upon us, in spite of the fact that they have been fully and finally visited on our Savior, the Lord Jesus. It is not living in anxious dread that divine wrath will yet find us out and bring death and eternal destruction to our souls.

One passage that particularly reinforces this truth is Psalm 130:3–4. It's the sort of text that is easily overlooked and ignored. On first reading, something seems terribly askew. Would it not have made more sense for the psalmist to say, "But with you there is *justice*, that you may be feared"? Is it not the prospect of God exacting payment for our transgressions that evokes fear in the human soul? If God should indeed "mark iniquities," then fear seems the only appropriate response.

But the good news is that with God "there is forgiveness." That being the case, would not all "fear" be eliminated? One would certainly think so. Yet the psalmist asserts that the result of forgiveness (perhaps even its purpose) is that we might fear God ever more fervently. So the meaning of this remarkable text must be found elsewhere.

Think deeply about what is being said. With God there is forgiveness. From him proceeds the grace that provides a propitiation for our sins. He has taken every step necessary to accomplish our redemption through his Son. As we saw in Psalm 103:10, he no longer deals with us according to our sins or repays us according to our iniquities. Indeed, our sins have been removed from us as far as the east is from the west (Ps. 103:12).

This is why the fear of God mentioned in this text *cannot* be fear of facing condemnation or fear of encountering and experiencing his righteous wrath. Do you see the psalmist's logic? If what we find with God is forgiveness for our sins, what grounds remain for us to live in terror of his judgment or wrath? If God has wiped clean the slate of our sin and guilt, then clearly he has chosen *not* to "mark iniquities" and just as clearly all reason for fear is gone. Therefore, if the "fear of God" in this passage were a reference to the dread of impending destruction, forgiveness is emptied of all meaning and value.

But according to what we read in verse 4, forgiveness is the foundation for fear. The unshakable knowledge that God will never "mark iniquities" (v. 3), which is to say, the assurance that our sins have been forever forgiven, is the reason why we fear God. There's no escaping the force of the psalmist's language: fearing God is the necessary fruit of forgiveness. This alone demands that fearing God entail something altogether other than being afraid of judgment.

Forgiveness, as much as any act of God, reveals his incomprehensible greatness and majesty. The infinitely transcendent God of holiness and truth has acted in grace on behalf of hell-deserving sinners. Once the reality of this is fully grasped, the only reasonable response is one of brokenness, humility, and breathtaking awe at such amazing love.

Certainly there is joy in the knowledge of our forgiveness, as well as gratitude and praise. But these are perfectly consistent with holy fear, that bone-shattering realization that it is by divine mercy alone that we are not forever consumed by divine wrath. One can simultaneously "taste" the goodness of the Lord (Ps. 34:8a) and "fear" him (Ps. 34:9a). In fact, "it is grace which leads the way to a holy regard of God, and a fear of grieving him."[4]

So let it never be said that holy reverence for the Almighty is incompatible with freedom and joy. For as Thomas Adams so perfectly put it, "no man more truly loves God than he that is most fearful to offend him."[5]

43

Omniscient

Psalm 139:1–6

O LORD, you have searched me and known me!
You know when I sit down and when I rise up;
  you discern my thoughts from afar.
                                    —Psalm 139:1–2

I had a choice today about what to eat for lunch. As I drove west on 135th Street, I was faced with the decision of whether to turn left into the Sonic drive-in or continue straight ahead to Subway for a roast-beef sandwich on wheat bread. Nutrition would be better served by the latter, but the allure of a chicken-strip dinner with fries and a Diet Coke ultimately prevailed.

Did God know which choice I would make prior to the moment that I made it? If I had chosen at the last possible second to forgo both the sub and the Sonic and opted for a Hardee's hamburger, would God have slapped himself upside the head and shouted: "Wow! I never saw that one coming"?

It sounds like a silly question, but I find little comfort in the suggestion that God was oblivious to my choice before I made it. Some would argue that, given his exhaustive knowledge of my previous decisions concerning lunch and the orientation of my taste buds, he could at least have projected with a high degree of probability the likelihood that I would end up at Sonic rather than Subway. But even then, I could have surprised him, or so I'm told.

David would have disagreed. The author of Psalm 139 takes great comfort in knowing that God knows him exhaustively—past, present, and future. David was strengthened and reassured by the fact that no thought, desire, plan, or purpose escaped the eye of his heavenly Father.

Psalm 139 is a glorious celebration of the multifaceted splendor of God and the imminently practical implications that it bears for you and me. The treasures in this psalm concerning the nature and activity of God are timeless and priceless and deserve our careful and considerable attention. Therefore, I'm going to devote three meditations to this psalm. First, we will look at God's *omniscience* in verses 1–6. We'll then turn to David's portrayal of God's *omnipresence* in verses 7–12 and finally to his comments concerning divine *omnipotence* in verses 13–18. I'm not ignoring verses 19–24, having already addressed them in conjunction with our study of imprecations in the Psalms in several earlier meditations.

That the first six verses are concerned with God's knowledge is evident from the repetition of the verb "to know" in verses 1, 2, and 4, as well as the noun "knowledge" in verse 6. But not everyone likes the idea of being utterly, exhaustively, and intimately known. They prefer to keep the secrets of their soul hidden from view. That God might know them in such pervasive detail is unnerving, to say the least. David, on the other hand, revels in this truth. As we'll note momentarily, such knowledge, he declares, "is too wonderful for me; it is high; I cannot attain it" (v. 6).

Let's look more closely at the extent of God's knowledge of David (and of us) and the joy it ought to evoke within us.

In the opening statement, "O LORD, you have searched me and known me" (v. 1), "searching" is obviously an anthropomorphic image, for "God knows all things naturally and as a matter of course, and not by any effort on his part. Searching ordinarily implies a measure of ignorance which is removed by observation; of course this is not the case with the Lord; but the meaning of the Psalmist is, that the Lord knows us thoroughly as if he had examined us minutely, and had pried into the most secret corners of our being."[6]

If it were the case that God was truly ignorant of David prior to his searching of his soul, this would mean that God is not omniscient at all, that he lacks not only knowledge of the future but of the present state of the human heart as well—something not even the most ardent open theist is willing to admit.

In order to demonstrate that God also has exhaustive knowledge of every position and movement, David employs a figure of speech called *merism*, in which polar opposites are used to indicate the totality of all generically related acts, events, localities, and so on. Thus: "You know when I sit down and when I rise up" (v. 2a). His choice of words is designed to encompass the totality of his life's activities. God's knowledge extends to every conceivable physical state, gesture, exercise, posture, and pursuit. "When I am active and when I am passive and everything in between . . . you know it all!" David leaves nothing to guesswork: "My most common and casual acts, my most necessary and trivial movements, are all seen by you. Nothing escapes your eye!"

Indeed, God knows every mental impulse that governs and regulates such outward behavior. We read in v. 2b that God "discerns" our "thoughts from afar." Every emotion, feeling, idea, thought, conception, resolve, aim, doubt, motive, perplexity, and anxious moment is exposed before God like an open book.

And all this "from afar" (v. 2b). Some take this as a reference to God's transcendence, the point being that the distance between heaven and earth by which men vainly imagine God's knowledge to be circumscribed (limited, bounded) offers no obstacle. Though God be infinitely high and we be so very, very low, he knows us thoroughly.

Others, such as my friend Ray Ortlund, read this verse in the light of verses 7–12 which focus on God's omnipresence. Thus he sees in it a *temporal* meaning:

> In verses 7–12, David makes the point that God is always present with him. The distance in view in verse 2, then, must be not spatial but temporal, as this word is also used in Isaiah 22:11, 25:1 and 37:26.

Long before any impulse wells up from within David's psyche, long before David himself knows what his next mood or feeling will be, long before he knows where his train of thought will eventually lead, God perceives it all.[7]

What follows serves only to confirm this truth: "you search out my path and my lying down and are acquainted with all my ways" (v. 3), that is to say, every step, every movement, every journey is beneath your gaze.

Should there be any lingering doubts, verse 4 utterly dispels them: "Even before a word is on my tongue, behold, O LORD, you know it altogether." Two things are important to note. First, God has knowledge of our words "before" they are spoken. Second, God has exhaustive and comprehensive knowledge of our words. He knows them "altogether" or completely. Spurgeon was surely right when he said:

> Though my thought be invisible to the sight, though as yet I be not myself cognizant of the shape it is assuming, yet thou hast it under thy consideration, and thou perceivest its nature, its source, its drift, its result. Never dost thou misjudge or wrongly interpret me; my inmost thought is perfectly understood by thine impartial mind. Though thou shouldest give but a glance at my heart, and see me as one sees a passing meteor moving afar, yet thou wouldst by that glimpse sum up all the meanings of my soul, so transparent is everything to thy piercing glance.[8]

How often have you blurted out, perhaps at an especially ill-advised moment, some word that you had no idea was forthcoming? Of this I can assure you: God wasn't in the least surprised or caught offguard. You and I may not always know what we will say, but God does.

Quite simply, God surrounds us. His knowledge has us hemmed in (v. 5). We are enveloped by his loving care. "We cannot turn back and so escape him, for he is behind; we cannot go forward and outmarch him, for he is before. He not only beholds us, but he besets us."[9]

How does all this affect you? Does it elicit fear in your soul? Anxiety? Anger? For David, God's exhaustive and all-encompassing knowledge of him is simply "too wonderful" (v. 6a). He lacks the necessary faculties of mind, spirit, and affection to fully grasp what is at stake. It is too deep, too high, too wide, too expansive and broad for his finite mind to entertain. Such knowledge not only surpasses his comprehension but his imagination as well. "It is high; I cannot attain it" (v. 6b). Again, I yield to Spurgeon:

> Mount as I may, this truth is too lofty for my mind. It seems to be always above me, even when I soar into the loftiest regions of spiritual thought. Is it not so with every attribute of God? Can we attain to any idea of his power, his wisdom, his holiness? Our mind has no line with which to measure the Infinite. Do we therefore question? Say, rather, that we therefore believe and adore. We are not surprised that the Most Glorious God should in his knowledge be high above all the knowledge to which we can attain: it must of necessity be so, since we are such poor limited beings; and when we stand a-tip-toe we cannot reach to the lowest step of the throne of the Eternal.[10]

So, yes, God knew from all eternity that I would end up at Sonic today, enjoying chicken strips and fries, and let's not forget the Diet Coke. And I rejoice and rest in the assurance that he knows tomorrow's menu as well.

44

Omnipresent

Psalm 139:7–12

Where shall I go from your Spirit?
Or where shall I flee from your presence?
—Psalm 139:7

salm 139 is all about God, simply and solely. If that doesn't interest you, I doubt that you'll find it of much help in life. That it *might not* interest you is, of course, tragic. That it *ought* to interest you goes without saying. But let me say it anyway. Better still, let Charles Spurgeon say it:

There is something exceedingly improving to the mind in a contemplation of the Divinity. It is a subject so vast, that all our thoughts are lost in its immensity; so deep, that our pride is drowned in its infinity. Other subjects we can comprehend and grapple with; in them we feel a kind of self-content, and go our way with the thought, "Behold I am wise." But when we come to this master-science, finding that our plumb-line cannot sound its depth, and that our eagle eye cannot see its height, we turn away with the . . . solemn exclamation, "I am but of yesterday, and know nothing.". . . But while the subject humbles the mind, it also expands it. . . . Nothing will so enlarge the intellect, nothing so magnify the whole soul of man, as a devout, earnest, continuing investigation of the great subject of the Deity.[11]

As we saw in the previous meditation, David's passionate concern in verses 1–6 is with God's knowledge of him: his exhaustive, comprehensive, infallible insight into his soul and spirit, into every movement and motivation of his life. In verses 7–12 he turns his attention to God's presence. His point is that God is inescapable:

> Where shall I go from your Spirit?
>> Or where shall I flee from your presence?
>> If I ascend to heaven, you are there!
>> If I make my bed in Sheol, you are there!
>> If I take the wings of the morning
>>> and dwell in the uttermost parts of the sea,
>> even there your hand shall lead me,
>>> and your right hand shall hold me.
>> If I say, "Surely the darkness shall cover me,
>>> and the light about me be night,"
>> even the darkness is not dark to you;
>>> the night is bright as the day,
>>> for darkness is as light with you. (Ps. 139:7–12)

Did David really want to escape God's presence? Is this descriptive of an actual historical event in which he sought to elude the Almighty? There's no evidence to indicate that such was his intent. In all likelihood David is speaking hypothetically: "*If* it were my intent to flee your presence, would I be successful? Where could I possibly go?" Of course, the answer is "nowhere. For you, O God, are everywhere."

If ascent were David's avenue of escape, it would be to no avail. No matter how high he goes, God is there. If he reversed course and descended into the depths of the grave, God is waiting patiently for him there as well. To seek to flee God's presence in any and every direction is to fly into the center of the fire to escape the heat.

Perhaps if David were to make light itself his chariot (at 186,000 miles per second) he could escape God's presence. Alas, not even the lightning-like rapidity with which the rays of the sun dart from east to west as they first break out over the horizon at dawn ("the wings of the morning," v. 9) are sufficiently speedy to outrun God.

There's one last chance (or is there?). If one might somehow sink beneath the depths of the sea, where no light can penetrate and no human has yet ventured, where strange and elusive creatures swim in utter anonymity, God would surely be absent. Think again.

Such extravagant efforts to escape God's presence have all failed. Perhaps, then, something less dramatic is called for. Why not simply turn off the lights, pull the drapes, close the blinds, and draw up the covers over one's head? No, again no, not even the most impenetrable gloom of night can shut God out. Darkness may conceal man from man, but not man from God.

Is there no secluded hideaway, some remote corner of the universe to which even the Deity has no access? Might we not there sin freely? Might we not there sin secretly? But where is "there"? Name it, find it on a map, describe it however you choose, and there you'll find God.

Let's be sure we understand the theological truth behind David's language. Theologians rightly make a distinction between *immensity* and *omnipresence* when they talk of God's relation to space. Whereas immensity affirms that God transcends all spatial limitations, that his being cannot be contained or localized, omnipresence signifies more specifically the relationship that God in his whole being sustains to the creation itself. In other words, omnipresence (being positive in thrust) means that God is everywhere present in the world; immensity (being negative in thrust) means that he is by no means limited to or confined by it.

This means that it is probably inappropriate to speak of God as having *size*, for this term implies something that is measurable, definable, with boundaries and limitations. It would seem, then, that the question "How big is God?" is unanswerable.

God, of course, is not *in space* in the sense that we or the angelic host are. We who have material bodies are bounded by space and thus can always be said to be here and not there, or there and not here. That is, a body occupies a place in space. Angelic spirits, on the other hand, as well as the dead in Christ now in the intermediate state, are not bound by space and yet they are somewhere, not everywhere. But God, and God alone, fills all space. He is not absent from any portion of space or more present in one portion than in another. To put it in other terms, we are in space *circumscriptively*, angels are in space *definitively*, but God is in space *repletively*.

Psalm 139 is hardly the only place in Scripture where this truth is found. Consider also:

> "Can a man hide himself in secret places so that I cannot see him? declares the LORD. Do I not fill heaven and earth? declares the LORD." (Jer. 23:24)

> "But will God indeed dwell on the earth? Behold, heaven and the highest heaven cannot contain you; how much less this house that I have built!" (1 Kings 8:27)

We should also remember that God is present everywhere in the totality of his being and not merely by the operation of his will. That is to say, he is essentially or substantially, not only dynamically, omnipresent. Some falsely contend that God is present in all places only by way of influence and power, acting upon the world from a distance, but not himself wholly present throughout. But as Herman Bavinck explains, "God is not present in creation as a king in his realm or a captain aboard his ship. He does not act upon the world from a distance; but with his whole being he is present powerfully here and everywhere with respect to his essence and power."[12]

Although God is wholly present throughout all things, he is yet *distinct* from all things. It does not follow that because God is essentially in everything that everything is essentially God. Pantheism asserts that the being of God is one and the same with the being of all reality, such that God minus the world equals zero. Biblical theism, on the other hand, asserts that God minus the world equals God. The universe is the creation of God and thus, in respect to essence, no part of him. The creation is ontologically other than God, a product *ex nihilo* of the divine will, not an extension of the Divine Being itself. Consequently, although all things are permeated and sustained in being by God (Col. 1:16–17; Acts 17:28), God is not all things. Again, God is not present *as* each point in space but rather present *with* or *in* each point in space.

What practical implications does this marvelous theological truth have for us? In the first place, there is in divine omnipresence a stern warning to the wicked. Stephen Charnock elaborates:

> How terrible should the thoughts of this attribute be to sinners! How foolish is it to imagine any hiding-place from the incomprehensible God, who fills and contains all things, and is present in every point of the world. When men have shut the door, and made all darkness within, to meditate or commit a crime, they cannot in the most intricate recesses be sheltered from the presence of God. If they could separate themselves from their own shadows, they could not avoid his company, or be obscured from his sight. . . . Hypocrites cannot disguise their sentiments from him; he is in the most secret nook of their hearts. No thought is hid, no lust is secret, but the eye of God beholds this, and that, and the other. He is present with our heart when we imagine, with our hands when we act. We may exclude the sun from peeping into our solitudes, but not the eyes of God from beholding our actions.[13]

Spurgeon agrees, and he reminds us that "this [truth] makes it dreadful work to sin; for we offend the Almighty to His face, and commit acts of treason at the very foot of His throne. Go from Him, or flee from Him we cannot; neither by patient travel nor by hasty flight can we withdraw from the all-surrounding Deity. His mind is in our mind; Himself within ourselves. His spirit is over our spirit; our presence is ever in His presence."[14]

If God's omnipresence frightens the wicked, it should console and comfort the righteous. No matter what the trial, no matter the place of its occurrence; no matter the swiftness with which it assaults, no matter the depth of its power, God is ever with us. His loving protection ever abides. "Even though I walk through the valley of the shadow of death, I will fear no evil, for *you are with me*; your rod and your staff, they comfort me" (Ps. 23:4).

Finally, Charnock reminds us of what a glorious and powerful incentive to holiness is the truth of God's omnipresence:

What man would do an unworthy action, or speak an unhandsome word in the presence of his prince? The eye of the general inflames the spirit of a soldier. Why did David "keep God's testimonies"? Because he considered that "all his ways were before him," Ps. [119]:168; because he was persuaded his ways were present with God, God's precepts should be present with him. The same was the cause of Job's integrity; "doth he not see my ways?" Job [31:]4; to have God in our eye is the way to be sincere, "walk before me," as in my sight, "and be thou perfect," Gen. [17:]1. Communion with God consists chiefly in an ordering our ways as in the presence of him that is invisible. This would make us spiritual, raised and watchful in all our passions, if we considered that God is present with us in our shops, in our chambers, in our walks, and in our meetings, as present with us as with the angels in heaven; who though they have a presence of glory above us, yet have not a greater measure of his essential presence than we have.[15]

Omniscient. Omnipresent. And now, on to omnipotent.

232

45

Omnipotent

Psalm 139:13–18

I praise you, for I am fearfully and wonderfully made.
                                                —Psalm 139:14a

S ome feel threatened by the sovereignty of God. They regard it
        as an infringement on their personal autonomy or fear that it
        will reduce humans to mere automatons, incapable of mean-
ingful and morally significant choices.

Others, yours truly included, cannot imagine life apart from the
comforting, reassuring, rock-solid confidence that flows from knowing that God governs all things, from the exalted affairs of heaven
to the seemingly random raindrops that plummet to earth. I think I
have David on my side. Or perhaps I should say that since David is
a defender of divine sovereignty, so too should you and I be.

To this point in Psalm 139 David has focused on two of the so-
called *omni's* of God: *omniscience* in verses 1–6, and *omnipresence*
in verses 7–12. But the questions might be asked: How do we know
that God truly knows? On what grounds do we embrace the notion
that he is always and ever with us?

The answer is found in what follows next in vv. 13–16. In fact,
the answer is wrapped up in the causal particle with which verse 13

opens. I'm referring to the word *for*. Don't overlook this word or fail to grasp its significance, for in it we find an answer to our questions, "How is it that God knows David so intimately? What accounts for his immediate involvement in the affairs of David's life?" The answer, quite simply, is that it is God who formed him in his mother's womb and ordained all his days. David's point is simply to assert that no one has a truer, more accurate, or more exhaustive knowledge of a person than the sovereign God who has made him and fashioned his days in advance of their occurrence. Thus he writes:

> For you formed my inward parts;
>> you knitted me together in my mother's womb.
> I praise you, for I am fearfully and wonderfully made.
> Wonderful are your works;
>> my soul knows it very well.
> My frame was not hidden from you,
> when I was being made in secret,
>> intricately woven in the depths of the earth.
> Your eyes saw my unformed substance;
> in your book were written, every one of them,
>> the days that were formed for me,
>> when as yet there was none of them. (Ps. 139:13–16)

Here we see an exalted portrayal, in extremely personal terms, of an abstract and often misunderstood theological term: *omnipotence*.

The Bible doesn't merely speak of God's power or his ability to produce effects. It clearly affirms that such power is without limitations. His power is infinite. It knows no boundaries other than what is required by God's nature.

Thus we read that God is "mighty in strength" (Job 9:4). He is "the Lord, strong and mighty" (Ps. 24:8), a "great and awesome God" (Deut. 7:21), "the Lord of hosts, the Mighty One of Israel" (Isa. 1:24a). "Ah, Lord God! It is you who have made the heavens and the earth by your great power and by your outstretched arm! Nothing is too hard for you" (Jer. 32:17). Creation is a testimony to "the greatness of his might," for "he is strong in power" (Isa. 40:26).

234

When Mary inquired of Gabriel how she, a virgin, could conceive a child without the involvement of a man, his response was "nothing will be impossible with God" (Luke 1:37). After comparing the difficulty of a rich man getting into heaven with a camel passing through the eye of a needle, Jesus said: "With man this is impossible, *but with God all things are possible*" (Matt. 19:26). Consider as well the following texts:

> Whatever the LORD pleases, he does,
> in heaven and on earth,
> in the seas and all deeps. (Ps. 135:6; cf. 115:3)

> For the LORD of hosts has purposed,
> and who will annul it?
> His hand is stretched out,
> and who will turn it back? (Isa. 14:27)

> "Declaring the end from the beginning and from ancient times things not yet done, saying, 'My counsel shall stand, and I will accomplish all my purpose.'" (Isa. 46:10)

> Then Job answered the LORD and said:
> "I know that you can do all things,
> and that no purpose of yours can be thwarted." (Job 42:1–2)

> All the inhabitants of the earth are accounted as nothing,
> and he does according to his will among the host of heaven
> and among the inhabitants of the earth;
> and none can stay his hand
> or say to him, "What have you done?" (Dan. 4:35)

Returning to Psalm 139, we see that David focuses on two manifestations of God's power in his life. He first declares that God has altogether shaped and fashioned him in his mother's womb (vv. 13–15). The word "formed" in verse 13 literally means "to possess," and "inward parts" is a reference to one's kidneys, which in Hebrew thought encompasses the most secretive and sensitive locus of the personality. "You knitted me together" actually means "to weave" or "to embroider" and would include not only David's physical features, such as hands, toes, ears, legs, etc., but also the psychological characteristics of his personality and temperament.

Here the mother's womb is described not merely as the secret place but "the depths of the earth." Perhaps this points to the remote and hidden place of fetal development. But others have seen here a retrospective reference to the formation of the first human body out of the dust of the ground, i.e., the creation of Adam himself. Delitzsch writes: "According to the view of Scripture the mode of Adam's creation is repeated in the formation of every man (Job 33:6). The earth was the mother's womb of Adam, and the mother's womb out of which the child of Adam comes forth (David) is the earth out of which it is taken."[16]

The second manifestation of God's power consists of his decree of all David's "days" (v. 16). "Every one of them," says David, were written in God's book. But "every one" of what? The King James Version looks back to David's "unformed substance" and thus translates verse 16, "in thy book all my *members* were written." Most other translations (NIV, NASB, NRSV, ESV) look forward to the "days" that were "formed" or "ordained." It is these days, then, that were written in God's book before one of them came to be.

Steven Roy points out that "this latter translation has the advantage of the grammatical agreement of the plural ('all of *them*') with the plural 'days.'"[17] Donald Glenn agrees:

> The reason David can affirm that the Lord knows his every thought, word, and action (and knows them beforehand—verse 2b), and the reason he cannot escape from this knowledge and consequent control is because the Lord formed him and foreordained the course of his life. Likewise, the reason that in verses 17–18 David responds with such awe about the Lord's thought and purposes is that the Lord's foreordination of his life proves how precious and constant are the Lord's thoughts about him.[18]

Both the number of his days and their content have been preordained by God (cf. Ps. 56:8). As each day of his life passes he may look upon it and confidently assert that everything that transpired had already been sovereignly orchestrated by the merciful and mighty hand of God.

But how are we to understand verses 17–18? David declares, "How precious to me are your thoughts, O God! How vast is the sum of them! If I would count them, they are more than the sand. I awake, and I am still with you."

Many argue that these "thoughts" are not all that God thinks about *in general* but primarily his intentions toward David *in particular*, which understandably would be extremely "precious" to the psalmist. If so, then David is referring both to God's preordained plan for his life (now inscribed in God's book, v. 16) and to the ongoing implementation of that purpose in the present. According to this view, verse 18b means something along the lines of "When I wake up from sleep I discover that nothing has interrupted your design for my life or put a distance in our relationship with one another." On the other hand, it must be noted that David's marveling at the "sum" of God's thoughts as exceeding "the sand" of the seashore makes more sense if it is a reference to the full extent of divine omniscience.

So, in conclusion, how does divine omnipotence strike you? What response do you find welling up in your soul? Stephen Charnock contends that it at least ought to awaken worship:

> Wisdom and power are the ground of the respect we give to men; they being both infinite in God, are the foundation of a solemn honour to be returned to him by his creatures. If a man make a curious engine, we honour him for his skill; if another vanquish a vigorous enemy, we admire him for his strength; and shall not the efficacy of God's power in creation, government, redemption, inflame us with a sense of the honour of his name and perfections! We admire those princes that have vast empires, numerous armies, that have a power to conquer their enemies, and preserve their own people in peace; how much more ground have we to pay a mighty reverence to God, who, without trouble and weariness, made and manages this vast empire of the world by a word and beck! What sensible thoughts have we of the noise of thunder, the power of the sun, the storms of the sea! These things, that have no understanding, have struck men with such a reverence that many have adored them as gods. What reverence and

adoration doth this mighty power, joined with an infinite wisdom in God, demand at our hands.[19]

There is also in divine omnipotence a warning to the wicked: "How foolish is every sinner," writes Charnock. "Can we poor worms strut it out against infinite power?" He continues:

> Oh, that every obstinate sinner would think of this, and consider his unmeasurable boldness in thinking himself able to grapple with omnipotence! What force can any have to resist the presence of him before whom rocks melt, and the heavens at length shall be shriveled up as a parchment by the last fire! As the light of God's face is too dazzling to be beheld by us, so the arm of his power is too mighty to be opposed by us.[20]

God's omnipotence is also a comfort to us, as it was to David, when we are persecuted and oppressed (Ps. 27:1). In it we find encouragement when we are tempted (1 Cor. 10:13). It is especially a comfort to us when we pray, for it reassures us that God is altogether able to do exceedingly abundantly beyond all that we either ask or think (cf. Eph. 3:20–21).

Well, there you have it: omniscient, omnipresent, omnipotent. What a God!

46

Finding God in the Cave

Psalm 142

A Maskil of David, when he was in the cave. A Prayer.
—Psalm 142, superscription

J ust when I think I might have God ever so slightly figured out, he pulls a surprise on me that shatters and confuses and discombobulates what little understanding I have of him.

I'm a theologian by trade, so it's my responsibility and calling (and joy) in life to do what I can to connect the dots of divine revelation and hope that the resultant picture at least looks vaguely similar to the God I read about in Scripture. But, sadly, that picture all too often ends up looking more like me than it does God and reflects more what I think should be true or false rather than accurately portraying what God says is true or false, good or evil. The fact is, when God and his ways are looked at from a merely human point of view, he can often appear quite strange.

Whenever I use that language I'm compelled to pause and say, "Hey, Sam, hold on. Be careful. You don't want to be guilty of sacrilege or, worse still, blasphemy in talking about God in such terms." But then again, God is a bit strange, in the sense that I don't understand why he does not do things the way I would do them if I were God.

Of course, the problem isn't that God is strange but that I am sinful. The warped perspective I have of the Almighty is due, not to his being odd or out of line, but solely to the selfish and often corrupt way in which I filter and interpret the data of human experience.

Having said that, I can't help but think that David would have agreed with me. Having spent considerable time in many of his psalms, I'm convinced that he was occasionally (often?) just as confused about God as we are, just as befuddled and puzzled about what he does and why, as we are these many centuries later.

In fact, I suspect that lingering beneath the words of Psalm 142 is David's suspicion that God is strange. I say this not simply because of what is in the psalm itself but from what we read in the superscription: "A Maskil of David, when he was in the cave. A Prayer."

What's so unusual about that, you ask? More than unusual, it's downright shocking. Remember, this is *David* speaking, David, the man after God's own heart (1 Sam. 13:14), the man singularly selected by the Lord, out of all the men of Israel, the man anointed by Samuel the prophet to be king over God's people. King! Anointed! But here he is sitting, and probably sulking, in a cave.

I could certainly understand this more readily if it were written by a few other odd characters in Scripture, such as Cain or Balaam or Saul or Jezebel or Judas Iscariot. We expect people like that to find themselves in caves, hiding from their enemies, fearful for their lives. But David? The man who waxed eloquent about "green pastures" and "still waters" (Psalm 23), the man who rejoiced to live in the presence of God where "fullness of joy" could be found, the man who wanted nothing more than to linger at God's right hand where "pleasures forevermore" are experienced (Ps. 16:11) and to spend his days beholding the beauty of God (Ps. 27:4). David, in a cave? God, you're strange.

As best we can tell, David twice found himself seeking safety in a cave. The first occasion was in a cave near Adullam, just west of Jerusalem. This is described in 1 Samuel 22:1. The second occasion was at En-Gedi, on the western shore of the Dead Sea, described in

1 Samuel 24:1. In both instances he was there to escape Saul, who had threatened to kill him.

Psalm 142 is probably describing the first of these two incidents. What a contradiction it must have felt like to this man of God. I can almost hear him in protest: "God, this isn't at all what I expected to happen when you anointed me king over your people. Hiding out in a cave for protection from my enemies wasn't in the job description. I'm supposed to be honored and revered and respected. I'm supposed to be sitting on a throne with servants at my beck and call. So what am I doing here with the spiders and snakes and wolves in a cave hiding to save my life?" Strange God.

To make matters worse, we need to remember that the cave was David's final destination, not his first. Before he ever got to the cave, he first had to jump out of the way when Saul attempted to impale him with a spear. He then had to escape a death threat by being let down from a window by his wife. After that he was forced to flee into the night to elude the soldiers who were dispatched to capture and kill him. For a time he hid out in the fields surrounding Jerusalem and eventually suffered the humiliation of being compelled to seek refuge in the city of Gath, the hometown of his old enemy Goliath. After all this, David sat down in a cave—disconsolate, discouraged, possibly depressed, and no doubt confused about this God whom he loved and served.

Before you dismiss all this as speculation, allow David the freedom to be human. Don't you think he had his doubts? Don't you think he wondered aloud about why God did what he did, as well as when and how and to what purpose this scenario had unfolded? Could it be that even David, on occasion, might have asked himself, "Is this God to be trusted with my life?" I don't believe this is speculation, because we have the words of the psalm that largely corroborate this perspective. We'll turn to them in the next meditation.

The bottom line, then, is that this psalm is here to tell us how to pray when God seems strange. This psalm is uniquely suited for people who need encouragement in the midst of trial and suffering, people who are wondering if God even knows where they are. It's a psalm designed to tell us what to do when we're in a "cave" of our own.

This *maskil*, a musical term, of David's was a prayer he uttered while in the cave. May I suggest that at least part of its purpose is to tell us that God is attentive to our needs and hears us no matter where we are? Our prayers, like David's, reach his ear and enter his heart whether we are on land, at sea, in the air, or stuck away in some desolate cave (whether literal or metaphorical). If God heard Jonah's prayer from inside the belly of a fish and heard David's prayer from inside a lonely cave, he will surely hear yours whether uttered in a church building or at home or in your office or car or while lying on your bed at night.

May I also suggest that David is telling us that God hears and answers not only *wherever* we may be but *whatever* we may be experiencing? In other words, although David's cave was quite literal, it also describes spiritually what David was feeling, most likely abandoned, alone, useless, defeated, helpless, embarrassed, but still hopeful, as we'll shortly see.

So, if God seems a bit strange to you at times (or a lot), especially when you find yourself in something of a "cave," or perhaps even on those occasions when you actually wish you could spend some time in one just to get away from life and the constant hassles it throws your way, then this psalm is for you. We'll look carefully at its content in the next meditation.

47

No One Cares for My Soul

Psalm 142

When my spirit faints within me,
   you know my way!
In the path where I walk
   they have hidden a trap for me.
Look to the right and see:
   there is none who takes notice of me;
no refuge remains to me;
   no one cares for my soul.
                              —Psalm 142:3–4

We now return to the cave where King David has sought refuge from Saul's homicidal rage. It's hard to envision a more bizarre and ironic scene than this, but having dwelt on it in the previous meditation, we now move to the substance of David's prayer.

Although David's cry is passionate, dare I say guttural, it has form and structure. He begins with a *plea* in verses 1–2, followed by a description of his *plight* in verses 3–4. Notwithstanding the precarious nature of his situation, God is still his *portion*, as verses 5–6 make clear. Finally, his *praise* is forthcoming in verse 7.

On second thought, I'm not sure the word *plea* is sufficient to communicate the depths of desperation in David's heart. It's a bit too tame. What we hear in this petition is more a shriek of helplessness. Still, we mustn't think of it as a random or meaningless cry, but one with purpose and focus. Even as David gives vent to his deepest concerns, he arranges or organizes his passion into intelligible supplications. He has a formal complaint to set before the Lord.

One thing is certain: David is far from self-conscious in his prayers. He shows no concern for how he might sound or appear. Image and style play no part in his cry to the Lord. He suppresses nothing but pours out his complaint and articulates his trouble. There's wisdom in this, for as Spurgeon reminds us, "an unuttered grief will lie and smolder in the soul, till its black smoke puts out the very eyes of the spirit."[21] If we can learn anything from David's experience it is that we must tell God everything: how we have sinned, fallen, failed, and broken down. We need to tell him how fickle our faith is, how weak and worn we are.

Don't think for a moment this will come as a shock to God or that it will offend him and turn him off to your needs. In fact, in verse 3 David affirms that God already knows his situation (his "way" or "path"), yet that does not inhibit his honest and open declaration. After all, "we do not show our trouble before the Lord that he may see it, but that we may see him. It is for our relief, and not for his information" that we pray.[22]

David here sets himself apart from what I call *prayer-sayers* and *prayer-players*. The former are people for whom prayer is a mere ritual, an artificially organized sequence of words that lack heart and spirit. They approach prayer mechanically, as if with the right words and tone and posture God is compelled to respond positively to our requests. The latter treat prayer as if it were a religious sport. They trifle with God, even toy with him. They don't honestly believe God is who he says or will do what he has promised, so prayer becomes a game, perhaps a way to parade their piety before others.

David, on the other hand, is a prayer–pray-er (verb), one who takes God at his word and pleads with the confident assurance that the Almighty hears and cares and will act in due course to achieve whatever will best serve his glory and our spiritual good. These are people for whom prayer is a whole-souled, gut-wrenching, heart-wracking outpouring of all that is within to him who sits on the throne.

David's plight (vv. 3–4) isn't a pretty sight. Honestly, he sounds depressed. It's as if a heavy, impenetrable fog of confusion and consternation has engulfed him. He feels drowned, smothered, crushed, and conquered by his circumstances. Now remember: this is David— yes, David—depressed to the point of despair.

He describes the nefarious tactics of his enemies in verse 3: "In the path where I walk they have hidden a trap for me." Perhaps they search for David's tender spots and exploit them. They set a trap in those areas where he is particularly vulnerable and then taunt him for having put his faith in a God who seems not to care. It may be that the "trap" is a reference to temptation. They bait him into betraying his commitment to God and then denounce him as a hypocrite.

"Look to the right and see," shouts David; "there is none who takes notice of me; no refuge remains to me" (v. 4a). This reference to the "right" may be his way of saying he lacks counsel for the defense. There is no one who will argue his case or defend him against unwarranted accusations. But there's another possibility. In the ancient world a man's shield was held in his left hand, and his neighbor stood to protect him on the right. But David stands alone. His gaze to the right is met by a silent void. No friend, no reassuring smile, no comforting word of encouragement.

Was there no one at all to help David? Well, yes, there were a few, but not the sort of folk you want when you're facing a crisis of this nature. We read in 1 Samuel 22:2 that when word leaked out of David's condition, "everyone who was in distress, and everyone who was in debt, and everyone who was bitter in soul, gathered to him." I can imagine David's reaction: "Oh, great, just what I needed. The only people who come to help are a pack of distressed, indebted, embittered malcontents. Thanks God."

Then he utters what has to be the most pathetic and disheartening cry of all: "No one cares for my soul" (v. 4b). People can usually endure any crisis so long as they know they're not alone. Our friends may not have money to bail us out or wisdom to dispel our confusion, but at least they are friends. At least they are there. I can't imagine anything worse than facing a dream-shattering, disillusioning, perhaps even life-threatening trial when no one is there who gives any indication that he or she truly cares. Oh, sure, people show up and smile and offer pious platitudes that are supposed to pass for compassion and concern, but you know better.

What is left for David? Only God. But that's enough! "I cry to you, O Lord; I say, '[They may not care for my soul but] You are my refuge, my portion in the land of the living'" (v. 5). Whatever David had lost, he still had all he needed. "God is my refuge, my strength, my portion!" There's still trouble at hand, says David, for "I am brought very low" (v. 6a) and my persecutors "are too strong for me" (v. 6b). But God is enough.

We see here in David's experience a principle, or perhaps better still a *pattern* of how God deals with us in crisis. So often when he wishes to make a man great he first breaks him. Before God lifts you up, he brings you low. "He makes nothing of you before he makes something of you. This was the way with David. He is to be king in Jerusalem; but he must go to the throne by the way of the cave."[23] The reason is obvious, or at least it should be: God does it this way to ensure that he gets the glory. "We are afflicted in every way," wrote Paul, "but not crushed; perplexed, but not driven to despair; persecuted, but not forsaken; struck down, but not destroyed" (2 Cor. 4:8), all "to show that the surpassing power belongs to God and not to us" (2 Cor. 4:7).

I think David understood this principle, which explains his declaration of intent to once again praise God for his bountiful provision that he is assured will yet come. He longs for deliverance because it will afford him the opportunity to once again thank God in the midst of the people (Ps. 142:7a). "The righteous will surround me," says David, "for you will deal bountifully with me" (v. 7b).

Thus we see that the prayer that began with a shriek ends with a song. There's no indication that David finally figured out the ways of this oftentimes strange God. But he refused to suspend his faith or obedience on his ability to decipher the mysteries of divine providence. You may still be in a cave of sorts, crying into the darkness, convinced that no one cares for your soul. But God does. Truly he does. Truly he is your portion, your hope, your strength, and ultimately your joy.

48

The Unsearchable Splendor of God

Psalm 145

> The eyes of all look to you,
>> and you give them their food in due season.
> You open your hand;
>> you satisfy the desire of every living thing.
>> —Psalm 145:15–16

I suppose there are as many different kinds of prayers spoken prior to eating a meal as there are families who pray. When Melanie and Joanna were young, the greatest problem we faced wasn't in getting them to pray but in getting them to finish before the food got cold. Neither of them was able to pray for the meal collectively but insisted on giving thanks for each individual item on the table. They thanked God for the potatoes, the fork, the milk, the salt, the napkin, the dessert, and just about anything else in sight. As time passed, we finally succeeded in getting our point across and were able once again to enjoy a hot meal.

At least one thing hasn't changed with the passing of centuries: people in the ancient world also expressed their gratitude to God before sharing a meal together. In fact, when they prayed before the midday meal it was customary for them to recite all or part of Psalm 145. This was largely due to the statement in verses 15–16.

But this psalm is important for more than what it tells us about where our food comes from. It is one of the most vibrant and expressive hymns of praise to be found anywhere in the Old Testament. Not only does it provide a marvelous declaration of the majesty and incomparable greatness of God, but it also instructs us on our responsibility to worship him as he deserves. Take a few minutes to read the entire psalm.

Our approach to this psalm won't be verse-by-verse or in recognition of some elaborate structure. I'd like simply to summarize what it says, first, about the *character* of God and, second, about our privilege and joy in *celebrating* him. So let's begin.

David begins with God's *greatness* (vv. 3, 6b), a word that is horribly overused in our day and applied to anything from deodorant to the most obnoxious professional athlete. Historically, many have taken the adjective g*reat* and made it part of their name: Alexander *the Great*, Peter *the Great*, Catherine *the Great*, and in our own day the comedian Jackie Gleason simply went by the title *The Great One.*

I beg to differ. God alone is great! Furthermore, his greatness is *unsearchable* (v. 3). No one ever has or ever will fully fathom the depths of his greatness. Not all the minds of all the ages using the most advanced scientific equipment can capture all that God is. He is utterly beyond and infinitely past finding out.

David also points to his *majesty* (v. 5), or better still, the *glorious splendor* of his *majesty*. There is a great light or luster or spiritual brilliance that emanates from the magnificence of his majesty. God's majesty is blinding and breathtaking and beyond comprehension or calculation.

Ah, but he is also *good* (vv. 7a, 9a). Can you envision how horrific it would be if this great and powerful and awesome God were *bad*? Don't take his goodness for granted but joyfully celebrate it and declare it aloud and rest confidently in it.

Our God is also *righteous* (v. 7b). To say that God is righteous is not to say he conforms to human standards of right and wrong.

Rather he conforms perfectly to the standards of his *own* perfections. But if he is holy and wholly righteous, how can unholy and unrighteous people like you and me enter his presence? The answer follows.

According to verse 8, God is "*gracious* and *merciful, slow to anger* and *abounding in steadfast love.*" Yes, God has a holy temper, but he has a very long fuse. Even those who deny and blaspheme his name are recipients of his patience and long-suffering. He permits his enemies to live, to spew forth their horrid sacrilege, all the while blessing them with food and air and earthly pleasures, affording them even more time and opportunity to repent (cf. Rom. 2:4–5).

"Steadfast love" is the translation of the Hebrew word *hesed*, elsewhere rendered by such terms as *mercy, goodness, lovingkindness, loyal love,* and occasionally by the word *grace.* Its primary emphasis is on God's covenant love, his steadfast commitment to his people.

All these qualities of character inform his deeds and give shape to his providential oversight of creation. So let's look briefly at what this great and majestic and good and righteous and gracious and merciful and long-suffering God does.

For one thing, he works (vv. 4, 5b, 6a, 9, 12a). David goes even further and speaks of his *mighty* works, his *wonderful* works, his *merciful* works, and his *awesome* acts.

More specifically, he rules (vv. 11–13). But unlike every other ruler or potentate, God is in office for life (see Dan. 4:3, 34). There is no transition team to move from one heavenly administration to another. There are no inaugural ceremonies (God has *always* been on the throne). There is no concern over the qualifications of a *vice-god* should the Almighty be unable to serve out the full extent of his term. There are no tearful good-byes to the staff, no waving "so long" from the steps of a helicopter, no cleaning out of the desk in the heavenly oval office to make way for his successor.

Among earthly kings, especially in British history, we hear of James I and James II and Charles I and Charles II and Charles III, etc. Not in the heavenly kingdom. There is no Yahweh I and Yahweh II, for God is first and last, and there is no other. None preceded him and none shall succeed him.

The everlasting ruler sustains (v. 14) all he has made. We should read this verse in connection with verse 13 and "admire the unexpected contrast: he reigns in glorious majesty, yet condescends to lift up and hold up those who are apt to fall."[24] He also supplies (v. 15) food and life and satisfies the desires of his creation (v. 16).

He is altogether righteous in his dealings with us (v. 17a). Of course, that's easy for us to believe when things are going well. But God is righteous in *all* his ways, not just in the circumstances that favor us. Nothing is more difficult to acknowledge when we are in trouble, or when he afflicts us, or when we feel he has been unfair.

And we must never forget that he is not only righteous but also "kind in all his works" (v. 17b). We don't typically put those two words together, for it's difficult to be both at the same time. We swing to one extreme or the other and are either rigid and demanding or excessively lenient and tolerant. But in God they find perfect harmony, as seen most readily in Jesus, who was simultaneously high and humble; both strong and tender; righteous, yet gracious; powerful and merciful; authoritative, yet tender; holy, yet always forgiving; just, yet compassionate; at times angry, yet also gentle; and firm, yet friendly.

Finally, he answers prayer (vv. 18–19), preserves the righteous (v. 20a), and destroys the wicked (v. 20b).

How does one respond to such a God? Needless to say, such splendor, majesty, mercy, and might call for the loudest and most passionate of praise.

We are to extol him (v. 1a), which literally means "to be high." God *is* high, and we acknowledge and declare it so. To extol is to exalt above all others, to set as preeminent over every other thing. We also bless (vv. 1b, 2a, 10b) and praise (v. 2b) and commend and declare (v. 4, 6b) and meditate (v. 5) and speak (v. 6a) and pour forth praise of his abundant goodness (v. 7a).

As if that weren't enough, we sing aloud (v. 7b) and give thanks (v. 10a) and make known (v. 12) his mighty deeds. And let's be diligent to do it every day (v. 2a), forever and ever (vv. 1a, 2b, 21b):

> Through all eternity to thee,
> A joyful song I'll raise;

But oh, eternity's too short
To utter all thy praise. (Adam Clarke)[25]

A heart flooded with thoughts of the splendor of God and what he does can no more conceive of an end of praise than it can conceive of an end of God himself.

One final thought: above all else, may our praise and honor and joyful celebration of this God be great, for "great is the LORD, and [therefore] *greatly to be praised*" (v. 3a). True worship must always be proportionate to the object of adoration. Great praise for a great God. "No chorus is too loud, no orchestra too large, no psalm too lofty for the lauding of the Lord of Hosts."[26]

So much more could be said, and more will be said, as we continue our focus on worship in Psalms 147 through 150.

49

Lord of the Stars,
Healer of Hearts

Psalm 147

Praise the LORD!
For it is good to sing praises to our God;
   for it is pleasant, and a song of praise is fitting.
   —Psalm 147:1

I've never witnessed the destruction of my city or place of worship or been driven from my home by pagan hordes and held captive for seventy years. Neither have you. There are no words to describe the physical, emotional, and spiritual devastation of such an experience. So I won't try. But let's look on the upside. Try to envision how you would feel upon your *release* from bondage, together with the opportunity to return home and rebuild your city and church.

If you find it hard to imagine such heights of exhilaration and ecstasy, you needn't worry. You would feel and respond and act precisely the way the Israelites did when they returned to Jerusalem following their seventy years' captivity in Babylon. We know how they felt and what they thought because Psalms 147, 148, 149, and

150 were most likely written at that time as an expression of their joy and celebration.

There is little in the Psalms that can compare with these final four hymns when it comes to the depths of delight and the heights of exultation they embody. Unlike many of the psalms we've examined, in these you'll find no lament, no sorrow, no complaint, not a shadow of doubt or fear or despair. They are pure, unalloyed exultation.

Psalm 147 is actually three psalms in one. The first hymn is found in verses 1–6, the second in verses 7–11, and the third in verses 12–20.

The first of these three hymns begins appropriately with a call to praise: "Praise the LORD! For it is good to sing praises to our God; for it is pleasant, and a song of praise is fitting" (v. 1). Don't be afraid to enjoy God. Singing and celebrating the supremacy of Yahweh is "good" and "pleasant" and "fitting," if for no other reason than that is what we were created to do. Fish swim in the water, birds fly in the air, and the redeemed revel in God.

Are there reasons for such reveling? What is it about God and what he's done that warrants such worship? The answer follows immediately:

> The LORD builds up Jerusalem;
> > he gathers the outcasts of Israel.
> He heals the brokenhearted
> > and binds up their wounds.
> He determines the number of the stars;
> > he gives to all of them their names.
> Great is our Lord, and abundant in power;
> > his understanding is beyond measure.
> The LORD lifts up the humble;
> > he casts the wicked to the ground. (vv. 2–6)

The reference in v. 2 is surely to the actual events that transpired in Nehemiah's day when the people returned to rebuild the city. What's truly remarkable is that God is not simply concerned with physical walls but with spiritual wounds. Earthly kings distance themselves from the lowly, but our God condescends to bring aid to the shattered and suffering. Said Spurgeon:

Behold, the Most High has to do with the sick and the sorrowful, with the wretched and the wounded! . . . Few will associate with the despondent, but Yahweh chooses their company, and abides with them till he has healed them by his comforts. . . . He himself lays on the ointment of grace, and the soft bandages of love, and thus binds up the bleeding wounds of those convinced of sin.[27]

This is your God: he lovingly heals the crushed in spirit and powerfully assigns the stars their place in the heavens. He knows every hair on our heads and calls the stars by name (cf. Isa. 40:26). Spurgeon again says it best:

From stars to sighs is a deep descent! From worlds to wounds is a distance which only infinite compassion can bridge. Yet he who acts a surgeon's part with wounded hearts, marshals the heavenly host, and reads the muster-roll of suns and their majestic systems. O Lord it is good to praise thee as ruling the stars, but it is pleasant to adore thee as healing the broken heart![28]

How wonderful that he is both the Lord over stars and the healer of hearts, but if he had to choose one or the other, there would be no hesitation. Our God would let every star in every galaxy disintegrate and disappear before he would abandon or neglect so much as one of his children, struggling and immature and frail though they be.

He is "great" (v. 5) and "abundant in power" (v. 5), and his knowledge knows no bounds (v. 5); yet he stoops to lift up the humble and to bring judgment on the wicked (v. 6). His greatness isn't an excuse to ignore the humble but the very reason why he regards them with such compassion.

Yet again, now in the second hymn, we are called upon to "sing to the LORD with thanksgiving" and to "make melody" "on the lyre" (v. 7).

This time the ground of our praise is rooted in the providential care God displays for the work of his hands (vv. 8–9). He causes clouds to form. He determines their shape and size and the duration of their existence. If they should give rain, praise him! If the grass should grow, praise him! If the beasts are fed, praise him! If the ravens should eat, praise him! Nothing is left to chance or happenstance. Mother Nature didn't do it; Father God did.

The temptation to be impressed with military might and human ingenuity is strong (v. 10). Resist it. God's delight is elsewhere. He "takes pleasure in those who fear him, in those who hope in his steadfast love" (v. 11). God revels in your holy reverence. He finds inexpressible joy when he, not money or power or political gain, is the object of your hope. God delights in this because it magnifies his supremacy and all-sufficiency to be and do for his people what mere earthly stuff cannot. And we delight in it because we find a satisfaction in him that nothing in this world could hope to supply.

In this third and final hymn (vv. 12–20), the focus continues on God's providential power among men and especially in nature. He is the author of peace, the source of food, the creator of snow, the origin of hail, and the one who breathes wind.

Even beyond that is the fact that his covenant people have been the unique recipients of his law. The revelation of his "rules" (vv. 19–20; cf. Psalm 119) is a far greater display of his affection for us than all the wonders of nature combined. Do you feel loved of God, knowing that he cared enough to speak truth and righteousness to your heart in his holy Word? Do you not see that his affection is deep and profound precisely because he has forbidden to you those things that would diminish your capacity to experience fullness of joy, things that would ultimately destroy your soul?

I say this because people are not naturally inclined to equate rules with love. They consider the many "thou shalts" and "thou shalt nots" of Scripture to be indicative of God's efforts to deprive us of joy through the imposition of all manner of restrictions and regulations. What we so often fail to see, however, is that God has commanded nothing but what is conducive to our maximum spiritual satisfaction. He forbids us only that which would diminish our capacity to enjoy him to the fullest.

And thus as the psalm began ("Praise the LORD!" v. 1), so it appropriately ends ("Praise the LORD!" v. 20). This is the pattern we will see yet again in the final three psalms, to which we turn in the concluding meditation.

50

Praise Him! Praise Him!

Psalms 148–150

Praise the LORD!
Praise God in his sanctuary;
   praise him in his mighty heavens!
Praise him for his mighty deeds;
   praise him according to his excellent greatness!
                                          —Psalm 150:1–2

The complete texts of Psalms 148–150 are too lengthy for me
to include in the text of this meditation but too important
for any of us to ignore. So I encourage you to open your
Bible and read them now. After you have finished, consider these
four themes that emerge.

1) *Worship is a universal privilege.* I could have said "obligation,"
for worship is a duty we are commanded to fulfill. But I don't want
to give the impression that it is burdensome or oppressive. Exulting
in the exaltation of God is an unparalleled privilege that is permeated
by joy and satisfaction. But it is the *universal* dimension that I want
you to note, especially as it is delineated in Psalm 148.

There are no people who are excluded or a place where praise
is not proper. In verses 1–6 the whole of the celestial or heavenly

universe is called on to praise God, and in verses 7–12 it extends to the whole of the terrestrial or earthly universe.

He is to be praised both "from the heavens" (v. 1) and "from the earth" (v. 7). "All his angels" (v. 2a) form an innumerable choir and join in the song (cf. Rev. 5:11). Even the "sun" by day and the "moon" by night (v. 3a) declare his power, never leaving their Creator without a witness.

All "shining stars" (v. 3b) add their voice to the chorus of praise. Billions and trillions and quadrillions of thriving heat and energy and blinding brightness testify to his immeasurable power and artistic skills. The Babylonians, from whose captivity these worshiping Israelites had recently been released, believed the stars were deities that controlled their destiny. But here we see that they are but one section in the celestial choir that echoes the glory of their Maker.

Every "creature" of the "sea" (v. 7) has a song to sing: whether diminutive perch or massive whale, be it the majestic dolphin or the ravenous shark. Stingrays and moray eels and starfish and barracudas and bass and trout and salmon together draw attention to him who is worthy of all worship.

As we saw in Psalm 147, so also in 148, "fire and hail, snow and mist," even "stormy wind" fulfill his word (v. 8). "It is a grand orchestra which contains such wind-instruments as these! He is a great leader who can keep all these musicians in concert, and direct both time and tune."[29]

By means of "mountains and all hills," whether the towering Himalayas or the foothills of central Kansas, be it Everest or an anthill, God is glorified (v. 9a).

"Fruit trees and all cedars" (v. 9b) testify to his splendor: yes, apple trees and cherry trees and sycamores and oak and elm and sweet gum and weeping willow and sequoia and pine and, well, you get the idea.

Let us not forget the "beasts and all livestock" (v. 10a), both longhorn and lion, both jersey and jackal, even simbrah and stallion.

For some of us it's hard to imagine that "creeping things" (v. 10b) such as tarantulas and ticks could praise God, but indeed they do; as also do all "flying birds," whether blue jay or buzzard, cardinal or crow.

Of course, we mustn't forget the human race. "Kings of the earth and all peoples, princes and all rulers" (v. 11), "young men and maidens" together with "old men and children" (v. 12) are to praise the name of the Lord.

All that have "breath" (Ps. 150:6) should praise him with every breath until they are out of breath.

> I sing the mighty power of God, that made the mountains rise,
> That spread the flowing seas abroad, and built the lofty skies.
> I sing the wisdom that ordained the sun to rule the day;
> The moon shines full at His command, and all the stars obey.
> (Isaac Watts "I Sing the Mighty Power of God")

2) *The focus of such adoration is always and ever God alone for who he is and what he's done.* We do not worship the world or revere the reflection. We fix our hearts on the Original, the Source, the First Cause of all subsequent causes (see Ps. 148:5–6, 13–14).

We are to "praise *him* for his mighty deeds" and "according to *his* excellent greatness" (Ps. 150:2). There is a limit to praise only if there is a limit to God. Ah, but there is an infinite plenitude to his greatness that our worship could never exhaust.

3) *Worship is an exhilarating experience, both for God and for us.* We are to "be glad" in our Maker and to "rejoice" in our King (Ps. 149:2). We are to "exult in glory" and "sing for joy," even while on our "beds" (Ps. 149:5b). Whether as we go to bed, or perhaps during seasons of sleeplessness, or as we rise up in the morning, or even when laid prostrate from affliction, let praise fill our hearts and mouths.

Why is worship so pleasing and satisfying? Because, as C. S. Lewis noted, "All enjoyment spontaneously overflows into praise unless . . . shyness or the fear of boring others is deliberately brought in to check it. . . . Except where intolerably adverse circumstances interfere, praise almost seems to be inner health made audible."[30] I think we delight to praise what we enjoy, said Lewis, "because the praise not merely expresses but completes the enjoyment; it is its appointed consummation. It is not out of compliment that lovers keep on telling one another how beautiful they are; the delight is incomplete till it is expressed."[31]

In worship *we see* and *God is seen*, and in both is unrivaled pleasure, ours and his. We enjoy him who is eternally enjoyable and he enjoys being exalted in our enjoyment.

God commands that we "praise his name with dancing" and make "melody to him with tambourine and lyre" (149:3) because he *"takes pleasure"* in his people when they do (149:4a).

4) *There can be no mistaking the extravagant and exuberant nature of godly worship of God.* It involves not only singing (149:1, 5) but also dancing (149:3; 150:4) and a wide array of musical instrumentation (149:3; 150:3–5). Said Spurgeon:

> Let the clash of the loudest music be the Lord's; let the joyful clang of the loftiest notes be all for him. Praise has beaten the timbrel, swept the harp, and sounded the trumpet, and now for a last effort, awakening the most heavy of slumberers, and startling the most indifferent of onlookers, she dashes together the disks of brass, and with sounds both loud and high proclaims the glories of the Lord.[32]

As this series of meditations on the Psalms concludes, what has been the central and controlling theme throughout? I think the answer is obvious: Big God . . . beautiful God . . . faithful God . . . great God . . . gracious God . . . powerful God . . . loving God . . . loyal God . . . righteous God . . . merciful God . . . majestic God . . . enjoyable God . . . joyful God . . . judging God . . . holy God . . . happy God!

And to top it off, he's *our* God.

Appendix

Understanding the Psalms

There are numerous books that provide the necessary tools for reading and interpreting the Psalms, and I strongly encourage you to take advantage of them. Most commentaries begin with at least a brief introduction that addresses principles for understanding these hymns and prayers of the Old Testament, but I'm particularly fond of three more specialized books, each of which is uniquely suited for its target audience.

The most exhaustive and moderately technical of these surveys is the excellent work by C. Hassell Bullock, *Encountering the Book of Psalms: A Literary and Theological Introduction* (Grand Rapids, MI: Baker Academic, 2001), 266 pages.[1] An excellent mid-level introduction to the Psalter is provided by Tremper Longman in his book *How to Read the Psalms* (Downers Grove, IL: InterVarsity, 1988), 166 pages. Finally, those who are delving into the Psalms for the first time will find especially helpful the book by Ronald Allen, *Praise! A Matter of Life and Breath* (Nashville: Thomas Nelson, 1980), 246 pages.

In what follows I make no pretense at originality but have drawn heavily on these and other resources that strive to bring alive the

Psalms for the Christian today. My prayer is that this brief overview will whet your appetite for more extensive and in-depth study of this most remarkable of biblical books.

The Title to the Psalms

The Hebrew title applied by the Israelites to their anthology of hymns used in temple worship is the term *tehillim* or *praise*. Although there are a variety of different songs in the collection, this term is the most appropriate insofar as most of the psalms contain at least an element of praise. The word *psalm* itself comes from a Greek term which in classical times meant "the music of a stringed instrument." However, with the passing of time the word took on the meaning "a song of praise" while the notion of accompaniment with a stringed instrument gradually disappeared or was altogether forgotten.[2]

The Genre of the Psalms

The word *genre* refers to the *type* of literature one is reading. When a group of texts share certain characteristics pertaining to literary shape, mood, content, or structure, we say they belong to a particular genre. The genre of the Psalms is poetry.

Poetry is clearly different from normal prose literature, given its unique tendency to stimulate the reader's imagination and to stir one's emotions. Prose, on the other hand, more directly addresses the intellect and challenges the will. Poetry is evocative. It makes greater use of literary structure and vivid imagery and figures of speech, some of which will be noted below in greater detail. In general, the language of poetry is more distant from everyday speech than is prose. Old Testament scholars have identified no fewer than eight different types of poetic literature in the Psalms.

1) *The Hymn.* Hymns are known for their exuberant praise and celebration of God (cf. 103:1–2). Most hymns share a similar basic structure which includes a call to worship, followed by the reasons why God is worthy of praise, and then a renewed call to praise.

Often in the call to worship, the psalmist will enlist the praise of others in the covenant community (cf. 113:1). The reasons for praise are the specific deeds God has performed on behalf of his people or particular attributes of the divine character (see 92:1, 4 and 96:1, 5). God is frequently extolled as creator (19:1–4) and as king (47:5–6). Good examples of the hymn include Psalms 33, 36, 105, 111, 113, 117, and 135.

2) *The Lament.* The widest gap in the Psalms, both theologically and emotionally, is the one between the hymn and the lament. As Tremper Longman has said, "The lament is the polar opposite of the hymn on the emotional spectrum."[3] The chief feature of the lament is its *mood* (see, for example, Ps. 22:1–2). Typical psalms of lament include Psalms 3, 6, 12, 13, 26, 28, 30, 42–43, 77, and 142, among others.

Scholars have identified two features of most psalms of lament: their passion and their progression. On reading these psalms one virtually hears the anguished cry: "I am hurting! My enemies are winning! And God, you don't seem to care!" The progression within these psalms is also noticeable, as the author moves from obvious pain to overt praise, from sighing to singing. Although he often appears helpless, he is never utterly hopeless.

The feeling of being abandoned by God is perhaps the most striking feature of these psalms. Students of the Psalms have identified at least seven elements associated with the lament: (1) invocation, combined with (2) a plea to God for help (see 12:1 and 17:1); and (3) complaint (22:6–7). Note well, however, that in virtually all laments there is (4) an expression of trust in God; (5) either a confession of sin or a declaration of innocence (69:5; 26:5); (6) a curse or imprecation on one's enemies (109:8–9); and finally (7) a hymn of praise in which the psalmist acknowledges what God will do for him, resulting in worship (26:12). On occasion the lament is national rather than individual, as the psalmist speaks on behalf of all Israel (see Psalm 83).

3) *The Thanksgiving Psalms.* When God does respond to the psalmist's lament and brings deliverance or healing or victory over his enemies, there is immediate thanksgiving. In other words, "the thanksgiving psalm is a response to answered lament."[4] See Psalms 32:1; 34:1; and 18.

4) *Psalms of Confidence.* Here the psalmist declares his trust in God's goodness and greatness and power. At least nine psalms seem to fall into this category (11, 16, 23, 27, 62, 91, 121, 125, 131).

These psalmists often employ vivid imagery to describe God's nearness (he is our shepherd, refuge, rock, help, fortress, etc.).

5) *Psalms of Remembrance.* Although the Psalms rarely refer to specific historical settings, they do make reference to the great redemptive acts of God in the past, most often the exodus and the establishing of the Davidic covenant (such as Psalms 89 and 132; see also 78, 105, 106, 135, and 136). God's wonderful acts are recounted so that the entire nation of Israel might praise him.

6) *Wisdom Psalms.* Here we read of the concrete and practical ways God wants his people to live. Psalms 1 and 119 are good examples.

7) *Kingship Psalms.* One form of kingship psalm focuses on the earthly king of Israel, such as Psalms 20, 21, and 45. Others proclaim the kingship of God himself, such as Psalms 47 and 98.

8) *Imprecatory Psalms.* The most disturbing and often confusing psalm is the one that contains prayers of imprecation in which the wrath and judgment of God are called down on a wicked and rebellious people. You will note that I devoted three meditations to such psalms, trying to grasp their meaning and significance for us today.

The reader will also often come across certain technical terms which describe the type of psalm in view: (1) "Psalm" (Hb. *mizmor*), a song accompanied by the plucking of the strings of an instrument; fifty-seven psalms are so labeled. (2) "Song" (Hb. *shir*); twelve psalms are labeled with this term. (3) "A contemplative poem" (Hb. *maskil*); thirteen psalms are described this way. (4) "A poem containing pithy sayings" (Hb. *miktam*); found six times in superscriptions. (5) "Prayers" (Hb. *tepillah*); found in five psalm titles. (6) "Praise" (Hb. *tehillah*); Psalm 145. (7) The term *shiggaion* occurs only in Psalm 7 and is of uncertain meaning. Perhaps it is a musical term or a literary designation, such as psalm of "lamentation."

The Superscriptions: Are They Inspired?

"The titles introducing the individual psalms give information about the author, the historical occasion which prompted the writing, the melody, the psalm's function and, occasionally, other matters."[5] Most psalms have titles; those that don't (e.g., Psalm 33) are called "orphan" psalms. Whereas most English translations place the title above the psalm, making it appear separately, in Hebrew the title is usually the first verse of the psalm itself. This explains why the verse numbers in the Hebrew text are frequently one higher than the verse numbers in the English versions. Generally speaking there are two types of titles: those indicating *authorship* and those describing *historical occasion*. Psalm 3 contains both: "*A Psalm of David* [authorship], *when he fled from Absalom his son* [historical occasion]."

It should be noted that the phrase translated in English, "of David," can also be translated "to David" or "for David." The argument has been made, therefore, that David did not necessarily write each of these psalms, but that they were written in the style which he established. However, I believe a close examination of the content of these psalms reveals that David was indeed their author. The denial of Davidic authorship often reflects theological prejudice: liberal scholars want to "late-date" the Psalms, placing their composition hundreds of years after David, usually during the post-exilic period.

Historical titles specify the event that inspired the writing of the psalm. See, for example, Psalms 3, 7, 18, 30, 34, 51, 52, 54, 56, 57, 59, 60, 63, and 142. Virtually all historical titles are connected with something in the life of David. More important is the fact that the title usually refers to David in the third person, whereas the psalm itself is written in the first person. This suggests that someone other than David later added these titles.

How should we understand these titles? Some, such as Longman, do not believe they are canonical:

> After all the evidence has been surveyed, it is best to treat the titles as non-canonical, but reliable early tradition. Practically speaking, the implications for reading a psalm are twofold. We should let the psalm title initially inform the reading of a psalm. However, we shouldn't bend the interpretation of a psalm unnaturally to make it conform to the title.[6]

Others, however, insist that nothing suggests that these superscriptions are anything but credible. Most conservative Old Testament introductions, as well as the commentaries, argue persuasively for the inspiration of these titles.

Here are the authors noted in the Psalter along with the compositions ascribed to them:

Moses: Psalm 90;

David: 73 psalms, all but 17 of which are in Books 1 and 2 (see below);

Asaph: Psalms 50, 73–83;

Heman, the Ezrahite: Psalm 88;

Ethan, the Ezrahite: Psalm 89;

Solomon: Psalms 72, 127.

The Groupings of the Psalms

The Psalter is divided into five books: 1–41, 42–72, 73–89, 90–106, and 107–150. Most believe the five books were created to parallel the five books of Moses (Pentateuch). Each of the five books concludes with a doxology (cf. 41:13). Each of the five books also shows a preference for a particular version of the divine name.[7]

Book 1: Yahweh (272x), Elohim (15x);

Book 2: Yahweh (74x), Elohim (207x);

Book 3: Yahweh (13x), Elohim (36x);

Books 4–5: Yahweh (339x), Elohim (7x).

Most of the Davidic psalms are found in the first two books of the Psalter. Psalm 72 closes with these words: "The prayers of David, the son of Jesse, are ended" (v. 20). However, a number of psalms before Psalm 72 are non-Davidic, and a number of psalms after Psalm 72 are Davidic. Evidently through time both Davidic and non-Davidic psalms were added to the Psalter in a way that ignored this grouping.

One grouping of psalms is based on their function: Psalms 120–134 are called *songs of ascent*. These were probably songs sung by the people of Israel as they ascended the temple mount.

We should also note the interesting fact that as we move through the Psalter we move from mourning to joy, from lament to hymns of praise. The last seven psalms not only are hymns of praise, but they also are psalms in which the whole of creation is invited to participate in the worship and celebration of God.

It is difficult to reconstruct the history of how the Psalter was formed, but Bruce Waltke, in an unpublished paper,[8] has suggested these four stages:

First stage (individual poems). It all began with poems and songs by individuals (a prayer by Moses, a song by David, etc.). Some of these were selected for use in regular worship while others were not. For example, the song of Miriam (Ex. 15), the song of Moses (Deut. 32), the song of Deborah (Judges 5), the lament of David (2 Sam. 1), the hymn by Jonah (Jonah 2), never became part of the anthology of songs used in the hymn book of the temple. On the other hand, a prayer by Moses (Ps. 90), a song by David (compare 2 Sam. 22:1 and Ps. 18; 1 Chron. 16:7ff. with Ps. 105:1ff.) were adopted for use in public worship and made their way into the Psalter.

Second stage (collection of poems). These songs were then collected. Evidence for an early collection of Davidic songs is found in Psalm 72:20. In 2 Chron. 29:30 we read that "Hezekiah the king and the officials commanded the Levites to sing praises to the Lord with the words of David and of Asaph the seer." This suggests that two collections existed in Hezekiah's time: "the words of David" and "the words of Asaph."

Third stage (the collection into the extant books). The collection of these smaller anthologies into the books as we now know them was the third stage. This probably took place by different people in successive periods spread over quite a space of time.

Fourth stage (the work of the final editor). The final collection of psalms as we know it reflects the work of one mind giving shape and definition to the many songs. We have no record of who this person(s) might have been.

The Hebrew Bible contains 150 psalms, and Protestant versions have followed this. The Greek Bible has an additional psalm at the end of the book. Also, two of the Hebrew psalms have been subdivided in the Septuagint (LXX), followed also by the Latin Vulgate, and twice a pair of psalms in Hebrew have been fused into one.

The Uses of the Psalms

The principal use of the Psalms was, of course, for the private and public worship of the faithful within Israel. The so-called psalms of ascent, noted earlier, were *procession* hymns, i.e., hymns sung by worshipers as they approached Jerusalem and the temple. Often specific acts of worship are mentioned in conjunction with a psalm:

> But I, through the abundance of your steadfast love, will enter
> your house.
> I will bow down toward your holy temple in the fear of you.
> (5:7)

> So I have looked upon you in the sanctuary,
> beholding your power and glory.
> Because your steadfast love is better than life,
> my lips will praise you. (63:2–3)

> I will come into your house with burnt offerings;
> I will perform my vows to you,
> that which my lips uttered
> and my mouth promised when I was in trouble. (66:13–14)

The notation "for the director of music" or "for the choir director" occurs in fifty-five psalms and "serves probably as a musical addition, marking the psalm to be a part of temple worship or to be recited by the leader of the choir."[9] The psalms truly were the "Old Testament Hymnbook." They were meant not merely to be read but to be sung.

The Christian (New Testament) Perspective on the Psalms

With the coming of Jesus and his death and resurrection, the Psalms are read in a new light. On the road to Emmaus, following his resurrection, Jesus spoke to two disciples and said: "These are my words that I spoke to you while I was still with you, that everything written about me in the Law of Moses and the Prophets and the Psalms must be fulfilled" (Luke 24:44). The reference to the Psalms is inclusive of the third section of the Hebrew canon, often called *the writings*. Clearly Jesus believed that the Psalter anticipated and spoke about his ministry, suffering, and glory. Indeed, the Psalms are quoted in the New Testament more often than any other Old Testament book (more than four hundred times).

This raises the obvious question about the so-called *messianic psalms*, which is to say, how and to what extent the Psalms speak of the coming Christ. A messianic psalm, in the general sense, is any psalm that alludes to the coming of Messiah. Scholars have identified several categories that oftentimes overlap.

In a number of psalms the author expresses in lyric verse some significant event in his life or experience with God which, while true of the psalmist, is typical of and finds its ultimate fulfillment (or antitype) in Christ (see Pss. 16:10 and 34:20).

Then there are instances where the psalmist describes both internal and external experiences that transcend his own individuality and circumstances and find their fullest historical expression in Christ alone. Often the language is deliberately exaggerated, by means of hyperbole, but becomes quite literal when applied to the Messiah (see, for example, Psalm 22).

Some also point to what may be called "indirect" messianic psalms in which a particular king is described in terms of what is hoped may come to pass but only finds its final fulfillment in the person of Christ (see Psalms 2, 45, and 72).

Finally, there is the "direct" messianic psalm that is wholly prophetic, most likely pointing to Jesus with little or no application to any contemporary figure. These are rare, Psalm 110 being the best possible example.

Parallelism in the Psalms[10]

The primary literary characteristic of the Psalms is *parallelism*. A good example is found in Psalm 6:1–2, where we read:

> O LORD, rebuke me not in your anger,
>   nor discipline me in your wrath.
> Be gracious to me, O LORD, for I am languishing;
>   heal me, O LORD, for my bones are troubled.

You can easily see the repetition in these two verses. In verse one, "rebuke" and "discipline" are parallel, as are the phrases "in your anger" and "in your wrath." In the second verse the psalmist twice calls on the Lord. He asks him to be "gracious" and to "heal" him, and in both cases a reason is given ("for I am languishing" / "for my bones are troubled"). This is poetic parallelism, which simply refers to the correspondence that occurs between the phrases of a poetic line.

There are three primary forms of parallelism in the Psalms. Perhaps the most common is *synonymous* parallelism. This is when there is repetition of the same thought in two different phrases using two different but related sets of words. A good example is Psalm 2:1–3:

> Why do the nations rage
>   and the peoples plot in vain?
> The kings of the earth set themselves,
>   and the rulers take counsel together,
>   against the LORD and against his Anointed, saying,
> "Let us burst their bonds apart
>   and cast away their cords from us."

Notice how each phrase is paralleled by a nearly synonymous phrase in the second part. Again:

> Wash me thoroughly from my iniquity,
>   and cleanse me from my sin! (Ps. 51:2)

> Where shall I go from your Spirit?
>   Or where shall I flee from your presence? (Ps. 139:7)

> I pour out my complaint before him;
>   I tell my trouble before him. (Ps. 142:2)

Second, there is *antithetic* parallelism. Again, the same thought is expressed in two lines, but this time the author uses antonyms (a word that has a meaning opposite of another word). See Proverbs 10:1 for an example ("A wise son makes a glad father, but a foolish son is a sorrow to his mother"). Consider the following:

> For the LORD knows the way of the righteous,
>> but the way of the wicked will perish. (Ps. 1:6)

> Blessed is the man who makes
>> the LORD his trust,
> who does not turn to the proud,
>> to those who go astray after a lie! (Ps. 40:4)

> For not by their own sword did they win the land,
>> nor did their own arm save them,
> but your right hand and your arm,
>> and the light of your face,
>> for you delighted in them. (Ps. 44:3)

Finally, there is *synthetic* parallelism. In this case, the second phrase appears to complete or supplement or further explain the idea contained in the first phrase.

> But his delight is in the law of the LORD,
>> and on his law he meditates day and night. (Ps. 1:2)

> Truly God is good to Israel,
>> to those who are pure in heart. (Ps. 73:1)

There are other, secondary forms of parallelism, such as *emblematic* parallelism. In that case, one of the phrases will use a word of comparison (*like* or *as*) to draw an analogy. Often one line conveys the main idea, while the second line illustrates it with an image. For example,

> As a deer pants for flowing streams,
>> so pants my soul for you, O God. (Ps. 42:1)

> For dogs encompass me;
>> a company of evildoers encircles me;
> they have pierced my hands and feet. (Ps. 22:16)

A good example of this is found in the book of Proverbs:

> Like a sparrow in its flitting, like a swallow in its flying,
>   a curse that is causeless does not alight. (Prov. 26:2)

Yet another category has been called *repetitive* parallelism. Sometimes this is also called stair step or climactic parallelism. It refers to those cases in which a statement in the first line is partially repeated in the second but is intensified or carried further than would be the case in synthetic parallelism.

> Ascribe to the LORD, O heavenly beings,
>   ascribe to the LORD glory and strength.
> Ascribe to the LORD the glory due his name;
>   worship the LORD in the splendor of holiness. (Ps. 29:1;
>   see also vv. 3–9)

Other Literary Characteristics of the Psalms

An awareness of four other literary features of the Psalms will prove extremely helpful in our efforts to interpret them properly.

There is, first, *chiasm*. This word comes from the Greek letter *chi* which looks like *X*. When written out, a chiastic line will take the form of an *X*. Psalm 1:1 is chiastic, and can be rewritten to reflect this principle:

> Blessed is the man who walks not
>   in the counsel of the wicked,
>   in the way of sinners,
> he does not stand.

Ellipsis occurs when the second phrase in parallelism will omit a part of the first phrase on the assumption that the reader knows to insert it. Usually it is a verb that is omitted.

> You have put me in the depths of the pit,
>   [*you have put me*] in the regions dark and deep. (88:6)

The italicized phrase is missing in the original text, but the author assumes you will read it as if it were there.

Inclusio involves repetition that opens and closes a poem in a way that binds its parts together. Note how Psalm 8 opens and closes with the phrase, "O LORD, our Lord, how majestic is your name in all the earth!" *Inclusio* provides us with a sense of closure in having read a complete poem.

An *acrostic* is a poem in which the first letter of each line forms a recognizable pattern, in most cases the alphabet. The most famous Old Testament example is Psalm 119, in which each stanza has eight lines that begin with the same letter of the alphabet. Thus the first eight verses of the psalm begin with words that have as their initial letter *aleph* (the first letter in the Hebrew alphabet, corresponding to English *A*). This pattern continues through the next twenty stanzas. Examples of acrostic psalms are 9, 10, 25, 34, 37, 111, 112, 119, and 145. Aside from the obviously aesthetic nature of such structure, the purpose of the acrostic psalm was most likely to facilitate memorization.

Figurative Language

The Psalter, as one might expect, is replete with figures of speech, perhaps more so than any other book of the Bible. It's not as difficult as some might think to discern the presence of figurative language, but Walter Kaiser has provided us with several helpful guidelines that are worthy of note.[11]

First, we should determine whether there is a "mismatch between subject and predicate" if the sentence were to be interpreted naturally. For example, "in the statement, 'God is our Rock' [cf. Ps. 18:2, 31, 46; 19:14; 31:3; etc.], an animate subject (God) is identified with an inanimate predicate noun (Rock)," alerting us to the presence of something that is less than literal. Bruce Waltke has referred to this as "juxtaposition," by which he means that the author "transferred a word or a larger piece of literature from its normal linguistic environment into a literary environment where it is not at home. For example, in the sentence, 'The Lord is my shepherd' (Ps. 23:1), the word 'shepherd,' which is at home with words which have reference to animal husbandry, is here transferred and juxtaposed with the 'Lord,' a word pertaining to a transcendent, spiritual being. . . . When David prayed, 'Cause me to hear joy and gladness' [Ps. 51:8], he juxtaposed objects that refer to an emotional state with a verb that refers to a physical activity."[12]

We should also take note when a colorful word is followed by one that immediately defines it and thereby restricts the range of its application. A good example would be Paul's declaration in Ephesians 2:1 that we were "dead" in "trespasses and sins." Or again, would the statement be absurd or inconsistent with the rest of inspired revelation or the normal order of creation if one took the statement literally? When we read, for example, that "the mountains clapped their hands" we are obviously dealing with a figure of speech.

Kaiser also asks, "Is there a reason for using a figure of speech at this point in the text? For example, does the text require a heightened feeling, some dramatic emphasis, or some mnemonic device for retaining the message?"

One of the best ways to detect the presence of figurative language is to be familiar with the wide variety of possibilities that exist. Someone has said there are as many as two hundred different figures of speech, several of which have from thirty to forty varieties. But we need only mention a few of the more prominent examples often found in the Psalter.

The most important category of figurative language is that which employs *comparison* to convey some truth or principle. In order to make a point, an author will typically explain the unknown by comparing it with something already familiar to his audience. Of course, there are obvious limitations in this. As G. B. Caird reminds us, "The description of manna given in Exodus is informative, provided that you are familiar with coriander seed (it is 'fine as the hoarfrost on the ground'; 'it was like coriander seed, white; and its taste was like wafers with honey' Ex. 16:14, 31)."[13] The problem we face is that we don't live in the world of the Bible and are often ignorant of what, to Isaiah or David, were everyday, commonplace realities.

We must also keep in mind that when two things are compared they are rarely, if ever, alike in every respect. We mustn't push the comparison beyond what is reasonable. For example, "when the psalmist tells us that a united family is like oil dripping down Aaron's beard on to the skirts of his robe, he is not trying to persuade us that family unity is messy, greasy or volatile; he is thinking of the all-pervasive fragrance which has so deeply impressed itself on his memory at the anointing of a high priest (Ps. 133:2)."[14]

When God is compared "to a dry wadi (Jer. 15:18), a festering sore (Hos. 5:12), or a panther mauling its prey (Hos. 5:14), the degree of correspondence is low. It is a little higher when the similitude is drawn from nature in her more beneficent guise: the security of the rock (Ps. 31:2–3), the sun as source of light and life (Ps. 84:11), a bird's care for its nestlings (Deut. 32:11; Luke 13:34)."[15]

The most common forms of comparison are the *simile* and the *metaphor*. The simile is an explicit or formal comparison that employs words such as *like* or *as*. A good example of the simile is Psalm 2:9 where God is said to break the nations with a rod of iron and "dash them in pieces *like* a potter's vessel." In the case of metaphor, there is an implicit or unexpressed comparison. If a simile says, "A is *like* B," the metaphor directly asserts "A *is* B." David, therefore, was using metaphor when he declared, "The LORD *is* my shepherd" (Ps. 23:1) or "The LORD *is* my light" (Ps. 27:1) or "you, O LORD, *are* a shield about me" (Ps. 3:3).

Another important figure of speech found often in the Psalter is known as *synecdoche*, in which a part is used for the whole or the whole for the part. For example, when David declares, "For you will not abandon my soul to Sheol" (Ps. 16:10) he isn't suggesting that other elements that constitute his being are left out. "Soul" is used for the whole of his being, both spiritual and physical.

Or consider the figurative expression known as *litotes*, in which a negative statement is used to declare a positive truth, or often a simple understatement is used to heighten the action being described. A classic example of this is found in Psalm 51:17. There David affirms that "the sacrifices of God are a broken spirit; a broken and contrite heart, O God, you will not despise." His point, of course, is that not only will God not despise such an attitude in his people, but he happily approves of it and will rejoice and celebrate it whenever present.

One final example should suffice. The figure of speech known as *personification* is often found in the Psalter, especially in hymns of praise and celebration. Personification is when things are represented or spoken of as if they were persons, or when an author attributes intelligence, by words or actions, to inanimate objects or ideas. In Psalm 96, the psalmist appeals for the "heavens" to "be glad" and for the "earth" to "rejoice" (v. 11a). Let the "field exult, and everything in it! Then shall all the trees of the forest sing for joy" (v. 12).

Countless other examples of figurative language could be cited, and I encourage you to avail yourself of the many excellent resources that identify and explain them.[16] I hope these basic principles will assist you in the reading of the Psalms and increase your appreciation for the literary and theological beauty of the inspired text.

Notes

Acknowledgments

1. All quotations are taken from *C. H. Spurgeon: Autobiography, vol. 1, The Early Years, 1834–1859* (Banner of Truth, 1973), 79–96.

Preface

1. Donald Williams, *Psalms 1–72*, Mastering the Old Testament (Dallas: Word, 1986), 18.

Part 1: Psalms 1–19

1. Jonathan Edwards, "Nothing upon Earth Can Represent the Glories of Heaven," in *Sermons and Discourses 1723–1729, The Works of Jonathan Edwards*, vol. 14, ed. Kenneth P. Minkema (New Haven: Yale University Press, 1997), 145–46.

2. Sam Storms, *One Thing: Developing a Passion for the Beauty of God* (Fearn, Ross-shire: Christian Focus, 2004).

3. Jonathan Edwards, "Christian Happiness" in *Sermons and Discourses 1720–1723, The Works of Jonathan Edwards*, vol. 10, ed. Wilson H. Kimnach (New Haven: Yale University Press, 1992), 305–6.

4. Jonathan Edwards, "Spiritual Appetites Need No Bounds," n.d.

5. Charles Spurgeon, *The Treasury of David* (Peabody, MA: Hendrickson, n.d.), 1.a.23; emphasis mine. Spurgeon's commentary on the Psalms is published in three volumes, each of which has two parts, independently paginated. Henceforth all citations from Spurgeon will indicate whether it comes from volume 1, 2, or 3, as well as the first half (a) or second half (b) of that particular volume, followed by the page number.

6. A. W. Tozer, *The Price of Neglect* (Camp Hill, PA: Christian Publications, 1991), 13.

7. Spurgeon, *Treasury of David,* 1.a.36.

8. John Piper, *The Pleasures of God* (Portland, OR: Multnomah, 1991), 217.

9. Spurgeon, *Treasury of David,* 1.a.45.

10. Ibid., 1.a.46.

11. Ibid.

12. Quoted in Piper, *The Pleasures of God,* 211–12.

13. Ibid., 212.

14. Ronald B. Allen, *Rediscovering Prophecy: A New Song for a New Kingdom* (Portland, OR: Multnomah, 1983), 90.

15. Ibid., 94.

16. Peter C. Craigie, *Psalms 1–50,* Word Biblical Commentary (Waco: Word, 1983), 127.

17. Donald A. Carson, *How Long, O Lord? Reflections on Suffering and Evil* (Grand Rapids, MI: Baker, 1990), 44.

18. Ibid., 31.

19. Ibid., 73.

20. Ronald B. Allen, *Praise! A Matter of Life and Breath* (Nashville: Thomas Nelson, 1980), 152.

21. Ibid., 155.

22. J. I. Packer, *Rediscovering Holiness* (Ann Arbor, MI: Servant, 1992), 217.

23. Ibid., 217–18; emphasis mine.

24. Tremper Longman III, *How to Read the Psalms* (Downers Grove, IL: Inter-Varsity, 1988), 26.

25. See Allen, *Praise!* 154.

26. The substance of this meditation is adapted from my book, *Pleasures Evermore: The Life-Changing Power of Enjoying God* (Colorado Springs: Navpress, 2000), 235–46.

27. Spurgeon, *Treasury of David,* 1.a.177.

28. Larry Crabb, "Fly on the Wall: A Conversation about Authentic Transformation among Dallas Willard, Larry Crabb, and John Ortberg," in *Conversations: A Forum for Authentic Transformation* (Spring 2003), 1:30.

29. C. S. Lewis, "The Weight of Glory," in *The Weight of Glory and Other Addresses,* ed. and intro. Walter Hooper (New York: Simon and Schuster, 1996), 31.

30. C. S. Lewis, *Reflections on the Psalms* (San Diego: Harcourt Brace Jovanovich, 1958), 63.

31. Source unknown.

32. Ronald B. Allen, *Praise!* 132–33.

33. Jonathan Edwards, "Personal Narrative" in *Letters and Personal Writings,* ed. George S. Claghorn (New Haven: Yale University Press, 1998), 16:793–94.

34. John Piper, *The Pleasures of God* (Portland, OR: Multnomah, 1991), 86–87.

35. John Piper, *When I Don't Desire God: How to Fight for Joy* (Wheaton, IL: Crossway, 2004), 184.

36. Ibid., 184–85.

37. Sam Storms, *Pleasures Evermore: The Life-Changing Power of Enjoying God* (Colorado Springs: Navpress, 2000), 191–94.

38. John Piper, "Wonderful Things from Your Word," January 11, 1998, http://www.desiringgod.org.

39. John Piper, "How Dead People Do Battle with Sin," January 1, 1995, http://www.desiringgod.org.

Part 2: Psalms 22–37

1. Charles Spurgeon, *The Treasury of David* (Peabody, MA: Hendrickson, n.d.), 1.a.324. Spurgeon's commentary on the Psalms is published in three volumes, each of which has two parts, independently paginated. Henceforth all citations from Spurgeon will indicate whether it comes from volume 1, 2, or 3, as well as the first half (a) or second half (b) of that particular volume, followed by the page number.

2. Ibid., 1.a.326; emphasis mine.

3. H. C. Leupold, *Exposition of the Psalms* (Grand Rapids, MI: Baker, 1969), 199–200.

4. John Calvin, *A Harmony of the Gospels: Matthew, Mark and Luke,* vol. 3 (Grand Rapids: Eerdmans, 1972), 194.

5. Jonathan Edwards, *Dissertation Concerning the End for Which God Created the World,* in *Ethical Writings,* ed. Paul Ramsey (New Haven: Yale University Press, 1989), 8:493.

6. Joni Eareckson Tada, *Glorious Intruder* (Portland, OR: Multnomah, 1989), 59.

7. Ibid.

8. Much in this meditation has been adapted from my book *One Thing: Developing a Passion for the Beauty of God* (Fearn, Ross-shire: Christian Focus, 2004), 46–48.

9. Much in this meditation has been adapted from my book *The Singing God: Discover the Joy of Being Enjoyed by God* (Lake Mary, FL: Charisma, 1998), 55–65.

10. Charles Spurgeon, *Treasury of David,* 1.b.82.

11. Much in this meditation is adapted from my book *The Singing God,* 99–110.

12. Charles Spurgeon, *Treasury of David,* 1.b.107.

13. John Piper, *The Pleasures of God* (Portland, OR: Multnomah, 1991), 208.

14. Charles Spurgeon, *Treasury of David,* 1.b.122.

15. Jonathan Edwards, *The Miscellanies,* no. 448 (New Haven: Yale University Press, 1994), 13:495; emphasis mine.

16. Here is a more complete list, in case you're interested in reading all of them: Pss. 5:10; 6:10; 7:6; 9:19–20; 10:2,15; 17:13; 28:4; 31:17–18; 35:1,4–8,19, 24–26; 40:14–15; 41:10; 54:5; 55:9,15; 56:7; 58:6–10; 59:5,11–14; 63:9–10; 68:1–2; 69:22–28; 70:2–3; 71:13; 79:6,10–12; 83:9–18 (cf. Judg. 4:15–21; 5:25–27); 94:1–4; 97:7; 104:35; 109:6–19, 29; 119:84; 129:5–7; 137:7–9; 139:19–22; 140:8–11; 141:10; 143:12.

17. C. S. Lewis, *Reflections on the Psalms* (San Diego: Harcourt Brace Jovanovich, 1958), 22.

18. Ibid., 25.

19. Peter Craigie, *Psalms 1–50,* Word Biblical Commentary (Waco: Word, 1983), 41.

20. Ibid.

21. Ibid.

22. James E. Adams, *War Psalms of the Prince of Peace: Lessons from the Imprecatory Psalms* (Phillipsburg: P&R, 1991), 52; emphasis in original.

23. Henry Mennega, "The Ethical Problem of the Imprecatory Psalms," master's thesis, Westminster Theological Seminary, 1959, 38.

24. James Dick, "The 'Imprecatory Psalms,'" in *Psalm-Singers' Conference* (Belfast: Fountain, 1903), 94.

25. John Piper, "Do I Not Hate Those Who Hate You, O Lord?" October 3, 2000, http://www.desiringgod.org.

26. Sam Storms, *The Singing God*, 169–75.

27. Dan B. Allender and Tremper Longman, *Bold Love* (Colorado Springs: Navpress, 1992), 211.

28. Ibid., 216.

29. Ibid., 224–25.

30. John R. W. Stott, *Christian Counter Culture: The Message of the Sermon on the Mount* (Downers Grove, IL: InterVarsity, 1978), 119.

Part 3: Psalms 42–63

1. Charles Spurgeon, *The Treasury of David* (Peabody, MA: Hendrickson, n.d.), 1.b.270–71. Spurgeon's commentary on the Psalms is published in three volumes, each of which has two parts, independently paginated. Henceforth all citations from Spurgeon will indicate whether it comes from volume 1, 2, or 3, as well as the first half (a) or second half (b) of that particular volume, followed by the page number.

2. Ibid., 1.b.274.

3. John Goldingay, *Songs from a Strange Land* (Downers Grove, IL: InterVarsity, 1978), 33–34.

4. Spurgeon, *Treasury of David*, 1.b.272.

5. Goldingay, *Songs from a Strange Land*, 35.

6. Ibid., 104.

7. Ibid., 104–5.

8. Edward Dalglish, *Psalm Fifty-One in the Light of Ancient Near Eastern Patternism* (Leiden: Brill, 1962), 104.

9. J. J. Stewart Perowne, *The Book of Psalms* (Grand Rapids, MI: Zondervan, 1976), 416.

10. Henri Blocher, *Original Sin* (Grand Rapids, MI: Eerdmans, 1997), 28.

11. Ibid.

12. Dalglish, *Psalm Fifty-One*, 121–22.

13. Ibid., 147.

14. Goldingay, *Songs from a Strange Land*, 168.

15. Gordon MacDonald, *Rebuilding Your Broken World* (Nashville: Oliver-Nelson, 1988), *xviii*.

16. I have lost track of the source from which this quote originated.

Part 4: Psalms 73–88

1. Charles Spurgeon, *The Treasury of David* (Peabody, MA: Hendrickson, n.d.), 2.a.249–50. Spurgeon's commentary on the Psalms is published in three volumes, each of which has two parts, independently paginated. Henceforth all citations from Spurgeon will indicate whether it comes from volume 1, 2, or 3, as well as the first half (a) or second half (b) of that particular volume, followed by the page number.

2. Ibid., 2.a.251.

3. D. A. Carson, *How Long, O Lord? Reflections on Suffering and Evil* (Grand Rapids, MI: Baker, 1990), 143.

4. Sam Storms, *Reaching God's Ear* (Wheaton, IL: Tyndale, 1988).

5. Portions of this meditation are adapted from my book *To Love Mercy: Becoming a Person of Compassion, Acceptance, and Forgiveness* (Colorado Springs: Navpress, 1991), 28–31.

6. C. F. Keil and F. Delitzsch, *Commentary on the Old Testament: Psalms*, vol. 5 (Grand Rapids, MI: Eerdmans, 1975), pt. 3, 23.

Part 5: Psalms 91–104

1. Charles Spurgeon, *The Treasury of David* (Peabody, MA: Hendrickson, n.d.), 2.b.90. Spurgeon's commentary on the Psalms is published in three volumes, each of which has two parts, independently paginated. Henceforth all citations from Spurgeon will indicate whether it comes from volume 1, 2, or 3, as well as the first half (a) or second half (b) of that particular volume, followed by the page number.

2. John Piper, *A Godward Life*, Book 2 (Portland, OR: Multnomah, 1999).

3. Ibid., 54.

4. Ibid.

5. Ibid., 55.

6. Ibid.

7. Christopher Hitchens, *God Is Not Great: How Religion Poisons Everything* (New York: Twelve, 2007).

8. Ronald B. Allen and Gordon Borror, *Worship: Rediscovering the Missing Jewel* (Sisters, OR: Multnomah, 1982), 132.

9. Sherwood Eliot Wirt, *Jesus, Man of Joy* (San Bernardino, CA: Here's Life, 1991), 74.

10. Ibid., 75.

11. Ibid., 89.

12. Ibid., 41.

13. Ibid., 42.

14. Ibid., 55.

15. Charles Spurgeon, *Treasury of David*, 2.b.233.

16. John Piper, *The Pleasures of God* (Portland, OR: Multnomah, 1991), 83.

17. Quoted in J. J. Stewart Perowne, *The Book of Psalms* (Grand Rapids, MI: Zondervan, 1976), 235.

18. C. Leupold, *Exposition of the Psalms* (Grand Rapids, MI: Baker, 1969), 726.

19. Charles Spurgeon, *Treasury of David*, 2.b.304.

20. Ibid., 2.b.305.

21. Ibid.

22. Leupold, *Exposition of the Psalms*, 731.

23. Joseph Addison Alexander, *The Psalms* (Grand Rapids, MI: Baker, 1975), 428.

24. Piper, *The Pleasures of God*, 94.

25. Ibid., 94–95.

Part 6: Psalms 115–150

1. Charles Spurgeon, *The Treasury of David* (Peabody, MA: Hendrickson, n.d.), 3.a.53. Spurgeon's commentary on the Psalms is published in three volumes, each of which has two parts, independently paginated. Henceforth all citations from Spurgeon will indicate whether it comes from volume 1, 2, or 3, as well as the first half (a) or second half (b) of that particular volume, followed by the page number.

2. Ibid., 3.a.54.

3. Henry Scougal, *The Life of God in the Soul of Man* (Harrisonburg, VA: Sprinkle, 1986), 62.

4. Charles Spurgeon, *Treasury of David,* 3.b.119.

5. Quoted in ibid., 3.b.127.

6. Charles Spurgeon, *Treasury of David*, 3.b.258.

7. Raymond C. Ortlund Jr., "The Sovereignty of God: Case Studies in the Old Testament," in *Still Sovereign*, ed. Thomas R. Schreiner and Bruce A. Ware (Grand Rapids, MI: Baker, 2000), 29.

8. Spurgeon, *Treasury of David*, 3.b.259.

9. Ibid.

10. Ibid., 3.b.260.

11. Charles Spurgeon, *The New Park Street Pulpit*, vol. 1 (1855; repr. Pasadena, TX: Pilgrim, 1975), 1.

12. Herman Bavinck, *The Doctrine of God*, ed. and trans. William Hendriksen (Edinburgh: Banner of Truth, 1977), 162.

13. Stephen Charnock, *The Existence and Attributes of God* (Grand Rapids, MI: Sovereign Grace, 1971), 174.

14. Spurgeon, *Treasury of David*, 3.b.260.

15. Charnock, *Existence and Attributes of God*, 179.

16. C. F. Keil and F. Delitzsch, *Commentary on the Old Testament: Psalms*, Vol. 5 (Grand Rapids, MI: Eerdmans, 1975), pt. 3, 350.

17. Steven C. Roy, *How Much Does God Foreknow? A Comprehensive Biblical Study* (Downers Grove, IL: IVP Academic, 2006), 33.

18. Donald R. Glenn, "An Exegetical and Theological Exposition of Psalm 139," in *Tradition and Testament*, ed. John S. Feinberg and Paul D. Feinberg (Chicago: Moody, 1981), 176–77.

19. Charnock, *Existence and Attributes of God*, 429.

20. Ibid., 437.

21. Charles Spurgeon, *Treasury of David*, p. unknown.

22. Ibid., 3.b.324.

23. Ibid., p. unknown.

24. Charles Spurgeon, *Treasury of David*, 3.b.380.

25. Quoted in Spurgeon, *Treasury of David*, 3.b.384.

26. Ibid., 3.b.376.

27. Charles Spurgeon, *Treasury of David*, 3.b.415.

28. Ibid.

29. Ibid., 3.b.439.

30. C. S. Lewis, *Reflections on the Psalms* (San Diego: Harcourt Brace Jovanovich, 1958), 94.

31. Ibid., 95.

32. Spurgeon, *Treasury of David*, 3.b.464.

Appendix

1. See also C. Hassell Bullock, *An Introduction to the Old Testament Poetic Books* (Chicago: Moody, 1979; 1988).

2. One of the more popular English titles to the book of Psalms is "Psalter." According to Bullock, this word "comes from Alexandrinus, a fifth-century AD copy of the Greek translation known as the Septuagint, which called the book *Psalterion,* meaning 'stringed instrument.' The word actually occurs several times in the Greek text of the Psalms where it generally translates the Hebrew word *kinnor* ('lyre'), and sometimes *nevel* ('lyre'). Alexandrinus elevates this word to the title of the book" (*Encountering the Book of Psalms: A Literary and Theological Introduction* [Grand Rapids, MI: Baker Academic, 2001], 22).

3. Tremper Longman, *How to Read the Psalms* (Downers Grove, IL: Inter-Varsity, 1988), 26.

4. Ibid., 30.

5. Ibid., 38.

6. Ibid., 41.

7. Ibid., 44.

8. Bruce Waltke, unpublished "Notes on the Book of Psalms."

9. Willem A. VanGemeren, *Psalms*, in The Expositor's Bible Commentary, vol. 5 (Grand Rapids, MI: Zondervan, 1991), 34.

10. Longman provides a most helpful overview of the various forms of parallelism. See his *How to Read the Psalms*, 99–108.

11. All the following citations from Kaiser are taken from his book *Toward an Exegetical Theology: Biblical Exegesis for Preaching and Teaching* (Grand Rapids, MI: Baker, 1981), 122.

12. Bruce K. Waltke, "Historical Grammatical Problems," unpublished paper, 56.

13. G. B. Caird, *The Language and Imagery of the Bible* (Grand Rapids, MI: Eerdmans, 1980), 145.

14. Ibid.

15. Ibid., 154.

16. Longman, *How to Read the Psalms*, 111–22, has a helpful section explaining the use and meaning of such images in the Psalms.